6-11-87

GIVEN BY ERNIE MARZO AT THE QUESTION AND ANSWER SEMINAR. TO BERNIE A. MARTINEZ AT THE OLYMPIAN INN.

The LADY'S MEN

BY KEN AND JEANADELE MAGNER

Credits

Art Director — Dick Gilpin, Graphic Art Center

Gary Hail's photo on Page 214
State Times and Morning Advocate, Baton Rouge, La.,
Patrick Dennis, photographer
Beavercreek NEWS, Page 53, May 8, 1979
Ada NEWS, Page.184, photo, July 11, 1969

Introduction

This is a true story about two men. Born in America, they were exposed early to life conditions they could not tolerate. Each decided to make a new path for his journey. There the similarity ends.

Each born to loving parents, John and Harland began life a thousand miles from each other. By pure chance, the paths they were cutting in the jungle, crossed. By some strange alchemy — divine providence, perhaps — two who are as different as night and day, developed an admiration and friendship, one for the other. As fate would have it, both men were attracted to the same lady. And, as that same fate would have it, both decided to do something about it. Out of their meeting, an alliance developed, leading to an explosive adventure some have called "the perfect marriage."

All the names used in this story are the names of the actual people involved, with the exception of four, to avoid what might be a painful memory. The four pseudonymns are Bill Marshall, Hal Lorain, Harry, the drug salesman, and Ernest.

In recalling conversations that took place several years ago, people rarely remember with exactness the words used, while the incident is unforgettable. Furthermore, the total conversation, with interruptions, facial expressions, hand gestures and partial sentences, often makes little sense when written. So the dialogue is reconstructed and edited. Every conversation has been shown to at least one of the participants for correction or approval.

With these two necessary restrictions, the authors submit that what you now read really happened...

Your old men shall dream dreams;
your young men shall see visions.
John 2:28

I am come that they might have life,
and that they might have it more
abundantly. *John 10:10*

Appreciation

Many intimates, close friends, and some not so close, and many business associates of Harland and John, were valuable witnesses to the two of us as we pursued this adventure as responsible, investigative reporters. For their willingness to talk with us, without time considerations or financial reward, and for their frankness and every effort at accuracy, we especially thank the following:

(listed alphabetically)

Lonnie Abbott — member of Legislature — OK
Wayne Ahart — insurance company executive — TX
Fran Alexander — TVC field executive — AZ
Woody Alexander — TVC field executive — AZ
Lois Hail Allen — homemaker — OH
Cecil Atchley — educator (retired), dairyman — OK
Merle Boatwright — college registrar, retired — OK
Vicki Hail Bogert — homemaker — OK
Steve Breed — construction company executive — OK
Tommy Bush — Pre-Paid Legal executive — OK
Chuck Cannon — executive — TX
Charles Carroll — farmer — OK
Nell Carter — school employee — OK
    (for Dr. Irvin Carter, who passed away during the writing of this book)
Jane Close — high school teacher — OK
Linda Coffee — homemaker — OK
Virgil Coffee — TVC President — OK
Lloyd Collette — insurance company executive — LA
Edgar Cross — rancher/farmer — OK
Stella Cross — homemaker — OK

Pat Long Davidson — Pre-Paid Legal executive assistant — OK
Carolyn Davis — librarian — OK
Nick DeGiacomo — dog breeder, mgf. dog food — OK
James Dunham — insurance company executive — LA
Mamie Farnum — Chamber of Commerce — OK
Paul Fortner — school superintendent, stock broker — OK
Mary Jo Cannon DeGregoria — pastor's wife — KS
Gerald Grimes — Insurance Commissioner — OK
David Hail — pastor — OH
Gary Hail — radio morning show host — LA
Helen Hail — homemaker — OK and AZ
John Hail — TVC Founder & Chairman — OK and AZ
Joe Hail — realtor — OH
Lloyd Hail — pastor (retired) — FL
Norman Hail — insurance company executive (retired) — OH
Don Herzog — pattern maker — OH
Pat Herzog — church secretary — OH
Jill Breed Hodges — office manager — OK
Ed Hood — public relations — LA
Leon Hooter — TVC field executive — LA
Sue Hooter — TVC field executive — LA
Frank Jaques — attorney-at-law — OK
Ken Johnson — Pre-Paid Legal President — OK
Henry Katz — owner, department store — OK
Maxine Keck — homemaker — OK
Don Kinard — TVC field executive — KS
June Lawson — legal secretary — OK
Wanda Haney LeMarr — homemaker — OK
John Locke — insurance company executive — KY
Denise Hail Loney — homemaker — OK
Dennis Loney — TVC administrator — OK
Doris Lowry — high school teacher — OK
Lefty McFadden — public relations — OH
Bev Morgan — homemaker — OK
Don Morgan — businessman (retired) — FL
Fred Morgan — TVC executive — OK
Marjorie Hail Morgan — homemaker — FL
Werner Pfennigstorf — research attorney — IL
Nick Pope — insurance company executive (retired) — OK
Kathryn Prentice — Pre-Paid Legal supervisor — OK
Myra Rainey — attorney-at-law — CO
Dorothy Hail Rex — nurse — FL
Lynn Ridenhour — TVC field executive — MO
Dave Roller — TVC field executive — GA
D. E. Romines — TVC executive — OK
Katie Rowland Scowden — homemaker — OH

John Shultz — TVC field executive — CA
Sheila Shultz — TVC field executive — CA
Wilburn Smith — TVC executive — OK
Ben Steen — pharmacist — OK
Allen Stonecipher — student — OK
Brent Stonecipher — student — OK
Harland Stonecipher — Pre-Paid Legal Founder &
     Chairman — OK
Shirley Stonecipher — homemaker — OK
June Teas — TVC field executive — OK
Bob Thompson — Pre-Paid legal executive — OK
Sharon Unkefer — TVC field executive — OK
Joe Sam Vassar — attorney-at-law — OK
Charles Walls — rancher, school principal, pastor — OK
LaVerne Walls — teacher — OK
Curt Wilson — TVC executive — OK
Ruth Wilson — homemaker — OK

In searching out the facts of this story, more than 30,000 miles were traveled by air and highway. More than 60 extended interviews were taped and more than 40 of these were transcribed to assist in clearly tracking further facts and to establish exactness in conversation of the participants in the action.

Finally, we thank Harland and John, who agreed to our request that their story be shared. That consent came one year before publication. At the onset of our search into their lives, neither they nor their families, nor the authors, were aware of the coming of many, many calls, often late at night, for facts, the scrutiny of family memorabilia, or the intrusion into intensely personal and sometimes painful experiences...and of many other encounters that demanded patience and frankness from the principals...and received it.

Thank you,

KEN and JEANADELE MAGNER

Table of Contents

PART ONE

Chapter One

He lay motionless on his back, studying the swift movement of the billowing clouds building high above the Kanawha River. The sounds of the ball game and the noisy shouts of his friends were clear just beyond the untended bush line at the edge of the cemetery. The first baseman's mitt lay on his chest and dropped to his side as he swatted at a horsefly trying to land on his damp chin.

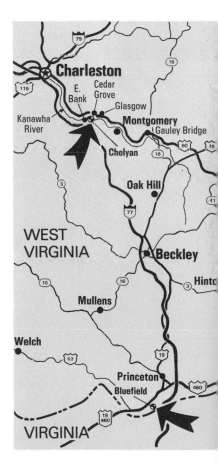

The sun was mid-August warm, but the trampled grass felt strangely cool against the sweat of his bare back. "Damn, anyway!"

Even as the frustration burst from his lips, he squirmed guiltily to look back in the direction of the parsonage at the far side of the cemetery. A 'damn' would be intolerable within earshot of his father — and a 'damn' on the Sabbath especially would be more than just trouble.

He rolled to his side and smiled a thin-lipped smile at the cluster of old gravestones around him, congratulating himself on finding a spot concealed from window view of the parsonage but close enough to the ball game to hear the action. And that was the best that Sunday would allow him with Dad spelling out the rules with puritanical precision.

"Hail! Hey, git yore butt ovah here, y'heah me? We gettin' our asses whupped an' we got two on! C'mon!"

"No way! Can't. Y'know that!"

"Hell! Jus' smack us a long 'un and y'can go back t'bein' Christian. Who's gonna know?"

Having pushed to an elbow to listen, Johnny slumped back to the ground. "Last time I did that, the ole man knew 'fore I got home and I took the whuppin'. So let's quit rechewin' the damned cole slaw an' see if you can't play baseball for a change!"

"So, wha's the glove for?"

The mitt rifled across the hedgerow over Dan's head. "Mike lent it t' me th'other night. Give it to him, will ya? I'll see ya later." He rolled to his other side away from the conversation.

A disgruntled set of epithets sputtered across the hedge as Dan scrabbled in the brush for the mitt. Then the glove whistled back and dropped at Johnny's feet. "Give it t'im yourself. Don't want 'im to know I been talkin' to a dayamn Christian!"

"Swell." The resentment burned fresh as it had many times before. This time Johnny let it burn. *Living was blocked, if having fun and having friends was supposed to be any part of it.*

He studied the etching on the ancient memorial that stood six feet tall in weathered limestone and offered perfect concealment from anyone looking across the graveyard from his latest home. Two nearly obliterated angels were carved above the inscription on the monument...

Happy Are They Who Die In The Lord
Ezekiel Stone
1844 — 1863
Gettysburg, Penna.

A tiny Confederate flag leaned wearily against the crumbling base of the memorial. Ezekiel Stone had been a soldier for the South, judging from the flag and the familiar rebel cap with crossed guns carved under the inscription. Johnny stretched to reset the little standard at right angles. There was something terribly forlorn about being born over a hundred years ago, getting to live nineteen years, and then winding up in this dreary cemetery in the beautiful, but hapless, poverty-ridden land of West Virginia, deep in the foothills of the Smokies.

At least Ezekiel Stone had a war he could go fight and even if his side did lose at Gettysburg, he fought for what he believed in and that's what mattered. Even if most of West Virginia had stayed loyal to the Union side, nineteen-year-old Ezekiel had lived life the way he believed he should. And someone had admired that in him enough to salute his guts in dying for it and to build him just about the largest monument in Cabin Creek. But the important thing was that he played the game the way he saw it.

And so would Johnny Hail. Someday. But right now, no way.

It wasn't Someday. It was Sunday — the most nothing day of them all. And Mondays and Wednesdays and Fridays and the others — always Revival Days. Seemed like the Nazarenes needed more reviving than anybody he knew. And he was stuck at fifteen, slave to whatever was right for the church, and his own life didn't matter.

Stuck at fifteen right in the same spot as Ezekiel Stone would have been, had he survived the War Between the States. And in lots of ways, he was lots worse off than Ezekiel, for at least his century-old counterpart had had the freedom to choose his route. And *so* he chose and lost. At least he exercised his right to choose! And now there was another war on. It made the Civil War look like a Sunday School picnic and he was fit and ready and tough, but this war wasn't being fought by fifteen-year-olds.

He remembered his reaction vividly, even now four years later, to the sneak attack of the Japs on Pearl Harbor. He was such a kid then. He'd been right in the middle of snap-the-whip with a bunch of other kids playing with that big old neon light pole and George Bader was the sucker they were picking on at the flip end of their line... and then the news came. The jerk kid world became a grownup's world. There was a burn in Johnny to get into this wild struggle to save a free world. He didn't understand it all, but he did understand freedom... and the lack of it.

He had followed the brutal brawl between free people like the British and the Free French and the Americans

Johnny at 15.

3

teamed against the Nazis and the Nips, out to make slaves of everyone. After Pearl Harbor, where his brother-in-law had been blown off the ship California, he'd agonized at how America kept losing in early months, but now the tide was turned. The Yanks and the Allies had retaken Europe and Germany had surrendered and it was all because of the muscle America had finally put together around the world to do a number on the dictators. Only mainland Empire Japan remained and that promised to be a wing-ding to take.

Why did he feel so rotten, when all he wanted to see happen for America was happening? That was exactly the problem. He'd counted on having a part, too, away from here, and that wasn't about to be his luck. The Nazis had wounded his oldest brother, Lloyd, and the fight was almost over without him. Take that and the home scene and what was left? "Damn!" and this time he didn't even feel halfway guilty. *Ezekiel would have said the same damn thing,* he reckoned.

• • •

Across the hedgerow, the baseball crowd was leaving. The happy yelping of familiar, carousing voices left no doubt the other team had won. *And so what? They needed his long ball, but who cared anyway?* Brother Hail's kids didn't play ball on Sunday. In fact, much as they all loved him, except for church and more church, there was very little the Reverend C. B. Hail's boys and girls — eleven of his own, others by his second marriage — fourteen of them altogether, *were* allowed to do.

• • •

He puzzled about his dad. You had to respect Charles Bruce Hail. He had once been out there in the real world where real people lived. He'd been an engineer with the Southern Railroad and you didn't make railroad engineer without knowing the scene. And then there had been that accident in the Cincinnati yards when the train he was switching had to brake suddenly and a box car door had flown open and wiped out this track man. His dad had blamed the man's death on himself.

There was no doubt about it. He had experienced a genuine call to the Lord's work and he had the courage as a middle-aged man to answer it. And with a wife and infant son, he'd studied for three years through God's Bible School in Cincinnati to ready himself for the ministry. Julia Dungan, who loved Charles Hail, was a very special mother to Johnny and all the other children they gave to the world. Julia was stricken with cancer at a young forty-seven and left a stunned husband and a disbelieving five daughters and five sons, eleven-year-old Johnny next to the youngest.

She always had been so much the center of the happy hours. Her spotless kitchen was the gathering point of social life of the parishes Brother Hail served, the only social scene of everyone in each little town. It was never her way to complain about the crowds around her home. The parishioners were drawn there to be with her and her kids and the pastor and even if often all that was on the table was flour and water biscuits with gravy, the Hail homes were happy places.

And there were lots of places Johnny had called home. At fifteen he already was into his ninth one, and again that was because of the ways of Brother Hail. He was a shepherd and wherever the flock was that needed him, that's where he went. Beginning churches from an absolute nothing but his commitment to do the Lord's work, he'd build a congregation till it could stand on its own and then he'd take his family and move on. And proud, stern man that he was, at Reelection-of-Pastor time each year, if he drew forty-nine affirmative votes in a congregation of fifty, with only one negative vote for his continuing as pastor, Charles Bruce Hail would pack up his furniture and family and leave. *He had the gas for it,* thought Johnny, somewhat irreverently, but he respected that in his dad. *C. B. always went at life on all eight cylinders.*

Sometimes it would be to primitive sections of East Tennessee where creature comforts were few. No matter. The Lord's children were there. So were outhouses and hand pumps, as well, *if* they were fortunate. Bluefield, West Virginia, where Julia left them, was a dirty little coal mining city. Brother Hail had to bury his wife and scatter his family to other parts of Hail clan back in Ohio while he put his own life together again. He and Julia had been so close.

And Johnny remembered the closeness he had felt toward his mother. All the kids in his family were that way and with so many of them, they all had to pull together. Mom had asked him when he was only four-and-a-half in Talahoma, Tennessee, if he would help older brother David, shy at the prospects of entering school. Would Johnny take him for her the first day?

It worked so well Johnny was allowed to stay on, too, and got a one year head-start. Shyness was never a problem for him, even then. He had wanted to help his father with worship at the church in those early pre-school years and when one of the elders offered to pay him if he would sing out a closing childish benediction, he grabbed at it. At the conclusion of the worship he would prance up the pulpit steps and, in full voice to the back row of seats where he was told his grandfather sat with poor hearing, he recited...

"We thank you for your offering, and kind
  attendance, too,
We hope our little program has stirred your hearts
  anew.
Please don't forget its message as you go away,
But work and pray for missions every single day."

Less than a year after they were sent to live in different homes in Ohio, young Johnny and David and Dorothy and their youngest brother Joe were called back home. His father had remarried and Ruth, with two young daughters and a son in the Marines, entered the Hail family. And then another girl, Mary Alice, was born to his new stepmother.

And here he was back in West Virginia in the Cabin Creek School District, definitely feeling like the misfit. His Dad had shown the love he had for his children in calling them back to his nest, but if he was stern with them before, he was forceful patriarch now.

• • •

And maybe he had to be, thought Johnny, pulling the gray tee shirt over his head. *Lots of family... Few dollars to go around... Couldn't be easy. But did he have to be so strict?* He winced against the glare of the afternoon sun for the first time, feeling the warmth as he remembered the embarrassment his father had put him to again last Sunday morning at worship. His nephew Charley was visiting from Ohio, like he always did in the summer. *Nephew! That was a laugh.* Uncle Johnny was only a month older than Charley. They'd been pals almost since birth, too. *Guys have to whisper, even in church, and Dad had really laid it on him in front of God and the whole congregation... including Charley.*

The stentorian voice barked from the square, boxy pulpit right in the middle of the reading from Revelation. "Johnny! You get up here!"

Johnny and Charley

He walked slowly from the back bench straight for the front row, to which he had been ordered many times before. It shifted as he slumped into it. It was a repeat all over again of Charley's last visit!

"Up here, young man! You will sit up *here!*" The finger pointed imperiously to the vacant, straight and hard, unfinished pulpit chair and Johnny marched. And he sat there through the whole service, staring at a worn spot on his pants knee, with his legs hanging and feet not touching the floor, not looking up at the faces all watching him. He was really resentful that life in the Hail family from stem to stern made him conform to church, or else. And that forced something in him to rebel. Not just to challenge the do-nots and the prohibitions of his father, but just as often the rules set down by other authorities.

"He tells you 'no' and man, you gotta be the first to try it," Charley chuckled as the two shuffled home from church that Sunday.

And now it was another Sunday...

He made his way morosely across the unkempt weeds of the burying grounds, seeing Dad's black Nash in the parsonage driveway. A twinge of discomfort traveled down his spine. He had counted on Sunday afternoon parish calling to take him a lot longer. It usually did. In fact, Johnny had carted the mitt along, really determined to cross that cemetery hedge and get in on the game. Baseball was like breathing to him. *So what could possibly be wrong with a little ball game?* He'd heard Dad often enough in the pulpit tell a Nazarene congregation that God gave man the Sabbath 'for rest and the renewal of the soul.' And *that was just what baseball did for him! It renewed him so's his soul could stand another week of boring awful school.*

As he passed the open garage, he debated tossing the glove in there out of sight, then gave up the idea. By now his father probably would have spotted it anyway and if the elder Hail and Johnny didn't see eye to eye on Sunday, they both were the same cut in facing a problem head-on without ducking. That and lots of other things he found good to admire in him.

The parsonage was deathly quiet when he slipped past

7

the kitchen screen door, holding it behind him so it wouldn't slam. In just about a second he expected that big voice of authority to cut through the quiet and to demand an accounting for himself. How had he dared violate a Sabbath canon, understood clearly by one and all of the Hail brood — there will be no competitive games on Sunday!...And no Sunday newspaper...and no purchases in a store on the Sabbath, or, in fact, let there be no using of any services thereby requiring some other child of God to violate the injunction of Holy Writ straight off Mount Sinai, 'Remember the Sabbath day to keep it holy.' Brother Hail and his flock were a loyal part of the Lord's Day Alliance and how could his son sabotage that loyalty?

But there was no sound of outrage from anywhere and he tiptoed to the hall. Distantly he heard voices out on the side porch. A lively exchange was going on. *He'd struck it lucky! Parishioners had come by. But wait! Didn't someone say something about 'Johnny...?' No matter. He was out of trouble.* He slipped into the tiny bath off the kitchen and toweled sweat from his chest, opting not to use the hand pump. It was so noisy and ancient. *Why risk calling attention to his presence?*

He studied himself critically in the mirror. Deep tan, slim body, a tumble of brown curly hair. *Why couldn't it be straight like the other guys'?* He drew himself up proudly, then leaned to brush his fingers across his jaw, wishing at least the start of whiskers was there. Even so, he looked five years older than fifteen and he could sure have kicked hell out of the Krauts, if he'd had a chance.

Shirt and tie in place again, he stepped back into the kitchen and peered into the ice box for something to tide over till supper. A dish of Brown Betty stood alone on the second shelf and that was all the ice box could offer. Idling over the decision, he chipped a thin sliver from the ice block and let it melt in his mouth.

He debated walking to the porch to say hello to Dad and his visitors. Then he reached impulsively for the dessert and dropped onto the kitchen stool. A few minutes later he rinsed the plate, remembering too late that the sound of the pump would carry to the porch. *Stupid! He could have made it to his bedroom and an hour's nap before evening church service. Now he might as well confront it.* The sound of a chair shifting carried to him. Dad would expect him to be courteous to guests.

One thing his father always did was to share the parish life with all his family. Maybe it was being part of all the business of the parish and being on the steps every time the church door opened that had motivated his brother Lloyd to follow his father's footsteps into the ministry. No such allure for Johnny. When he was a little kid it was fun to get up on a box out back and play like preaching, but so far for him the church promoted much too many 'do nots' and too many 'must dos' that flat made life a drag.

"Hi, Dad." He sauntered out onto the porch and smiled at the visitors. Both were men and neither returned his smile.

"Take a chair, son. Where've you been?"

"Oh, jus' out takin' it easy." He felt the negative vibrations and shifted uneasily, looking from his father to his stepmother. *She would never take the place of his mother for him.* Mom had been the one whose hugs and affection made tolerable the prohibitions and constant church and the revivals and more revivals, and the straight and very narrow. He looked across the two Sunday-dressed visitors and half-smiled at Ruth and though for a second she tried to return it, her face was tight and drawn as she looked past him. He knew it before his father said a word — *Johnny Hail was definitely in trouble — again.*

"Son, Mr. Ames and Mr. Burton are part of the Cabin Creek school administration." He gave Johnny that special searching look which meant honesty was expected. "Mr. Burton is the attendance officer. He tells your mother and me that you have not been in the classroom for the past two weeks. Please explain to all of us if there is truth to this and if so, what you have been doing."

Johnny wanted to flail. He was sure they knew all. He was sure Ruth, the newcomer to the Hail house had as much right to the title 'Mother' as he had any right to expect mercy for his truancy.

"Yes, sir. It's true. I haven't been there for a couple o' weeks. I've been drivin' a cinder truck up at one o' the mines. I really need the money an'..."

"But you don't even have a license to drive a truck!" interrupted an impatient father.

"We understand this was a semi, not just a little truck," added Mr. Burton.

"Well, yeah...but..."

"That will be all!" The command crackled across the porch and he flushed. The look from his dad was the one and only look Johnny felt of all four stares focused on his face. He had been a disappointment to his father and that hurt. *Why was he always getting caught?* "You will be at your desk in school tomorrow!"

"Yes, sir." He stood to walk across the porch, passed the two from the school without a word, passed his stepmother, then caught a glimpse over her shoulder of one of her daughters eavesdropping just beyond the living room door, wearing a smile of pure pleasure at his troubles. *There was no way any of the newcomers to his family could care about him, except as a target for torture,* he thought nastily. Johnny knew in that moment something was going to have to change in his life. There was no way he could tolerate Cabin Creek, West Virginia any longer.

"You are not dismissed! Sit down."

He dropped to the old rattan rocker by the door and felt the prickle of the worn out bamboo seat needle at his tail.

Mr. Ames cleared his throat. "There is one other thing I feel I must speak to your son about, Brother Hail." He cleared his throat again nervously. "It keeps coming to us from the recess supervisors and the lunch room monitors that wherever you go at break periods in school, John, a group collects. I need to ask you frankly, what in tarnation is going on?" He fixed Johnny with a stony, near-accusing stare. "I'll tell you honestly, boy, there's been a lot of vandalism going on in Chelyan. More'n just one does it, too. The police have asked us to watch for anything that looks like a gang in the Cabin Creek School District. Let me tell you, some of the faculty are nervous that you seem to be a ringleader. What have you to say for yourself?"

'Damn' would have been a good start. Johnny swallowed it and felt the fury surge up his neck as he met Ames' stare with open-eyed amazement. "I jus' like people, sir. Is that a wrong thing? We ain't hurtin' nobody. The kids like me. I don't even know what a gang is, 'cept that gang o' Nazis we jus' whipped." *So why was he having to apologize for kids liking him,* he wondered.

"Just as long as that's what all this is about..." Mr.

Ames measured out the words, then frowned uncomfortably, anxious now to break off the conversation. He turned back to Johnny's father, sitting with his hands folded on his belly. "I will say for your son, Brother Hail, the report shows, as you know, he's almost a straight-A student. Now, if he can keep off the cinder truck and try to use those talents sensibly..." He rose to leave and Johnny, because he had been trained to stand in respect to adults, stood slowly from his chair. A moment later the visitors were gone and he braced for the worst.

Johnny and Hupmobile

"So, why do you need money, son?" his father asked in a surprisingly conciliatory tone.

He sat back down. "I jus' gotta have some, Dad, to get that old Hup in shape. I mean it would make things a whole lot simpler 'round here. I could drive David and Joe to school and do things I gotta do. Helpin' Ruth with errands..." He winced inwardly at the abrupt change in his father's expression at the use of his stepmother's first name. It was a slip. He had been told several times that that was unacceptable. *No way could he call her 'Mom.'* He braced for the worst.

"And just how would two cars look in the parsonage driveway?" At least he had ignored the first name affront. "And what makes you think you could get any gas allotment stamps at all?...Why, you're just a student..." He sniffed impatiently and snapped, "That is, when you've a mind to be! No, I will not permit it and until I hear that you have attended school for one clear month without missing a day, you are not permitted to play ball."

"Aw...Dad! No baseball? It's right in the middle o' the league!"

"Enough!" His father gave that imperious sign that signalled the end of discussion. "You have a few short years to make good. I know, because I was deprived of school, that you will make more from the classroom, than from the baseball diamond."

He rocked silently on the old rattan, reaching for words that wouldn't come. A sting worked at the corner of one eye and it hit him abruptly that this old rocker, uncomfortable as it was, had been his mother's favorite chair through the years. He squinted at the floor so the tear wouldn't be seen as it became a trickle. She had used this chair on warm Summer days and evenings as her favorite place to cuddle and feed and rock the newest infant in the family. The rocker had always been a part of the pile of furnishings that moved from parish to parish with them and it was suddenly very special.

"You may go now, son." There was a kindliness in the dismissal. *Did his dad see the damned tear?* He hoped not.

He shuffled through the door to the living room and made his way upstairs. In the small bedroom he shared with Joe, he dropped onto the mattress and lay staring moodily at the white paint chipped in a crazy quilt pattern across the ceiling. *What to do?... Get up and leave?... Run away?... He could slip out of the house tonight... head straight for Route 60... Be easy... Couple hundred miles to the East was Norfolk and Newport News and the biggest Navy in the world... It was just about time for the last boat to Japan and nobody but nobody would doubt he was eighteen and fighting trim... Orphan, he'd tell 'em... No parents... They'd let him enlist... Bullshit, they would!... They kept turning kids just like him back every day in the recruiting stations... You couldn't make that orphan crap work...*

Try the other direction, needled his restless thoughts... *Take out West for no more'n ten miles and you're free and clear in Charleston... And then it's a beeline right on 77 for a hundred, maybe two hundred miles and you're back in Beavercreek... And how long would Dad sit still for that?... Maybe it's worth a try askin', though... The Morgans had liked him and told him to come back anytime and there was his buddy, Charley, and most of the guys he really liked were back in Ohio... He could get a job in Dayton... Wright-Patterson must be hiring every day with the war like it is... He could lie about his age... Judas Priest!... No baseball for a month!... Boy, Dad really stuck it in and broke it off that time!...*

The August heat held the temperature in the room at a stifling plus-100 and he drifted to and fro, half-asleep, half-awake. *What to do?... Where to go?... Did Hell get this hot?... Maybe that's where he had already worked himself into...*

"Johnny? Supper's ready!" It was one of Ruth's daughters. "Come straightaway, y'heah? Church in just one owhwahhh."

He staggered to his feet and straightened his navy blue string tie. *Sure good news that church was coming in one hour. Just for a minute he thought he'd died and gone to hell.*

❖ ❖ ❖

It was late that evening and Dad and Ruth were outside on the porch and all seven of the brood were in the three bedrooms upstairs.

"Could I speak to you a minute, sir?" He stood pajama clad and unsure of his resolve at the door.

"Yes. What is it, son?" There was warmth in his father's voice and that reassured. Almost always after worship services there was an afterglow that made this his dad's most approachable time.

"Well, I been thinkin' 'bout everything and I don't want no one to git me wrong or anything..." The request tumbled out. Was there any way possible he could be allowed to go back to Ohio for a spell? It had been in sister Marge's last letter to Dad that they sure missed him and he was such a big help around the place and a whole lot of the kinfolk up there keep talking about how they missed him, she wrote. Just last week. "Well...Dad...how about lettin' me go back there an' finish up high school there? It's a whole lot bigger school an', heck, I'd get a lot better education, prob'ly."

There was a wall of silence for what seemed like hours. Then there were questions. And some of the time he sensed hurt feelings and other times he felt his dad was listening.

"All right, John. Your mother and I will discuss it. Goodnight."

• • •

Credit Dad Hail, he sensed in his next-to-youngest son a special quality that could easily be nurtured or destroyed in an unusually gifted boy. And he certainly insisted in always trying to go just beyond the line of permission in everything. Ruth found him studying a photo taken of himself with his five sons. "Y'know, dear, every one of my boys is separate — just like every one of my daughters. But looky here at Johnny. I mean, everything about him is different than the rest. Look at this picture. He stands so proud; or is it rebellious? I wonder if he'll make it?"

He fell silent, ruminating over the boys. *If David showed some signs of hearing that mystic call from the Lord, as*

13

Lloyd had, there were no trumpets being heard by Johnny. Quite the opposite. If anything, he seemed working harder at his rebellion. Had he reached that age where any authority was a thing to challenge for any reason?

Couldn't fault the boy for laziness, not by a long shot. He chuckled, remembering how Johnny had taken Charley daily, during one of those first summers the boys were together down in Tennessee, and showed him how to sell. Healing salve, it was the first time. They'd go right to the front doors of total strangers and Johnny would ask if there were any achy people or sick people inside. They would tell all to a six-year-old. Well, Johnny had just the healing salve in this flat, round can to cure their problems — all of them. They even sold some, too, for 10¢ till a parishioner recognized the preacher's kid and brought the report home to the Hail kitchen.

Johnny had been working ever since. It seemed to C. B. that he was always into something. But this truancy from school...He'd picked up that old Hupmobile at the junk yard and had a corn cob under the pan holding the oil in.

Yes, it was time for a change of scene for Johnny. The boy's request made sense. Marge and Don could get him to a school where he wouldn't play hooky. Don would certainly see to that! After his implied promise to finish high school if he went back to Ohio, his father was sure that would happen. One virtue he was absolutely sure about in this son was that Johnny's word was his bond.

C. B. carried the picture of his sons back to the living room table, shaking his head in wonder. It was a good idea, this shift to Ohio for Johnny. And how much deliberation had gone into it before the notion was proposed? If he had discovered one trait in this young man, it was the way he thought things out. C. B.'s thoughts went back to the cinder truck incident. There was no way Johnny could think he would get away with truancy. Do you suppose he just had set up this whole business to get his point across?

"I'm going to call Marge," he announced, finding Ruth in the kitchen.

"If that's what you think best."

❖ ❖ ❖

The return to Ohio was arranged in that special way of the Hail and Morgan clans. Both patriarchs of the families, Charles Bruce Hail and Frank Morgan, had an intense respect for each other, and the whole North edge of the Hail family which had gravitated toward Dayton after marriage and after the death of mother Julia, would be unanimous in welcoming back this different one of the clan. Where other families might read such a shift in mid-adolescence as some kind of disciplinary step, there was a special love that pervaded those families that made it invitation, not punishment.

"Done," announced C. B. "Marge and Don say to bring him right up."

Ruth straightened from her search of the ice box with a sigh. "I was saving a Brown Betty for you tonight and it seems to have vanished."

"Ten guesses."

"That's exactly right."

Chapter Two

"Ready, Dad," Johnny called to his father, who was dozing in the shade of the large roadside maple. He hefted the bald tire into the trunk of the old Nash, wondering whether the cold patch he'd applied to the slash in the inner tube would hold. It had better. It was the only spare they had and they'd already had two flats since Chelyan.

"Good job, Johnny!" C. B. watched him anchor the spare into place and wrap the jack in the stained, old faded bath towel. "Now if the Lord will steer us away from any more nails, we'll make it by nightfall." As the trunk closed, he heard a muttered "Amen to that!"

His dad slid behind the wheel and Johnny wondered if he really had taken note of his know-how with worn-out tires. Slumping against the seat with half of his shoulder against the passenger door of the ancient rattletrap of a car, he watched his father through partly-closed lids, pretending to sleep. Forever neat in his uniform of the clergy — black suit and white shirt — C. B. seemed oblivious to the heat. The black tie in place, he had pulled the worn jacket on for the last leg of the trip. *Had to be sweltering, but always the minister,* thought Johnny as he shifted position to take in the horizon. Distantly he could make out the faint welcome silhouette line of a city.

There was that special feeling of coming home as they got closer to central Ohio and neared Dayton. It wasn't because he remembered that much about his birthplace. He hadn't really lived a full year in Ohio, even counting the seven months with his sister, Marge, immediately after his mother's death. But those few months around the Morgans and the Hails of Ohio had given him a home feel that none of the many parsonages ever could.

It was where Charley lived, too. Charley Cannon — 'Bee-bee' some called him, since 'he wasn't big enough to be a Cannon'. He came most every summer to Johnny's house, to wherever the parsonage of his grandparents was that year, and the two had become more friends than relations. Charley lived outside East Dayton in the area called Knollwood, with the rest of the family.

His father turned the Nash onto Route 35 in an Easterly direction as they approached the South edge of the city. A four-engine bomber from nearby Wright-Patterson Air Force Base wheeled overhead and traffic paused at a red light in the middle of a shopping district. It all felt good — like real people lived here. Not just more people, or city people, but here was a place where he could be his own man and where the world seemed freewheeling.

And Marge and Don wanted him back. So they said. He mulled on that as they turned up the unpaved street toward the house that was to become his new home. *He was older now. Had they agreed because it was a family thing to do? He didn't get along with Don so hot, but they made him sound wanted, as his father reported it. But who in the family wouldn't agree to a C. B. request? C. B. had most of them intimidated,* thought Johnny irreverently.

He saw Marge's house. Long red brick ranch with lots of room inside. He'd choose to believe the invitation was real. It was a clean start. The air was so clean. It was country, with acres of open ground separating neighbors. The cinders and the filthy soot were left behind in West Virginia with everything else he'd gotten away from.

The screen door sprayed open, disgorging a mixed crowd — young and old of Morgans and Hails. And when Marge flew across the lawn with her apron flying loose, to clutch him in a maternal welcome and announced with obvious delight, "Here's my next-to-baby brother!" Johnny knew an emotion of family he'd not known for years. He watched her loving embrace of their father and even as he extended his hand gratefully to Don, he puzzled about the warmth the rest of the kids seemed to feel toward Dad. Of course, he loved him, too, but he resented the institution his father had laid on his back...or so it felt. *Was it only him? Didn't anyone else resent it, too?* Now there would be a chance here to sift it all out and come to some sensible conclusions without pressure.

Or would there? Marge was hurrying them into the house for a quick bite of supper before evening church. Johnny glanced at Don to see how this member-by-marriage of the clan, recently out of the Air Force, reacted to the announcement. No visible sign that a service on a *Monday* night was anything out of the ordinary around here.

A honking serenade of arrivals rounded the corner and the driver leading the parade was in uniform. It was his brother, Lloyd, who had been with General George Patton's Army after graduating from the chaplain's school at Harvard. He was on medical leave from the service and arriving with him was Frank Morgan, patriarch of these Morgans of Knollwood and Beavercreek. Babies and small fry seemed to pour out from all directions. Johnny's sister Edith was hugging him, too, and Velma and Edna were having an intense conversation about Velma bringing so much contribution to the covered dish supper. It was happy. It was family. It really was like coming home and Johnny realized just how much he had missed it. *Dad must, too.*

"Well, Charles," heavy-jowled, jovial 'Grandpa' Morgan said, "you're going to have yourself quite a congregation tonight. The word's out you're preaching a special revival, you know."

The senior Hail chuckled. "I've got quite a congregation right here in the house. Fact is, Frank, since we started this church here in your basement, we've never had it any better for the Hails. The way you folks did for us — I'll never forget that."

C. B. and Julia, and their children

"Neither will we. And it's an extra special memory to us since it was your first church. You left us a strong one, C. B.; Parkview Nazarene is just mighty respected all through Dayton."

"That's good to hear. You folks made it all possible. We just moved you from one basement to another and you took it from there."

The men laughed together over the underestimating the parsonage committee had done. After they bought the Dayton property on the corner of Watervliet and Revere, the church planners dug the basement of the church-to-be and closed it in at the top as a worship house till they could afford the rest of the building. Then they attached the parsonage to that basement. A plain white frame, two-story house with three small bedrooms upstairs. Quite a bit too small for C. B. and his family of nine. And along came baby Johnny then, just to keep anybody from feeling like there was too much elbow room.

"Same thing's been happening with all those umpteen other churches you've started up since then in Kentucky and Tennessee and West Virginia. And you know what? Nothing makes me happier than that you aren't too proud to come right on down to the car lot and help me sell cars when things get tight and you can use extra money. I admire that in a real man of the Lord. Not afraid to get his hands dirty.

"And now the Hails are comin' back to Beavercreek one after another. We have Marge here and Edith and Edna and Norman...and now Johnny, too." He clapped an affectionate arm across Johnny's shoulders.

"Thank you, sir. It's good t' be back," And it was. Whatever else, he was clearly welcomed as much a part of the Morgans as the Hails.

That night after church Don Morgan sat alone with his young brother-in-law in the kitchen. Johnny sensed that Don was different than he'd been during that seven months visit years earlier. *Had it been because Johnny was a child then who had just lost his mother? Or was it that Don was back from the war now and maybe that experience had changed him?* He was crisp and tough. No humor. Johnny could feel the room bristle with tension verging on hostility as Don laid it on the line to him. "I'm goin' to spell it out for you, Johnny. We can have good times t'gether or it can get rough, if you mess with the simple rules in my house! If I get any flak from you, we're goin' to have trouble!"

As he got the word, Johnny sized up the situation. *This was definitely a different man welcoming the newcomer, but not about to take crap from a kid.* He wondered *who had advanced him to make it sound like he would be a problem? Dad? Ruth? What the heck, the guy wasn't much older than he was and he'd probably had a lot of stuff happen to him while he was gone...*

"Listen, sir, I sure do understand. You won't get no flak, nossir!"

"Jus' so's we understand each other...And listen, when I get a place for you, how'd ya like to make a few bucks up in the city from Morgan Motor Sales after school and weekends maybe, preppin' the new cars?"

"Oh, man...I mean, that's swell! I sure do like that new Kaiser wagon. You mean it? I maybe can work for you?"

"Well, I hope you're gonna work! Gotta pull your own weight. I'm sure Bob and your brother Norman would agree with that. We all run the place together, ya know."

• • •

It still was good to be here. He walked outside with Marge and Don and she pointed up the hill to the farmhouse at the crest. "You know, I'm glad you and Charley are such good friends, Johnny. Since Edith has been taken so sick, he's had to be a father to his brothers and Mary Jo. His dad is off on that bread route twelve hours a day. You'll be good for him, being here."

❖ ❖ ❖

So home it quickly became. Not just in the Morgan home with Marge and Don and 5-year-old Freddy and Mary Jo, too, when her mother was going through a bad week or more. But home was all through Beavercreek and Knollwood and Dayton and all its spreading areas. Everywhere he went it was like a new start at living.

When the space for him didn't open quickly at Morgan Sales, he found a job with the father of one of his classmates. Naomi, one of twenty-eight in his class at Beavercreek High, casually mentioned her father was looking for someone to work at his gas station up the road. The next day Johnny was there pumping gas at Scowden's Service Station, glad to have the job, even if that little Naomi, perched atop the empty pop cases, came along with it. For being a Junior, too, she really was a little one — must be only four-feet-something-or-other and she was a merciless tease and minimal help but at least the customers enjoyed her. She was always hanging around, usually sitting there with her legs swinging and calling something to him or someone else. Widower Howard Scowden groused about the fact that the traffic flow for gas and for oil changes always seemed to get heavier after school when Johnny was there and Naomi was, too. Johnny made some mental notes about her and about what happened with the upbeat atmosphere she made around the place.

• • •

"I can use your help down in Preppin' now, if you feel like goin' to work," Don offered some weeks later.

"Gosh, I don't know, Don. Mr. Scowden's kinda countin' on me. I'd hate to let him down."

"Aw, g'wan! Pump jockeys are a dime a dozen. 'Smatter? That pretty little daughter got your eye? Tell you what, boy, you prep my new cars right and you'll make some real pocket change. An' jus' to get you there, I'll give ya a set o' wheels. How 'bout that?"

That did it. Johnny was total commit to Morgan Sales. Don teased him about maybe taking delivery on his new car the next day and for that night Johnny entertained dreams of a demo Kaiser Manhattan. It was more than let-down when Don thumbed in the direction of the Model-A Ford and chortled, "There she is, boy. Heard you did a real job in West Virginia on an old Hupmobile. Let's see ya put your classic antique into first class shape."

And he did. If it was an oldie-goodie, it still was his alone. And so was his opportunity at Morgan Sales. He sized up the four-story red brick building at 555 South Main in Dayton. The first floor show room was all glass: easy to maintain high visibility, if he wanted Norman and Don and Bob Morgan to see his worth. And he certainly did. But the prepping work was done upstairs and well out of sight of any action. The only time he'd be seen by the bosses was bringing a car one way or the other by the elvator. But when they saw him, he'd be remembered.

He was. First among the many to know a new prepper was on the job was Ruth Reay. She was a member of Parkview Nazarene and someone had told her there that Johnny was a son of one of Parkview's former ministers. Ruthie was Girl Friday at Morgan's and very much at the center of the action in the fish bowl show room. She was the total secretarial force and with bright red hair that tumbled the full length of her back, it was easy to see why shy but pretty, petite, and always stylishly dressed Ruthie was the choice of four of the car salesmen as their personal secretary. And Ruthie had then the enviable ability of being able to down half-a-dozen doughnuts at coffee break with the men and then having lunch an hour later, without gaining an ounce. She admired slimness and neatness and personalities that matched her own quietness.

Johnny Hail was noticed from the first day of his working at Morgan's. Especially by Ruthie, who found it refreshing to have someone in the dirty end of car work arrive in neatly clean pants and work shirt, a stand-out contrast to the rest of the mechanic and prepping crew. She wondered how long that would last. He was positively skinny around a sea of portly figures, and was curlyheaded and also very quiet. Another plus. When he spoke, he had the ready smile and the easy manners of a very well-bred young man. He stayed that way.

Heavens, young is just what he was, compared to 20-year-old Ruthie. No way could she accept his bid for a date when inevitably, he tried. Besides, she had just met a handsome 22-year-old. An honest-to-goodness Dayton hero who had been the centerfielder for the one and only USA national championship amateur baseball team in 1944. Curt Wilson, who now captained a bowling team and brought his men to league nights different from all the other teams — wearing dashing white shirts with the team name on their backs — was introduced to her one night at the bowling alley. The choice was obvious. No skinny seventeen-year-old had a chance against an established hero with a Charles Atlas bod and such absolute self-assurance.

But she knew Johnny Hail was on his way to somewhere good, whenever he grew up. She was delighted when the Morgans asked her to do a television commercial for the company with a Kaiser wagon opening from the back to show the ease of packing and how much it could hold. It carried everything, including a canoe, picnic gear and family and it was such fun when Johnny was one of the men to do the commercial with her. He was definitely on his way.

By now everyone was aware that thirty-seven-year-old Edith was dying from what was suspected to be undulant fever. It was a long and agonizing tortue for her and was caused, some said, by unpasteurized milk or contact with infected cattle or dairy products. Johnny wondered if it went back to the early parsonage days and one of those back-hill churches C. B. felt called to serve in the poverty of Tennessee. His father's dismissal of Edith's condition as the "Will of the Lord" was *consistent*, thought Johnny in bitter times. *If he wasn't preaching hellfire and brimstone, he was explaining away the suffering of good people like his daughter, with a cop-out explanation like "God's Will."*

And now Johnny was watching more of the impact of poverty on the Cannons. Noah, Charley's Dad, had a baking company delivery route. So wide-spread was his territory that he had a forty-mile drive before he delivered his first loaf. He'd leave early, come back late and what did it get him? He still couldn't even afford to fix the farmhouse they all lived in with any basic conveniences. No electricity. No water. No toilet indoors. As a matter of fact, they had chickens and a milking cow and unpasteurized milk there, too.

In desperation to make his wife comfortable, Noah had taken his family all the way to San Diego one summer where he'd hoped the humidity was lower and would be helpful to this vicious brucellosis or undulant fever 'or whatever they called it.' San Diego hadn't worked either and Edith just worsened with wracking aches and pains and chills at night and fever in the day. Slowly, inevitably, energy and life withered from her youthful body.

It crushed Johnny to watch this happening to his sister. And all the while in his heart he felt a massive resolve growing. *There was no way he would allow HIS family — if he ever had one — ever to go through this sort of hell. If God's heaven made it blessed to be meek and poor and broken, so's the best you could do was sit around the parsonage kitchen table and gossip about those who HAVE and count the stars in your crown for having NOT, then he wanted none of it. No way in hell or heaven could he accept that as the Will of God! Give HIM the chance and the world was going to meet Johnny Hail — living the abundant life Jesus spoke about — loving his family with his active presence. Not being so dirt poor in some parish that the best you could do was to cop-out with something about God's Will. Forget it, Lord! HE was going to love and live and his way that took wealth, not poverty.* And he had a gut feeling that success, not failure, was closer to God's Will and so was wealth.

❖   ❖   ❖

As the weeks raced on a new Johnny began to emerge at Beavercreek High. He never had had trouble in the classroom absorbing new material. Now he began to shine as a student who could score high grades and never have to study after school. He was a classroom achiever, blessed with a near photographic memory. It was a source of annoyance to other kids to see the freewheeling, fun-loving Johnny head for home, taking no books along. His Model-A Ford was always loaded with the ever-present tagalongs. People just liked to be around Johnny-of-the-ready-wit-and-the-funny-stories, the-shared-buck-whenever-he-had-one, and the-constant-eye-for-a-way-to-challenge-authority, which he seemed expert at finding.

There were those in the family who saw in the impulses and the compulsions of this dynamic teenager signs of hope that a truly unique and gifted leader was emerging. Others in the same family, living on the same street, watching the same actions, avowed there was more trouble for Beavercreek's Off-Limits pool hall from this youthful Pied Piper than from the older crowd of ne'erdowells who always hung around it. Some prophesied Johnny was a cinch to be the family black sheep, picking up the title from the antics of older brother Norman, who had claimed the title, then put it down to go straight. Don was taking bets this kid was not about to graduate from high school. Even Johnny himself wasn't giving odds on that likelihood.

"So, why are you so attracted to John?" asked Edith Cannon of her son, shortly before her untimely death. "I love him myself, but he's *always* getting you into this kind of trouble!"

"Wasn't him! It was me who did it." Charley twisted uneasily on the stool in the kitchen and sipped the welcome glass of root beer his mother had poured for him. He shifted the tender cheeks of his buttocks, raw from the latest heavy hiding received from his father, and stared at the chunk of ice in his drink. "I love him, too, Mom. He's like my brother 'stead o' yours, an...an...an' he didn't make me go into the pool hall. We both done it."

"But, Charles, you were forbidden to go into that awful place. A very tough crowd hangs out around there. It's not safe!"

"We were jus' funnin', Mom. It's only a game and it don't cost us nothin', 'cause we always win."

"You mean you actually gamble for money?"

"Not with no money. It ain't gamblin'. We jus' got a system. We always win." His mother's sudden silence let him know that trouble was approaching and an instant later his father strode into the kitchen and stared in annoyance at the root beer.

"I punish him for wrong and you pat him on the head for it, huh?" Edith kept her silence.

And so did Charley. He respected the hard week's work and the long miles his dad put on the truck. Coming home to hear from one of the cluster of Hails living down the street that his son and Johnny were seen hustling the regulars at the pool hall, had to have been a jolt. *But did he have to lay the whip on his tail so hard?...without allowing an explanation?*

He sighed in resignation. *What was to explain?* He and Johnny had a great system with pool that couldn't lose and it was big adventure to beat older guys at their own game. It was all in playing "keep away," placing themselves one-two in the shooting order and the game was theirs. And if it was Johnny's idea to go put the hit on the pool hall, it was Charley who could've said, "No!" if the family stand against billiard parlors had really rubbed in. Truth was, as Charley knew, he just liked the way Johnny was. Let some authority figures say, "Don't!" and Johnny, likely as not, was the first one to challenge the prohibition. He had the guts to do what Charley *wanted* to do.

Like down at the school running track the week before. That time Charley thanked his lucky stars he was just spectator to the caper, even though it probably got him psyched to tag along with Johnny into the pool hall and punishment. That reminded him... *Wonder if Johnny being in the pool hall had been reported yet to Don and Marge?... There was one guaranteed switching, big as he was, if Don ever heard...Good luck, Johnny,* he thought. After that school track fling, this pool hall bit should *really* keep him on a leash!

The word had spread through the halls of Beavercreek High like wildfire. Johnny Hail is going to throw a fling-around after school. Charley wandered down to the athletic field to watch the action. Fling-around was just about what it was, too. The antique classic Model-A was jammed with classmates hanging on inside and out. All over the running boards and the spare tire and even sprawled across the hood of the car. Crazy bunch and wild and every one of them there because Johnny Hail had this neat idea: Let's play Suicide Ride! Was there anything they wouldn't do, if Johnny suggested it? Round and round the fifth-of-a-mile track with total laboratory disregard for life and limb, they tested the theory of centrifugal force. Kids flying off running board and hood the faster Johnny drove, tumbling happily into the grass. Why it took a responsible adult so long to get there, Charley couldn't figure out. Suddenly, roaring in from the opposite end of the field came Don Morgan, yelling furiously and blazing mad in a new Kaiser-Frazer. The party was over fast.

Sure, it was crazy to the grown-up world. But for the youthful Piper of Beavercreek, it was something new and interesting to try. Call it terminal curiosity.

• • •

Grounded from that incident for two weeks, he had escaped report for the pool hall caper. With Charley he was upstairs in the basketball court in Don's big barn. "Okay, hot shot!" he praised as Charley whistled one through the hoop from thirty feet out. He took the ball and tossed it to kindergartener Freddy. "Here, kid...practice! Maybe you'll get t' be as big a show-off as Charley-baby when ya grow up."

He flopped onto the patch of hay left in the mow that served as spectator row. "Man, I'm shot down! Listen, Charley, c'mon over here and we'll coach Freddy while I tell you 'bout this neat deal Don's got cookin'. I mean, it's the greatest! Babes an' a blimp an' a whole bunch o' stuff. We're gonna set this town on fire! Y'ever hear of a blimpburger?"

"Heck no. What's that?" Johnny was in his element when he was breaking the word of a new caper to pal Charley. There was something enviable about the solidness of Charley Cannon. He was the kind of a guy you could always count on when you were in a jam. And he was the kind of friend who fed Johnny's impulse-to-madness. He'd always be there at his elbow, watching and urging the madness on, as long as the party didn't go to insanity where the odds on physical harm coming to someone were too large, like that recent fling around the school track.

Charley had watched from the track edge and loved the

madness of Johnny. But him be aboard, too? No way! It went against the grain of Charley's built-in need to organize and test any big risk first. Charley often thought it probably was from his reaction to becoming a father-to-three before his time, though he envied Johnny's daring. Whatever else Johnny had of many great qualities, Charley loved the way he always swung at life. He was never cheated on a swing in baseball or whatever. Pitch him the ball and he attacked it like it was his last shot. Miss a lot? Sure. But when Johnny's bat met the ball, it was surefire a home run.

And, given a fairly safe madcap adventure, like the theater escapade a few years earlier, Charley quickly grabbed the daring that Johnny radiated when he challenged, "Let's go to the movies." That one was on another of Charley's summer visits to the parsonage, then in Moundsville, West Virginia.

You need to feel the weight of the prohibition from Dad Hail and Noah Cannon about the movie theater, to pick up the risks involved. Hollywood had damned more children to perdition than sucking thumbs had damned them to looking like Eleanor Roosevelt, said C. B. (As an unforgettable touch of C. B. Hail humor, the dyed-in-the-wool Republican, ever looking for a point to assault FDR, found it in the picture of the President's wife. With no regard for Christian charity, he hung the smiling Eleanor in each of their parsonages as a warning to his children that if they sucked their thumb, they could count on prominent teeth like Roosevelt's wife.)

But on the movies, the preacher was even more vocal. So it was sheer, forbidden adventure when Johnny strode to the ticket window, unafraid and able to convince the most critical observer that he, Johnny Hail, was an inveterate moviegoer. It was his first one, too, and it was too good to leave after the first showing of Roy Acuff in Night Train to Memphis, so the wild pair stayed on for the second showing. To Charley it had all the thrill of a declaration of independence as he kept watching around for someone to recognize him the dark. To Johnny, it was just another day.

And now here in the converted loft, Johnny regaled his audience of two with word of a great new restaurant about to open its doors to the benighted citizens of Beavercreek and Knollwood and just all of Dayton.

First, he oriented Charley to the product. It was the answer to the prayers of all the world who read Popeye in the daily comic strip. The cartoonist never did say what was in the favorite burger of Wimpy, one of the characters. Just called it a blimpburger. But Don Morgan had it figured out. He was going to introduce this fabulous burger to Ohio and to all the world in a way they wouldn't forget.

Scouting the best location, he found an available hilltop owned by his father, just outside Beavercreek. He also found a used car sales office, saltbox size, and currently unused. He made a deal to buy and haul the office to the hill. Presto! A restaurant was born.

Then he found a blimp left over from the Battle of Britain, brought back by a returned vet and stuffed away in a barn, together with a winch and hundreds of feet of chain. $180 worth of helium filled the 30-foot balloon. Huge letters on the grey canvas spelled out BLIMP. The restaurant was practically in business.

The blimpburger already had been invented. They started with ground beef, added chopped eggs, chopped lettuce, pickles, tomato and things uncommon to the plain garden variety hamburgers of 1946. So much topping crowned this gift from the gods that they decided on a radical departure and chose to skip the "lid" and serve blimpburgers open-faced.

"It's jus' the beginning, Charley-baby...Here, kid, go!" He tossed the basketball again to an impatient Freddy standing spreadlegged before the best shot on Beavercreek High varsity. "Gotta talk man-talk to Charley here."

"Please, Charley, c'mon an' play." Now it was Charley's younger brother John, who also had come into the loft.

Charley swiped at a leg and dumped the youngster to his backside. "Sit, Buckshot! C'mon, let's you'n me listen t' man-talk." He turned back to Johnny. "I call 'im Buckshot cause he's too little t' be a Cannon... That's a joke, y'know! Sounds like a lousy hamburger to me, if you really wanna know."

"Yeah, but the best part is the babes. You believe this? Don's gonna have carhops!"

Charley's eyes widened appreciatively. "Ya mean them girls prancin' 'round in sassy shorts and takin' burger orders?"

"No shorts. Slacks. You know Don! But ya got the rest right...only th' best lookin' girls in town. So, let's you'n me go help him move that ole building and get us a good job at the Blimp. Beats preppin' cars. Money, Charley, money!"

"I'm ready," agreed Charley.

"Wish I could get that Naomi to be a carhop. You know, I gotta have the plague with her. I tried to get her to be one of 'em and she said it was the same as datin' me. No way will she. Not till I 'grow-up-and-start-acting-like-a-responsible-adult.' I mean, she kills me!"

Charley commiserated with him, pointing out that Naomi had probably seen those girls he liked to be seen out with. They were the best lookers around and they had hellacious reputations. He rubbed it in that she was probably up on everything Johnny did or tried to do on a date.

"Whyn't you go play with Freddy," growled Johnny, sinking lower into the hay to end the conversation and turning his thoughts to ways to get Don to give him a key location at the upcoming opening of the drive-in.

The Blimp opened to the kind of public attention any budding restauranteur should love. To be sure, it captured the attention of the countryside. Attach an old defense balloon to a long chain and send it up into the night skies above rural Ohio, then aim a searchlight at it and what can you expect? Especially when you tell the world that a new delicacy called a blimpburger is in the making at the source of the light.

Only in rural America! Cars flocked from every direction, following the light with all the devotion of the Wise Men for the Star over Bethlehem. But this was a blimp over Beavercreek and it made the sheriff mad as hops. It gave the controller in the military airfield five miles North, near cardiac arrest to have that airborne obstacle in his traffic pattern. He gave the sheriff even more ammunition to use in ordering down the wonderful gimmick. With Morgan tenacity, Don hollered, "Restraint of trade!"

Meanwhile, Johnny Hail, loving every minute of Don's scrap with the authorities, worked feverishly at his role as blimpburger chief chef. Beside him Charley pumped away at the handle of the ice cream churn. Outside, cute carhops darted from car to car, reassuring waiting customers their burgers were coming and explaining to irate farmers that the blimpburger was too good to hide under a lid, hence only half a bun. The girls reported that half the customers demanded a lid or their money back. (Ray Crock of McDonald's fame would have loved every bit of the fabulous opportunity.)

And right at the height of second night chaos, the cry went up outside — "The blimp...the blimp! Where'd it go? Hey! Don, it's gone!"

Minutes later Wright-Patterson Airfield, a key center in our nation's defense, shut down from the threat of an unmanned balloon endangering aircraft in night flight around Dayton. National press coverage descended on the scene and when it was discovered that the chain had been cut deliberately, rumors of mischief and worse began to fly. Two logical contenders for possible accusation had the perfect alibis: they were highly visible in the kitchen. Another Hail in the neighborhood, whose exploits rivalled Johnny's, pleads innocence to this day.

If the blimp did any one thing, it opened the door for Johnny to demonstrate his quality of leadership. He got off to a rotten start! The quality was sorely tested within weeks. In charge of the grill and chief of burger production, Johnny brought his friends and followers into the kitchen and the carhop scene. All went so well at first that Don was impressed enough to leave this kid in full charge while he turned his attention back to the car dealership. With the Kaiser-Frazer firm in trouble, it needed his attention.

Then the rumor drifted in: Johnny and his team were doing more partying than burger production. With stealth worthy of a CIA agent, Don climbed quietly to the upper branches of a nearby tree and spent an evening watching everything. Johnny was learning a routine of production to free up his pressure and increase his fun. So was Charley. But it was the fun mood they were creating that stripped the Blimp of any organization as carhops and kitchen help headed out on fast rides in the moonlight or repeated walks down a path to the field.

"You're all fired!" An irate Morgan, fixed his glare on Johnny as he walked into the kitchen and grabbed him by the collar. "I been watchin' everything all night from that tree 'cross the way! Sittin' up there on a branch the whole time! Come back t'morrow for your pay. But I don't want none o' you around here no more!...And where do you think you're goin'?" he demanded as Johnny broke free and steered his current girl toward the door.

"She's gotta get home," he replied. "I'll take her in my car."

"Your car? Who says *your* car? Gimme the keys! I'll do the drivin'!"

For a long, silent minute Johnny and Don stood nose-to-nose, waiting for the other to swing first. It was the ultimate humiliation to Johnny in front of the girl. It was a flat dare from Don, who blamed all that he had watched happening on something more than inexperience in Johnny.

He was wrong. Credit his willingness to admit that the next day when he rehired Johnny and put him back in charge of the Blimp operations.

Call it a truce or call it a part of the learning curve for both about each other. Whatever, something helped a creative seventeen-year-old understand more about the world of people management in the fleeting episode of that summer at the blimp. It also helped a skeptical twenty-five-year-old veteran to appreciate the curious directness and honesty of Johnny Hail. He would not back off or run when the going was rough or when his ego was assaulted. He stayed and toughed it out.

When Edith's illness finally took her, Mary Jo came to the Morgan home and Johnny moved to another home in the family in Beavercreek — his sister Edna's. But his years with Marge and Don had planted something in the pair that had grabbed them and they missed his presence in the house instantly. There was a joie-de-vivre about him and a delight he took in every day as a special gift for him to use to the hilt.

The high school years were ending. He was a cinch not to graduate, if he had problems with a single course of study. Once again it was his irrepressible sense of humor that turned his status as highest grade student in the class to abject failure. The teacher was a heavyweight of gargantuan proportions, "like four ax handles broad," and inescapably the object of a lot of classroom humor. She lumbered by our hero on a morning when the only boy in the class should have known better than to say it, but whispered anyway, "She looks better comin' than goin'!"

If she was heavy of weight, she was not hard of hearing and within the hour Johnny was before the disciplinary principal, who happened to be the teacher's father-in-law. "That does it for any chance for you to graduate from this high school!" smirked the principal. "You have just flunked the course and you needed those credits." Obviously he hoped Johnny would stumble broken-hearted from his office.

"But look, sir, I've had straight A's for the last three months!"

"And you had a big mouth this morning. That's all! No more discussion!"

• • •

Twenty-four hours later in typical commitment to the day at hand, he was auditioning for a role in the Senior play, Don't Take My Penny. With him in the selected cast was Naomi Scowden. No question that she had graduated from little girl stage in her last year of school.

"Are you going to graduate, Johnny?" she asked after dress rehearsal.

"You kiddin'? Course I'm gonna graduate."

"I'm glad. Someone was saying something that scared me for you...I'm sorry about your sister."

"Yeah, well, maybe it's better. She was sick for a lotta years."

Naomi's graduation, 1948

Somewhere, somehow in the end of the year tally, whether motivated by mercy or fair play, the faculty put together credits from gym and Phys. Ed and concluded that to deny this student graduation, would be unfair. And so Johnny was graduated from Beavercreek High.

❖ ❖ ❖

"So, watcha gonna do, Chuck?" He laid the accent on the name and crinkled his nose disdainfully at the request from his buddy that he drop the 'Charley.'

"Wide open, Johnny. Been thinkin' 'bout the Marines. You know there's a big war cookin' up in Korea."

"You wanna be a Marine in that dumb scene? Man, you'll get your ass shot off for nothin'!"

"Not likely, but I'm not needed here anymore."

"Listen, man, let's you'n me go check out Nashville. David's got himself a hot dog stand or somethin' over there. He owes me one. I got him through kindergarten. We could work for him and maybe look at bein' college boys, now that I'm an honest-to-God high school graduate."

"How do we get there? You got any money?"

"We got thumbs, man! Let's go look 'er over."

Typical Johnny Hail, thought Charley. The heck with sending off for college catalogues or talking to David to be sure he could afford two helpers. Go see and maybe try it on for size or walk away, if it's a lousy idea. No way to go but try it and heck, it's only a four hundred mile hitchhike. Charley knew he could change his name to a more grown-up "Chuck" and put on that what-the-hell beautiful Marine uniform and he'd still himself go cautiously and weigh all the risks before getting involved. Ohhh, to be like Johnny and chance it sometime! "Okay, I'm with you. So how much money you got?"

"Johnny emptied his pockets. "Two dollars and thirty-nine cents," he reported gleefully. "So what're we waitin' for?"

"Yeah, sure." Charley could already feel the hunger pangs. "Okay, let's go. We're loaded."

Johnny's graduation, 1948

Chapter Three

They really hadn't decided whether to be college students or short order cooks at David's College Grille, or just what to do when they started hitchhiking from Ohio to Tennessee that hot summer day. The trip was a long one and traffic was light, but they were doing okay on getting lifts. One thing for sure, they had reached a turning point back home and were happy to be going — even with short, local rides from town to town. They were men now. Young adult males. And there was a war nearing in Korea. Though many made light of the situation, the military option was back again.

Charley's mother was dead and the three young ones he had cared for were scattered. He worried about them, but their future was out of his hands. Mary Jo, at 13, was with Don and Marge, and his brothers, John, 11, and Harold, 9, were with a family named Shultz in Indiana, who even intended to change their names. The boys hated it there, he knew, and both had already run away more than once. It was a time for new beginnings though and both Johnny and he felt pressure to get a college education. High grade students and good athletes, they were a cinch to do well, especially at a small college.

The church's denominational college in Nashville made a lot of sense, with David there running a little lunch stand, as well as going to school. At least it made sense to a lot of oldsters in the family who knew a college opportunity was probably seized now or never for these two young men of such promise. So, with nothing to lose and a need for a fresh start, they went South.

As they stood on the corner of Lester and Hart, watching students go by and studying the sign across the street — TREVECCA NAZARENE COLLEGE — both Johnny and Charley felt the sedateness nestled around them on eighty acres of the city. Old stone and brick classroom buildings and library and dormitories created an environment neither was ready for. Higher education looked far out of it, very ivy tower and pristine pure. *But there was a gym, so maybe there was hope,* Johnny thought.

Fulfilling a promise made back in Ohio, they crossed the campus and shuffled into the Admissions Office. There was an instant change of status.

"Why, you're another of Brother Hail's sons, John!... and you're a grandson, aren't you, Charles? Welcome to both of you! Welcome to Trevecca!"

Any family of a Nazarene pastor had celebrity status and the boys were given the grand tour, climaxing with a stop in the Office of the President. Heavy red draperies hung behind a massive reception desk and the large, imposing photos of sober-faced men in academic robes hanging on either side of the room gave the impression of dignity and wisdom.

"This will probably be the only time you visit Dr. Mackey's office during your matriculation," intoned their deep-voiced faculty guide as they awaited audience with the school's head.

"Uh...we're not sure we're stayin'," replied Johnny. "We really jus' came by to see David and maybe work for him awhile till we make up our minds." He was ready to leave then and there and knew Charley would be right behind him.

"Well, young man, you better realize the only people who get ahead in today's world are college educated." Mercifully, at that instant, the President of Trevecca was ready to see them.

It was a short visit.

It did little to help either boy make up his mind. Matriculation was a word they could neither spell nor understand. And any pompous ass declaring that only college people could make it in today's world had just waved a red flag in front of the two. Maybe it was the lure of fun at

David's on-campus grille, more than the attraction of a college degree, that kept them there even one night. David promised them work after their almost-illustrious careers in another family restaurant. Whatever the motivation, once on campus, without dedication to becoming a student again for the sake of just being a student, Johnny knew he was in trouble.

Five short weeks later a violent intramural football game gave both Charley and him the escape they wanted and with honor. It was followed by a command visit back to Dr. Mackey's office. The pair had been defensive backs in the game and a long pass was thrown to an opposing player sandwiched between them. They ate him for lunch, Johnny hitting high and Charley low with a sharp one-two. The player suffered a concussion. The next day they were summoned to the inner sanctum where cries of "Foul!" had reached all the way to the President.

"Boys, let's face it. You aren't really interested in college, are you?" The speaker didn't wait for an answer. "Already numerous escapades are credited to you that Trevecca won't tolerate. Not the least of them took place yesterday on the playing field..."

"Sir! We didn't mean no harm to that boy!" interrupted a furious Johnny Hail. "We both jus' tackled him at the same time. We didn't see each other comin'."

"It's the truth!" echoed Charley.

"No matter. It has caused quite a furor. We have taken the matter under consideration with the faculty and decided that in the best interests of all, you should postpone your college education here. Maybe later...Or, maybe someplace else. After all, you haven't really begun attending classes yet, have you?"

• • •

"So watcha gonna do now, Johnny?" asked Charley as they measured the future over cokes at the grille.

"Tell you what *I'm* gonna do." Johnny grinned that irrrepressible grin. "I'm gonna pack my bag and head for the Air Force. They're gonna draft me anyhow and I don't wanta be in any Army. I'm gonna enlist and go find me a war. Why don't we both go do it?"

"Not the Air Force. But we been thinkin' the same way. I'm gonna join the Marines. Wow, I've always wanted t'be a Marine! That's number one for me... Comin' back home in a Marine Corps uniform...everybody sayin', 'Boy, look at him!' "

It had to be Naomi. He couldn't get her off his mind. Through all the months of basic infantry training he'd had time to think. This war in Korea was a different war without neat lines of the front drawn. Everyone learned to be a combat foot soldier first, because the gooks from North Korea were everywhere South of the 38th Parallel. So it was back to basics for every G.I. — Air Force or whatever — to learn one-on-one survival and to do a lot of basic thinking.

And here in Wichita Falls, Texas, he felt the full impact of his feeling for Naomi. He could see her perched on the empty coke cases in her dad's gas station or always on the edge of the group anywhere, watching, laughing. He could see her across the aisle in the classrooms and, worse the luck, with the alphabetical seating, he didn't get to see her nearly enough with H's forward of S's. But he saw her now in his mind's eye. *Some romance!* Oh, he had kissed her once. He'd never forget that stage kiss in their Senior play with everyone around snickering. *Some romance, for sure!* Not a single date with her in all that time.

Now at least a thousand miles separated him from this girl who had suddenly become as important to him as living. It seemed he hadn't a prayer of having her attention now either. He sat down to write her again, as he had done before and before and before that. She *had* to know from all his letters that he'd grown up by now!

"Hail!" The Mail Call sergeant pressed a letter to his nose and whistled. "Ask her if she's got a sister who uses that perfume, Hail!"

He was on his bunk devouring Naomi's response. Suddenly the world around him began to move, slowly, concentric circles widening and growing wider till all at once an Air Force corporal named John Hail was off the bunk, flying into a wild blue yonder hysteria of skies with horizons unlimited because Naomi Scowden had just written her love for him for the very first time. Yes...Yes...YES! She did love him. YAHOO!! The Hail howl richocheted from barrack's wall to barracks wall. *Naomi Scowden loved Johnny Hail!*

'But what can we do about it?' the letter ended.

The certainty was that once his training at Sheppard Air Field was done, he would go overseas. And everywhere, especially toward the Orient, war clouds were gathering just as heavily as they had before Pearl Harbor. A sneak attack from someone seemed imminent. How could our country be on the edge of war all over again? And this time with Russia or one of its Communist satellites? We had been allies so recently...But there it was and who so newly in uniform could make plans?

Months passed before Naomi had a Christmas visitor. On leave from his base, Johnny was in Beavercreek with a single purpose. The question came as no surprise. He'd written it in letter after letter. "So, will you marry me?" He held her left hand, with his right index finger and thumb nervously balancing the engagement ring.

"Yes, I will. I love you, Johnny."

"Want me to ask your dad if it's okay?"

She giggled. "He might say no. You know these wartime romances. I mean, what if there *is* another war? You said yourself you're going to go overseas." She suddenly got quiet and her eyes moistened. "I'm serious now and you're about to crack up! Now stop it! You know he might insist we wait till you come home and, honey, I just can't."

Johnny seated the ring on her finger and nodded agreement. "Let's tell him later. I'm due for another two weeks' leave in June. So why don't we plan kinda private like that we'll get married then at the base chapel back at Sheppard. Okay with you?"

"I love it." She turned the diamond to the light and glowed happily. "I'll never be able to wait."

• • •

It was New Year's Eve at Norman Hail's home. The families and friends of Naomi and Johnny cheered the news of their engagement. Norm shook his head in mock disappointment as he clapped an arm across his kid brother's shoulder. "Sure happy for you, Johnny. She's a wonderful girl, but what's the Hail family goin' to do with the last of its black sheep going straight? First me. Now you."

A little black Ford with Ohio plates turned off Highway 171 and headed a few miles North to Sheppard Air Base. Naomi was one month earlier than planned, but the truth was neither of them had been able to wait until June.

When she had given the news to her father about her plans, Howard raised the questions she knew he would. Less than an hour from Johnny now, she reviewed a last time the objections he had raised and smiled contentedly at the love she felt behind them.

"Listen, honey, you know I want what's right for you, right?" He hurried on at her nod. "To tell you the truth, I really wish you'd wait till Johnny's discharged and gets his feet planted on the ground again. I mean, right now he's a fly-boy and you know how he used to be in school — had more dates than any other guy — you said that yourself. He's foot-loose now and about to go overseas for at least a year or two. And everything is right on the brink of a big knock-down-drag-out over there. Can't you wait? If your mother was living, I'm sure she'd ask the same thing."

She shook her head solemnly. "We've thought about that, Daddy. We really have. Here's the way Johnny looks at it…and, well, I do, too. He says, 'You live for today. Can't do anything about yesterday and nothing about tomorrow. Do it today.'"

"But, there *is* a tomorrow and what's he shown he can do yet? He was kind of a hell raiser in school. And he's done nothing but pump gas for me and fool around the shop over at Morgan's. Don't misunderstand. I like Johnny. He sure is a sharp kid, but what's he shown us? Didn't he go down Tennessee way to start college? What happened to that?"

"College wasn't for Johnny. Now, Daddy, you have to trust us. We've known each other three years and I know he's going to take care of me and make you very proud."

Directly before her, Naomi saw the impressive main gate of the base. It looked so huge. So intimidating. And inside there was a guy in an Air Force uniform who must be as important as all the other soldiers around as she pulled to a stop before the upturned palm of the M.P.

"Someone expecting you, miss?" The smiling PFC held her door and steered her toward the Visitor's Desk.

"Yes, sir. Corporal John W. Hail at the 3672nd Tactical Support Wing is. We're getting married," she added proudly.

"You are *what?* Did you say you are a-gonna marry a corporal from the Three-Six-Seven-Two? Miss, 'scuse me. I've gotta see your driver's license t'be sure you of age!"

"Cut it, Olsen! Give Miss Scowden her pass."

"Yessir! Jus' funnin', sir."

"Well, knock it off."

Olsen reached across the counter to clip the Visitor's Pass to Naomi's blouse and caught his C.O.'s glance. "Here, m'am. Be sure to wear this at all times. You go thattaway t'get to the 3672nd. Eleven blocks down, you take you a right turn all the way t'the flight line. You'll see this line of hangars and they's a Nissen hut right by the road. Listen, it's kind o' complicated... Sir, request permission to show the visitor to the 3672nd."

Johnny in the Air Force

"She can find it, Olsen! Miss, did you understand those directions?"

"Yes, I think I did." She followed PFC Olsen to her car and smiled her appreciation as she drove away from his airy salute.

Johnny and Naomi after wedding

He followed her departure wistfully... *The petite blonde with the very pretty and the vulnerable femininity needed protection in a jungle like Sheppard. Hail sure knew how to pick a woman! And he sure looked after the woman he picked...* The guy had been by the guard gate three times already in twenty-four hours, checking every shift at the gate to make sure they knew car make, license number and appearance of the lone young lady in the black Ford from Ohio... "She's comin' to marry me, so treat her right," he'd alerted all of them.

And suddenly Naomi was in his arms.

They walked together to the suntan frame chapel and stood before the bespectacled chaplain wearing the pinks and greens with the crosses on his lapels. It was simple and brief and it was everything the two of them needed. Another couple stood up with them and a crowd of his buddies from Wings were there with a raucous, shouting welcome to greet husband and wife as they walked down the steps of the chapel into the bright Texas sun and the first day of their lives as one.

"Ever been to Oklahoma?" he asked as they drove through the gate in her Ford and headed North.

"I think so. Didn't I just cross through it? I was too excited to know where I was."

"Well, we're goin' back right now. Wait'll you see where. One o' the guys told me about it. It's called Turner Falls and it's only a couple hours from here. 'Sposed t'be real neat."

"Do we need reservations?"

"Never fear. Hail's here. Whattaya mean? 'Course we need reservations! You know me. I'm the detail man. Plan it. Nothin' by accident."

"I thought you lived for today, or something like that?" she teased.

"It's today, ain't it?"

• • •

And it was. In two weeks it would be separation time with Johnny going across the ocean and Naomi back to Ohio. But at this moment the two had brought private longing and what seemed the impossible dream into focus and reality and the day was theirs.

❖ ❖ ❖

The North Koreans poured across the 38th Parallel the day Corporal John Hail arrived at the staging depot in Japan. Within hours the First Cavalry Division was being shoved back and still further back toward the water's edge in South Korea. All at once that very day it was a full blown war. A member of the 49th Fighter Bomber Wing, Johnny was into a war, the likes of which no one had ever seen before. No clear lines of enemy as Ezekiel Stone had at Gettysburg...or his descendents in Europe in World War II. Here in Korea the enemy was everywhere. It was a war loaded with frustration for Americans used to winning their wars. They could go so far and that seemed to be an end to looking for victory.

It filled one Johnny Hail with more frustration than he had ever known before. His mindset was fixed on winning. There was no almost-winning. You won! He played baseball... he studied tech manuals...he worked with one goal: Win at what you're doing. In Korea, the leaders of his America seemed set on something much less. And so many of them were little more than martinets, commissioned to order their soldiers into ridiculous situations — sometimes up a Hamburger Hill where the North Korean could make ground beef out of thousands of them...other times to the banks of the Yalu River and a chance to really turn the tide to victory... only to call back the assault and fire the general who thought to win.

If Korea had any value for Johnny, it was to teach him about real leadership. Most of what he learned was the power of leading by example and not by simply issuing commands. The 90-day-wonder with his short-term commission to glory and often long-term commitment to issuing orders and demanding a salute to the gold bar on his shoulder, was a special trial to the one-time Hellion of Cabin Creek.

At twenty-one Johnny was a different young man than that boy in a faraway parsonage. Now he was watching intently, choosing for himself the elements he would one day build into leadership. Long-gone was the rebel scrapping with authority. Emerging in him was the already established conviction of ways to lead and to inspire others to want to follow. It didn't come from pulpit invective or parade ground command. The leader had far subtler and more effective tools at his command.

He was missing his bride fiercely one year later when he sat alone on Christmas Day, remembering how she looked as he'd slipped the engagement ring so nervously on her finger. He was out on a lonely perimeter hardstand at an airfield at Taegu, waiting word about a Christmas Day mission. Parked against the nose wheel of the B-29, he wrote the note, seeing her with the Hails 6,000 miles away.

Johnny's pin-up girl

My dearest, darling wife,

I only wish I could deliver this personally, darling, but since that is impossible, I'll only live for the day when we'll never spend another Christmas apart. Let's only hope and pray that day comes in the New Year —

May you have the merriest of Christmases and the happiest of New Years.

> All my love
> All my life,
> Your husband

> JOHNNY

Johnny at Christmas

They weren't to be together the next Christmas either or the Christmas after that. For Naomi, survival was finding a position at Wright-Patterson Air Field and an identification to what her Air Force husband was doing in the months and the miles that separated them. She had excelled in office skills at school and now she was secretary to the commanding general at the base. The best she got from Korea was that it probably was going to be a long, dragged-out war.

· · ·

But finally the great word did come. Her man was coming home to finish his military tour in Texas. Leaving a note on the general's desk to please get her a transfer to Kelly Field, Texas, if there was any way possible, she left for California and reunion. It was Valentine's Day, 1952.

It was never a consideration of the commandant to let his secretary go to the likes of Kelly Field. Immediately on getting her note, he reached for the phone and began the process that ended in Staff Sergeant John Hail being redirected to Wright-Patterson Field, Dayton, Ohio, with Naomi remaining as the general's secretary. For a short while.

Johnny never knew a half-way temptation to remain in the military. He felt the lure of the new age of flying dawning with its incredible speed and its revolution in avionics. And there was an unforgettable test flight at Boeing when he had the opportunity to be a flight observer and to have talk time with Tex Johnson, a go-for-broke-pilot-legend of the Air Force. He listened to the free-wheeling maverick in a regimented life and Johnny knew there at Boeing Field in Seattle that the Air Force had no way to cooperate with his restless aspirations.

Abruptly his military service was ending. When he returned from the temporary duty in Washington State, of course Naomi was waiting for him. As he embraced her in the crowd waiting for all the servicemen pouring from the plane, he suddenly started to laugh.

"Johnny, whatever is so funny?"

"Don't look now, but I think the draft board is finally gonna get me!" He turned her around and smiled that crooked smile. "Remember the old geezer who ran the board for Beavercreek and let it out to the papers that me and Charley and another guy weren't available anywhere to do our duty for the country? Well, there he is in the flesh! C'mon... I wanna go shake his hand."

"Now, don't you dare!" She tugged him furiously and he gave it up.

"Well, anyway, he owes me an apology."

And he did. The old man had raised all kinds of hob trying to find 'that Hail kid and the Cannon kid, too.' He even went so far as to suggest they might be draft dodgers. Nobody at the recruiting stations in Nashville had bothered to tell the two volunteers that they should let their hometown draft board know of their signing in. A year later, with the 49th in a faraway combat zone in the midst of a rough and tumble fight for which he was being paid less than fifty dollars a week, Johnny got a letter forwarded from this man, demanding that he surface and do his duty for America in this war.

So much for duty. He had done it and Naomi tucked his Honorable Discharge, along with pictures of Mustangs, Jeeps and good buddies, into a soon-to-be-forgotten album. He took a final look at the baseball team on which he had played in his squadron's free hours. Great team and they even played on Sunday! Sabbath Blue Laws, Cabin Creek, revivals, teachers and principals who couldn't laugh at themselves or at youth enjoying its few years, were behind him. And it was another beginning.

Beavercreek had given him its very best and her name was Naomi. There a loving family had wrapped him in its arms and hung onto him during the rebellious time and seen in his mischief that it really was as he said — he never got anybody else in trouble intentionally, only himself. That was his hometown. It was Naomi's town. There the Morgans, tuned to the coming population explosion East of Dayton, had platted off a development. On Johnny's return they worked out a time payment program with him for a piece of ground in their planned community and sold him a little pre-fab ranch house with three very compact bedrooms. 'Dinky,' Don called it later, but dinky or not, it was the first home for Naomi and her husband, and a raft of friends from high school days rallied to help them wire and plumb and landscape their pre-fab.

Beavercreek was the place where Johnny had learned that even the lumps in living were part of the learning curve. He promised himself he wouldn't forget them when he and Naomi began their family. That he wanted to do in Beavercreek, Ohio.

David, John, C. B., Norman, Lloyd, and Joe.

Chapter Four

It was still pitch black outside as he drove down familiar Linden Avenue past Cosen's Little Corner Store out into the countryside.

He groped his shirt pocket and felt the nearly-empty pack of Chesterfields and wished the store was open. *Sure, he could live without the cigarettes...and someday he damn well would. It would make Naomi a lot happier if he'd chuck his beer and the coffin nails.* Even though he kept both vices out of their home and even though she never needled him about them, he knew in her heart she wished he would give them up. *How she worried about his welfare! Everything was for Johnny. She did their books. She managed everything around home and never made it feel like she was a bossy wife. Somehow she sensed what was needed and did it. What a girl! How lucky could one man get?*

He still could use a fresh pack! He grunted and pushed the flattened one back into the shirt pocket...*And her thing about smoking and drinking; that didn't come from some Nazarene No-No book. She wasn't even a church member, much less an evangelist for the straight and narrow, though they went to church and Sunday School every Sunday morning. He knew he could bring beer or smoking into their home and never hear a word. It just didn't seem to fit. If she didn't do it, then he didn't want to do it around her.*

It was greying over the horizon to the East and he drove slower now, watching. There it was — the corner involved in the deal between himself and the Morgans.

He'd have to sell Sohio Headquarters on the idea himself and that was already kayboshed with the letter he'd just received.

'Sorry, we don't believe a service station will ever work in that section East of Dayton. There is not sufficient traffic and there is no evidence of any dramatic growth.'

Well, that was just their first response up there in Cleveland. They hadn't heard the last of Johnny Hail. He drove slowly past the vacant corner in the Knollwood section of Beavercreek. "The Knollwood section of Beavercreek" really sounded very suburban and very settled and it was far from that. It was country. But if the Morgans had their way, it would be a community one day soon. For the moment, it was about as country as you could get. *No wonder Sohio had said what they did about little promise. Even the farmhouses were still dark at this hour. But the Blimp had drawn a crowd and that was out in the country, too. All they had done was to put a big searchlight beside it and the crowd came out of the bushes.*

A car approached, dimmed its lights and passed him. An early morning worker hurrying into Dayton, likely for a 7:00 a.m. shift. Then another one and in five minutes half-a-dozen had passed Johnny. *Where'd they buy their gas? Where did the drivers get that second cup of coffee or that first one with a cheery "Hello"? Likely not from their wives, at this hour.*

He swung his car in an excited 180° and headed back to the corner. *Just suppose he'd light up this corner by 6:00 in the morning...REALLY light it up...Make it the friendliest stop anywhere in Ohio...Man! he could put all that sorry second-guessing right where it belonged, back in Sohio Headquarters...*

He parked the car and got out. *Nothing here yet and that was for sure...A beat-up building and some left-over corn stubble in the field and a lot of worn macadam where the secondary intersected Route 35...Have to get that sharpened up...*He stared at the nothingness around him and saw the old building become a station...*Knollwood Sohio Service, it should say, but it would be Johnny Hail's brand of service. He wasn't about to wait for the traffic to build up and make this corner profitable for Sohio. He'd bring the traffic in! He'd light up the corner like a Christmas tree and whether it was night or day, there'd be lots of action on this back acre...*

Two hundred bucks, he reflected. *That's what he had* and at that, it was borrowed capital for his new venture. What he'd saved in Korea went into paying for that pre-fab and for finishing it. *But he was two hundred better off than being broke and he had friends. Man, he didn't realize how many friends he'd made in his two-and-a-half years before service. And Don and Frank; how do you beat a deal like that? They'd finance the land and the service station building and only need a penny a gallon to satisfy them that he was paying off fair and square.*

All he had to do now was to turn Sohio around and there was just one fellow to see who could make it happen. The President of the whole Sohio Oil empire, was *who.*

Hail, you won't get the business going sitting here with cow chips, wishing it would happen. Let's get going! Only a couple of hundred miles from here to Cleveland. I'll buzz Naomi from Columbus.

The President of Sohio Gas studied the slender young man with the flat top hair cut, the tanned features and the eager expression, seated at the corner of his richly-carved, glass-topped walnut desk. How rarely did a mere applicant for the right to sell Sohio Gas ever get through the door to his office? Especially one who already had been denied the privilege of the franchise. But something in this Korea veteran with the easy-going smile and the refreshing confidence that he had something different to discuss with the president, had persuaded his personal secretary to press a good word for Johnny Hail.

"Mr. Hail, you've got to give me some better reason than your excellent military record to risk Sohio's money out there in the Dayton boondocks. Our engineers' report here says if you're real lucky and work very hard, you might be pumping 12,000 gallons every three months. You can hardly live on that."

"You're absolutely right, Mr. Sparr. I've got every bit of respect for your engineers, but they don't know me. And they've also missed one big point." He paused dramatically.

"What's that?" Sparr watched his visitor with intense interest. Here was an enthusiastic man! These vets had been given a sorry war to fight. Some of them kept wearing that disappointment after coming home. Not this one. He had a solid pair of feet on the ground, willing to walk to Cleveland on them, if he had to, to present his conviction. It was a very special attitude.

"Dayton's going East fast, sir. We've got no competition anywhere in that area for six...seven miles. If I can suggest something, Mr. Sparr?" Johnny paused again and Sparr nodded the go-ahead.

"Well, I'll be putting my life savings into this station, so you know I believe in it. Now, if you put any gas you allow me on a prove-it basis, you can watchdog me all the way and if I don't do what I promise, you can kill the deal."

Sparr chuckled. "You're not only asking me to go against my engineers, but also to go against Sohio law and give you your gas on contingency? Is that what you're saying?"

Johnny's confident nod matched his wide-eyed, unblinking grin and Mr. Sparr returned the smile. "Be darned if I don't think you just might do it! You got yourself a deal, young man." The meaty hand stretched across the desk and as Johnny grabbed it, he knew he had turned a key corner. "Don't forget. You've got to do better than 12,000 gallons in three months to keep my support."

Within his first year back in Beavercreek he opened that Knollwood service station and it was an incredible success from its start.

One of his earliest customers, Don Herzog, pulled in for gas, sporty in his green convertible Chevy with its top down. "I'm glad you're here," he told the attendant who trotted to his car. "I've just now moved to Beavercreek and Sohio gas is my favorite, so I'll be a regular." The thing that caught his eye was the mood around the place. The customer was the only reason for there being a gas station, but most stations got pretty complacent about the source of their business. Not at Knollwood Sohio. As he watched the half-dozen eager youngsters at the pumps, he knew he was seeing something different than any station he'd known.

"You mind if I vacuum your carpet, sir?" A hand reached toward Herzog. "I'm Johnny Hail. Billy here tells me green

Service station ad

super Chevys puke on anything but Sohio."

"Mine does," grinned Don. It was the owner himself, hose in hand, smiling back at the newcomer. Trying to make an impression, thought Don. We'll see in a couple of months how they change.

He was wrong. The mood around the place just got better and better and he didn't even mind having to wait in line to get to the pumps. The whole place just gave him a lift.

"Hail, what are you doing down there?" It was Mr. Sparr himself. "You've been at it six months and we're sending 12,000 gallons to you every day! You giving away bootleg or something that's going to embarrass Sohio?"

Johnny laughed. "Just good service, sir. By the way, thanks for those engineers who showed up to measure us for the new tanks. Are they...uh, the guys who thought we'd sell about 12,000 gallons in 3 months?"

"The very ones," laughed Mr. Sparr. "Listen, Johnny, I'd like to have you share some of your ideas on a regular basis. Would you be one of the members on the Sohio Dealer Accounts Committee?"

"Be honored, sir."

It was the start of an incredible success story for Sohio and for Johnny Hail. Within three years the questionable little countryside gas station was doing more business than any other Sohio station in Ohio. Soon it was bettering all stations East of the Mississippi.

Before he was 22, Johnny was elected President of the Dealer Accounts Committee. "If he's short at age, he's sure long on service station experience," praised Sparr as Johnny took the office. That day the Sohio President gave the word that whenever Johnny called in, his call was priority. "This fellow is a marketing genius," he enthused, reviewing the latest antics in Knollwood on 5835 Linden Avenue.

It wasn't really a holiday — just the station's first anniversary and Johnny's way to celebrate was to make it a giveaway day to benefit the Lions Club Eye Fund. Lions and

Service station celebration

53

celebrants from the Dayton television station ran the service station from dawn till the usual 10 o'clock close and not for just a share of the profits. "It's all yours," Johnny told the fifty club members who had been pumping gas and directing traffic, expecting a piece of the profit. It was typically Johnny Hail. A floodtide of people had rolled in all day long, some even coming with not yet empty tanks, just to visit and leave a cash donation to Lions.

Johnny at work in service station

It was not a different day in the life of Knollwood Sohio. So busy were the pumps and filled were the bays that two off-duty policemen were hired to direct the traffic in and out of the driveways at peak hours. Every day the popularity grew for this out-of-the-way station six miles East of Dayton. The biggest giveaway daily was superior service and lots of honest friendliness. And Johnny had hired his sister, Lois Ann, to help Naomi with the records and to call customers in advance to remind them of the times for the regular car servicing. Fresh coffee was always brewing and lots of good-natured humor let the customer feel it was worth the difference to travel to Johnny's, even if it did mean waiting in line.

Lefty McFadden had signed into professional baseball ranks with the Cleveland Indians as a 16-year-old. He was a youngish baseball retiree and when he left a great pitching career a decade later, he returned to Dayton. He watched the atmosphere around Knollwood Sohio with interest. He had seen no one quite like this tireless, innovative young owner and he'd seen many hucksters of imagined and phoney goodwill. It wasn't like that with Johnny. His every move seemed a genuine aim at another's betterment and at making someone else important because of his effort. When a customer drove into the service station, that customer left knowing that for the time he was there, he was Johnny's most important customer. And everyone who worked for Johnny followed his cue. A dozen attendants manned the pumps and they all reflected the atmosphere Johnny believed in. And he wouldn't hire them, no matter how lowly the job, if he wasn't willing to know them personally and to welcome each employee into his home.

It was just as he planned it. A bright spot in the darkness on the road Westward into Dayton. A place where a hand wasn't out for every service rendered. There were even movies-for-free playing in the room behind the office and Freddy Morgan, now a bustling 12-year-old, made the only money earned back there by selling soda pop, since he was too young to legally pump gas.

Outside, parked near the air pump, was the Community Car. You didn't rent the Crosley or sign up in advance for it. You just had a worthy purpose and if you were a citizen of the community, it was yours as a loaner with no questions. Charley Lafino had responded to the crowd that was always moving in and out of the station, deciding it was time a grocery came to Beavercreek, next to here where Johnny Hail ran his business. It was no time at all before Hail and Lafino had teamed up on project after project to keep the three-ring-circus jumping.

Marge and Don Morgan were awed by the phenomenon in the little 4,000 population area of Beavercreek. Johnny, who once they despaired of ever finishing high school, had personally turned a miracle on a back pasture of Ohio. It didn't matter what he was doing when cars rolled in, Johnny got to the pumps on the run, while an attendant pumped the gas. Most often he personally cleaned the windshield and he was forever light-hearted, kidding and being kidded. It said something that the station owner cared enough to wipe your windshield, when he had boys he was paying to do those menial things.

Other gas stations through the Dayton area would declare gas wars. Johnny was always the last to drop his prices. He even charged a penny more to cover the green stamps he gave. He refused to believe you brought the customers to the station because of pennies saved. They were drawn because he gave them something other stations never caught as the magic.

"We ought to expand this whole thing." He was home from just closing out the station day. "We've got one place going right. Let's go for two. We've got an avalanche of competition showing up. I count six stations now in this area since we got going. What do you think?"

Naomi read her husband loud and clear. Boredom was grabbing Johnny. It had to find an outlet. It had been a fast five years and it was now a very profitable business. But the edge was off and she could see it from his restless wakefulness in the wee hours of the morning. She encouraged the second station.

Sohio didn't. It was one rule they wouldn't bend. It was just like his effort to get them to permit him to have a self-service island for customers who wanted to save pennies on the purchase by pumping gas themselves. "Ohio forbids it and will never allow that," he was told very bluntly by the same engineers who years earlier had seen no profit on Linden Road in Knollwood. Even with ready audience to Mr. Sparr whenever he wanted it, as the leader in sales for the company, Johnny could not persuade the committee of engineers that a second Sohio station would work in the East Dayton area with him running it, too.

That was their first mistake — to decide any owner as successful as Johnny should be content to settle back and enjoy his earnings.

There was a second fundamental error being made by the armchair generals in Cleveland who decided when Sohio would expand and when it would stand still. They failed to see that Johnny's motivation never was and never could be money. He had to have the green light to new adventure for the life of Johnny Hail. As the producer of so great a sales volume, with an impeccable record of paying all his debts and on time, this one should never have had his appeals for larger horizons ignored. They were.

And a morning came shortly after the turn-down when Johnny, dead-ended for expansion and new challenge, stood outside the Knollwood Sohio Service, staring at the ancient farmhouse a few properties down Linden.

"Yeah, Johnny, Dad and I just picked the property up for the heck of it. Goes way back, that old farmhouse does."

"Sure can see that. What are you going to do with it?"

"We figure it ought to make a darned nice commercial property, with all the action you're stirring up out at this end o' town. I'll guarantee you someone will want it, once it's fixed up. Maybe an antique dealer. The farmhouse was a stagecoach stop back before the Civil War. They tell me they called 'em weigh stations just like..." His voice drifted off. Johnny wasn't listening but striding away toward the old house. He trailed him silently.

"Okay, Don, I've got a proposition for you. Why not make money on this old heap while you're fixing it up? See, I've decided to open a furniture store and it might as well be here as in Dayton. We'll bring 'em out here for stuff like that."

"Won't work," Don opinioned solemnly. "Take it from a Morgan. You got the gas station to work, but furniture's a whole different ball game. People won't travel five miles to a furniture store out in the country. I know what I'm talking about!"

"I'll make you a deal." Johnny was in full pursuit. "You'll get a percentage of gross sales. Let's fix up the front of this old place. Here's my notion. Tell me how you'd do it better. You've got the know-how. What would you think about running a nice glass display room across the front, maybe three times wider than the first floor...and then put a nice brick second story front on 'er? Now wouldn't that look pretty classy?"

"Yeah...could," acknowledged Don, slowly catching the excitement of a campaign he knew Johnny had long been pre-planning. The sure clue was always that nonchalant, off-handed manner. He never ramrodded his plan. He just made it the other guy's. "What do you suppose you'd call it?" He had no doubt that that, too, was also pre-planned.

"What do you think about Johnny Hail's Home Furnishings?"

"Can't beat it. Let's talk about how you're gonna make money and make it worth our while to put this old heap into a commercial building. We can't do it on any bigger percentage of gas sales. Take too long to get our money back, even if you keep on selling like tomorrow's the last day for car drivin' in Ohio. You got any specific ideas on how you're gonna pay me for this?"

"Some. Let's talk about a percentage of gross on our furniture sales beyond a minimum rent. Say 5%. Got any idea what you'd need?"

Don's brow furrowed. Johnny had him with the offer. He liked a piece of any action. He reached for the best minimum guess. "Okay, how about 5% of gross and, say, $750 a month?"

"Make that $500 and we're on our way." Johnny shook his head in disbelief. "I can't believe I'm offering five percent! I'm a strugglin' family man. Got two kids to feed. I'm gonna ask my counsel about that."

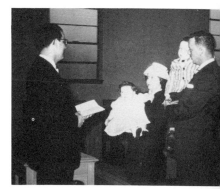

Denise's baptism with Uncle David.

"Counsel? You got a lawyer?"

"Naw. I got better'n a lawyer. You know the guy who walked off your car lot with Ruthie Whistle-winner? Remember Curt? He's a wheel at McGranahan's now and he told me, now that you've got me over a barrel with payments on my home and a penny-an'-a-quarter-a-gallon on gas and now this, I shouldn't go a nickle over five hundred a month, plus one other thing..."

"I don't believe I'm hearin' this!" grumbled Don, wondering now if Johnny himself somehow had maneuvered the Morgans' purchase of the old weigh station property without Dad or himself ever being the wiser. "So, what's the one other thing?"

"No big deal. I was gonna ask, while you're putting my furniture store together next week and you already got your men down here with the tools, how about putting in two more bays in the station? I'll give you another quarter-cent again on every gallon. Got so much demand for lube and oil and repairs now...It'll solidify your investment."

"I'm gettin' outta here!" groaned Morgan. "And, listen, you stay away from that guy Wilson, y'hear? You don't need any more advice!"

"Sure, Don. It's a deal then?"

"Yeah, if Dad says okay."

Naomi had not been instant enthusiasm when Johnny first pounced through the kitchen door of their new Central Avenue home with the news. "Honey, we're entrepreneurs in the furniture business! How about that?"

She looked up from her preoccupation with feeding a Gerber's spattered face. "How would you like to entrepreneur feeding one terrible one-year-old for me? It's one-for-the-mouth and one-for-Mommy-day."

"You betcha, babe." He took the sticky jar of mashed peas and straddled the stool, facing the high chair. "Here, see? Easy as pie." He stuffed the spoonful into Denise's mouth. "She just wants to be treated like an adult."

An explosive gurgle sounded and a wounded cry of surprised fatherhood burst from a thoroughly spattered Johnny Hail. Naomi choked back the giggle and when she finished mopping her husband's face and shirt, said solemnly. "When you two adults are done talking to each other, tell me about the furniture business."

Johnny glared at Denise. "First thing we sell is a high chair with a kid in it." He leaned close to look at his beautiful daughter. "Y'know, both our children look like you and this cute little nose gives me an idea." Spoon in hand, he reached thumb and forefinger to clamp tenderly on the tiny nostrils, then shoved another spoonful of peas through outraged lips.

"It won't work. I've tried that." Naomi shrugged and turned from the inevitable. Denise was now beet-red with fury.

"She's gotta swallow. Ohmigosh!..." The pea barrage took him squarely between the eyes the instant he took his fingers from her nose.

Gary and Denise

"Here! You don't need this after twelve hours at the station." She pushed his shoulder to move away. "Dinner's almost ready. Tell me what we're up to now." She dropped the towel in his lap.

That was Naomi — always ready, thought Johnny as he stood behind her, mopping the latest barrage and sticking his tongue out at Denise as he gave her the love/hate look. "Where's Gary?"

She pointed toward the living room with the spoon. "Watching television with Jeff Herzog. You ought to go listen to him. He's got a football game on with the volume down and he's playing announcer. Honestly, he's something else for three."

Johnny grinned and dropped into the chair out of range of Denise. "I know. He's done it to me. He makes the team he wants to see win, have the players doin' everything right, even when the other side scores.

"Okay, here's the big new deal. And listen hard, 'cause you're the accountant."

Naomi listened hard. She had learned much in the seven swift years of their marriage. She had known he had marketing brilliance ever since she watched him working for her father when they were sophomores in high school. Even then when he was just a pump jockey, he would nonchalantly check the oil and air cleaner and the battery fluids without waiting for the customer to ask. In those two months parts and service sales quadrupled. And when Johnny left, they fell flat.

She had been watching his marketing intuition bring incredible results in his own station, too, and it wasn't because he was a hustler of what the customer didn't need. The genius in her husband was his genuine interest in people. He liked them. He listened hard. He cared about them. And he was honest through and through. It was that simple. When he told them plugs needed replacing, it wasn't that Champion had a special dealer incentive that week; the car had fouled-up plugs. That said it all for Johnny Hail and honesty. From then on, you just multiplied and pretty soon you sold the largest amount of gas of anybody because the customers knew you weren't just a plastic funny man. You were for real.

How could anyone miss seeing that their best man was going to walk away because he couldn't be stifled? She sighed inside, listening to his enthusiasm for the new venture in furniture which she knew she was going to support. By her bookkeeping it was a little too early to try it. And furniture sales was a risky business. She had called a number of furniture stores in the Dayton area in the past week since Johnny had begun to really talk the new business seriously. She wanted background information about how they had to pay for inventory; about floorplanning and what banks thought about furniture stores and customers as credit risks. All very skeptical. Some said it took a far better credit rating for the store owner or the buyer to buy furniture on time than to get a house mortgage. The most unnerving thing she found when she called other stores, was the number of operator responses advising her, "...that number is no longer in service." But as she listened now to Johnny, she made herself remember one thing — her man was different.

"Tell me, dear one," she smiled that special Naomi way, "This isn't what they call the seven-year-itch, is it?"

"The seven year...what? Oh yeah...we have been married seven, haven't we?" He was puzzled for only a second then dropped to the breakfast nook bench. "C'mon, Naomi... be serious. That stuff is guys playin' around and never bein' home. You're my Marilyn, you know that. So how about it? Tell me when you're ready. We don't go if you say no. Okay?"

She knew he meant it. She was his life and lots more than his wife or the mother of their children. He'd home-worked the furniture store project himself and really wanted to go with it, but he'd never, not without her support, and he'd never try to force her to agree.

"Gotta go close the station," he called from the garage. "Back in an hour." She blew a kiss from the kitchen window and in the gatepost light saw his hand wave.

For a time after she had Denise tucked in, she mulled the ledger at the table-desk in their bedroom. *Wonder what Pat would think of the new venture.* The Herzogs, Pat and Don, and the Hails had become very close friends over the last five years. Even though Don and Johnny were such opposites, they enjoyed each other's company in church affairs and even vacationed together every summer. Don was the pattern-maker and very orderly in his lifestyle. But one great passion both men had — their home.

Through all the growth of his station, Johnny never let his first commitment, his family, be crowded out. It was a commitment that began with that "Yes" from Naomi and it surfaced again and again. Like that day they brought their firstborn, Gary, home from the hospital. They circled past the ballpark where Johnny's church team was playing and the cry went up for their missing third baseman to take a turn at bat. "Hit a homer for Gary!" yelled Don and Johnny did exactly that. Nothing in this man, caught in the whirlpool of building his empire, ever got in the way of trying to belt out a homer for his family. Neither Johnny nor Don had become members of the Nazarene Church when Naomi and Pat did, but they usually were there at worship with their families and always ready with time and money for the projects of the congregation.

Boats had become Johnny's passion. The 16-footer with the Scott Atwater engine had to go when a 19-footer with sleeping accommodations for six came to a Dayton Boat Show. By now little Vicki was with them, too, and the Herzogs and the Hails covered most of the waters of the Mississippi and the Great Lakes together.

Maybe a different viewpoint or just a listening ear from Pat might be the best help Naomi could find on this furniture business. She shook the thought from her head and turned out the lamp. This was their personal decision. In the quiet darkness she reflected the years that had passed. *Johnny was always consistent. Before he broached a new idea, he had thought it through thoroughly. Why should she doubt this was a good idea now?...*

"You okay, honey?" She swung in surprise with a startled gasp. She hadn't heard him turn into the garage.

"You surprised me." She was in his arms and she felt secure. "I must have been a million miles away."

"So what were you thinkin' about? My seven-year-itch?"

"I think we should call it Johnny Hail's Home Furnishings."

❖   ❖   ❖

From the beginning, it was obvious that the new enterprise was a welcome addition to the Beavercreek scene. The small school district was beginning to grow and the

Johnny Hail's Home Furnishings

appearance of the second ambitious Hail project was perfectly in keeping with what they had come to expect from a young man who one old-timer called, "The Personality of Beavercreek." It augured well for the growth of the community and everything Johnny touched turned to happiness for everyone. And so should this.

People cited what happened when he opened that gas station against the recommendations of professionals. He not only had made it work, but no less than thirteen stations now were clustered in the same service area. Where Johnny Hail went, people followed.

With his furniture store, Johnny made very *sure* they would come. Building on the lure, "Where Hundreds Save Thousands!", he launched the project. It was open Mondays through Saturdays till 10 p.m. and Sundays from 1 to 6. And with a new sensitivity to the power of advertising the legitimate media way, he let the world of greater Dayton know where the best buys in furniture were. "In the heart of Knollwood, hundreds save thousands!" proclaimed Phil Donahue, a young talk show host just getting an interview program going on a Dayton station. The call to "Shop your furniture needs at the unique store in the building that once was a stage coach stop" was echoed by game show host Gene Barry, and other soon-to-become-nationally-known personalities getting their start out on the road selling time for their station and honing their announcing skills. During Dayton University basketball games, at the breaks of the evening movie-for-TV, everywhere Johnny Hail's Home Furnishings was advertising.

A young man, still wearing the flat top of his military years, was determined to spread his own fortunes beyond the bounds of Knollwood/Beavercreek. The bigger market was an irresistible lure within the year. TV, radio, newspapers had brought in the customers, skyrocketing sales. The same spirit that made his gas station so successful was at work again. People liked Johnny Hail and his store. He was a fun guy, a direct guy who stood behind what he sold. He clowned with spontaneous cool, doing his own live television commercials, and at times using the budding announcer, 5-year-old Gary and sister, Denise, on a swing set which came as his gift to you with your purchase at Johnny Hail's Home Furnishings.

There was no way not to expand into Dayton itself and so the second store opened downtown on Dayton's Third Street just a year after the first one. How can you resist the manufacturers' willingness to quadruple-and-more the leverage of your home equity and give you all the inventory you need? It was going absolutely swimmingly. A private pre-showing opened the Dayton store with crowds coming for cocktails and buffet to introduce the new shop on the block in this most thriving marketplace in central Ohio.

It was going *too* well. No way to see warning signs

Newspaper ad 1957

63

when so many experienced pros in the furniture world urged him on to more and more commitment to larger and costlier inventory. Advertising was bringing the shoppers in. And hosting a regular Sunday morning Western movie to tap the Sunday stay-at-home audience did even more to bring out weekend buyers, too.

But there was no way he could be everyplace — the gas station, the Knollwood furniture store and the Dayton one. Sure, Bobby and Tom were great managers of Knollwood Sohio but Johnny still was there to open and close every day and there was less and less time for that. Then a new, irresistible lure surfaced. Good neighbor Charley decided to open a new IGA in Huber Heights, North of Dayton, and said, "Hey, Johnny, great opportunity for you to buy out a combination hardware store and post office out there..." Johnny looked and thought so, too, and yet another part of the business complex of Johnny Hail was in place.

Many friends and family benefitted from the enterprise of galloping Johnny. One sister was typical, working both the post office and the hardware store and maybe seeing Johnny-on-the-run for lunch or a stop-in to handle some problem. He couldn't do it all. Beyond running the businesses, planning the next advertising campaign, doing commercials and entertaining people for even greater business, Johnny was often stopping in for a drink or two late at night at the country club. Often too late to wake sharp for the next day's decisions.

Meanwhile the clouds were collecting over the Ohio scene. Even heavier advertising, more hands-on management and the partying couldn't slow the tightening circle of creditors. The balance sheet was *out* of balance and the handwriting was on the wall.

"Johnny, I wish you hadn't hired that girl." Naomi hated to add to his mounting worries. "Don't you remember who she is?"

"Sure. I know her. We all graduated together, right? She needs work. Don't worry."

"Darling, you have such a short memory. She didn't like you back then and hasn't changed now. She almost caused you not to graduate. Don't you remember? She's the one who tattled to the principal."

"No kidding? I sure enough did forget. Hey, what the heck, that's history. She needs a job. Don't worry. Just tell me how to keep my pride with all our inventory bonded and the sales manager demanding my signature for every piece we sell, before he'll bring it out."

The events flowed fast in the next few weeks. An inventory called for by creditors showed a $17,000 shortage of stock from the display rooms. Someone had been systematically stealing in Dayton. It was the breaking point. Johnny Hail had suddenly gone bust.

"What will you do?" Naomi watched him carefully as he weighed the answer. They had sweated through long hours taking last steps that might help...and nothing could help. He heard the last discouraging negatives from creditors on the phone. Then it was four a.m. and the empire had folded.

"Gonna go grab some sleep," he replied finally. "The station opens in two hours. I wanna be there." He reached for her hand. "Come on. We're back to square one. I for sure don't want no one in Beavercreek to think Johnny Hail's hiding 'cause he took a kick in the can."

• • •

The next morning early Don Morgan came looking. Johnny Hail's Home Furnishings was padlocked, but there was a free spirit in the air. Just down the street busily polishing the car windows of his customers, Johnny was highly visible and typically lighthearted.

"So, how you doin'?" he asked sympathetically. "Hear you got problems?"

"I'm doing fine! I got the finest customers in the world and that's a fact."

And it was his finest moment, thought Don as he drove away. There's no way anything in his life would ever show off the real Johnny Hail any better than the way he carried himself in this defeat.

Inside Johnny it was crunch time. He hadn't come back to Ohio and to the area that nurtured him through the high school years, to lose. He hadn't put in the years of military service practicing up to sign papers of surrender. If there was heartbreak going on inside him, it was never visible to the outside world.

• • •

They came like a swarm of locusts. The impatient creditors, the lawyers hired by the even-more-impatient creditors to pluck the last visible penny from the young man they had urged merrily onward to extend his buying power with or without equity. The sheriff came to auction their house and property. Family was there in the persons of the Morgans and others to salvage what dignity could be salvaged in a bankruptcy and foreclosure action. But it was inside hurting time for a proud man who knew his abilities.

What do you do when you're taking a licking? Where do you hide when the I-told-you-so types show up for gas and the chance to gloat? Here was one man who didn't hide or run. He was John Wesley Hail and they hadn't even begun to hear from him yet! And if someone wanted to come, it didn't matter who — creditor, needler, Internal Revenue Agent — he was going to be out there in plain view and they could take their best shot! This was *his today* and he was going to enjoy it.

• • •

He seemed to. Chuck Cannon spotted it was for real when he came by. Chuck had returned from his years with the Marines and was on the threshold of what was going to be a great career with Frigidaire.

"So what's next, Johnny?" he asked his buddy of more than thirty years.

"C'mon, Charley!" Johnny punched his arm. "Hey, sorry 'bout that...been calling you Charley so long, I forgot you want Chuck now. Man, the gyrenes really screwed you up! Well, let's see, you'n me could go back to sellin' that miracle salve in Tennessee."

"Sure we could. How's Naomi? She doin' all right with all this mess?" He wasn't about to let go of his worried look as he tilted back in a well-worn customer chair, facing the carefree smile on Johnny's face. "Man, how can you be so don't-give-a-damn?"

"I give a big damn!" Johnny spun his swivel chair to stare out the door and down the street at the building that housed his once thriving business. "See that out there? That's today! You know I feel cruddy about the stores and you know I'm stoney broke, but *I* know something a lot more important. I have a chance in this country I don't see any other man have in Japan or Korea or anyplace else. *I've got just as much right to fail as I got to succeed.* I made a few good decisions that turned wrong and I don't have to go cry about 'em. You want a coke?" He headed for the line on a trot and Chuck watched him wiping down a windshield and chatting with the customer, seemingly without a care in the world. Johnny was the same Johnny he had always been. No way was he going to stay in this trap.

Chuck reached for change as he took the chilled coke. "Put it away," grunted Johnny. "You want a busted arm? Here, have a Hershey bar, too, and while you're gettin' fat, lemme tell you something about Milton Hershey. You know how much it took Mr. Hershey to make his first million on chocolate bars?"

"How much?"

"Only four bankruptcies, that's all. It just took him going broke *four times* and it took never stoppin' believing in himself or his family believing in him till he made it. And here we sit a hundred years later eating his candy bars. Bet he's laughin' up a storm up there. Let me tell you, Chuck, I'm going to be rich again — just like that!"

"I believe you, buddy. Hey, let me buy dinner and let's go talk old times."

Johnny shook his head. "Gotta go sign some papers. See that old building over there beside Charley Lafino's? Naomi and I are going to open a breakfast-lunch restaurant. She's gonna cook and serve and I'm gonna help her. You know, all that Blimp experience and two weeks at David's joint, fella, I got restaurant experience! It'll be good for her, she says. Gives her a chance to help us get a new start."

Chuck nodded as he walked to the door. "I know she's a neat girl. Always have thought you over-married." The empty pop can narrowly missed as it whistled after the retreating figure. "Pick it up yourself, turkey," laughed Chuck. "I got other things to do."

• • •

Johnny sat alone and thoughtful in the emptiness of his hideaway manager's office. There was no feeling of defeat and he didn't need to dissect any longer the problems that caused the disaster. That was history. He could lick his wounds and agree with some of the critics that he got too big for his britches, that he was just a country boy from West Virginia who got suckered by city slickers. He could moan at the pile of rubble that once was Johnny Hail's furniture stores and hardware store and post office — and even this gas station that was practically no longer his. Its ownership had been signed over to one of the family to keep it from being padlocked like the rest. His own home bought at auction right on the sheriff's steps by another of the family. Humiliating. Now he was back at square one — emptyhanded.

"Like hell I'm beat!" he growled at the empty room. "Y'ain't seen nothin' yet!" One of the day shift managers caught the words just as he was steaming into Johnny's office with the word that Sohio must have heard about the furniture failure. They wanted cash on the barrel head for the gas truck load that had just arrived. The manager paused — waited...decided not to interrupt his boss's thoughts and moved quietly back down the hall. Johnny didn't need one more kick at the moment. At the outer desk he wrote the check for the delivery.

"Hey, man, I gotta have cash! I told ya! Dispatch will send me back with a hose in my ear to take it outta the tank, if I leave it for a check!"

"Look, fella, just come call your dispatcher! You ask him if he ever got a bum check from Johnny Hail. He'd better damn well remember who sells more Sohio than anyone else in this state, so get off his back! Johnny don't need no flak after all he does for this company!"

A grumbling set of epithets followed the retreating back of the manager, but none of it was heard. Tom had scored one for Johnny and that felt great. He wondered why that made him feel so good. Would have been easier to just dump the problem on the owner and walk away. Johnny wouldn't expect him to get in the middle — it wasn't his headache. But there was something about working for this guy after all these years. You really wanted to perform a lot better than what was expected.

Back in his office Johnny kept hearing that melody needling at his thoughts. It had been planted there as he drove to work and it was one of those haunting things that wouldn't get out of his head. "Da...da...Tum...ta... tum...tum...de...da...Dream...that was it...dream the impossible dream...that was it...That was exactly it!"

He grabbed for the phone and waited impatiently for Naomi to answer his dial. "Honey, Charley just came by here and says I over-married. Whatcha think?"

"I think he's right. But you should have three wives right at the moment to take care of your three offspring. How are you doing, darling?"

"Doin' fine, if I can just figure out a way to stay awake. We musta been up till five o'clock."

"Three-forty-five, to be exact," she corrected. "Listen, Lois just called. She said that since we won't be needing her at the hardware store, she'd love to come sit with the kids any time she can help us."

"Get her right away, why don't you? Then come on down here and let's go see what we gotta have to open up the Blimp."

Naomi giggled. "You sound like you haven't a care in the world, Johnny. By the way, I really have a great name for our restaurant. How about The Family Room?"

"That sounds good. I been thinking about help for you, since you're so dead-set on running it yourself. What do you think about Carl? You know he'd be one heck of a gofer and he's got a great attitude around people."

"But what about his heart? Would it be safe?" She had the feeling that her husband had already researched all that.

"No problem. I asked his family if we ever had a spot for him, would he be able to work. They'd love it."

"Johnny you never cease to amaze me. Wherever did you find the time to talk to his family?"

He yawned audibly over the phone. "Listen, we may have had our clock cleaned, but that ain't keeping most of Dayton and Beavercreek from coming out here to buy their gas this morning. Oh, and incidentally, since today is...whatta they say?...the first day of the rest of my life, I'm changin' my name. I ain't no Johnny no more. People are always coming around here asking where the jonny is. So I'm changing my name like Charley's done. From now on, Mrs. Hail, please address me as John W. Hail."

There was a squawk in the background...one of the kids wasn't buying the breakfast fare. "I don't think Vicki likes your new name," Naomi said, "but I like it okay. Why didn't you switch to Wesley? Aren't they still going to ask for the jon?"

He snorted. "You kidding? Why would a good old Nazarene want to be a Wesley? Anyway, the W is going to stand for WINNER for me, 'cause, Mrs. Hail, you're lookin' at a winner all the way!"

"And you are, John."

"Well, I'm gettin' out front. Got to polish some windows and get some action going. I'm gonna tell them that The Family Room will be open for breakfast and lunch within thirty days. Can we do it?"

"Of course. Before that."

That song kept needling his mind after he hung up. He had a dream. Thank God for Naomi who really gave him a reason for keeping it. He stabbed the moisture at the corner of his eye as he headed out the door. *Look out, world! Here comes John Winner Hail!*

Chapter Five

The Family Room was a good idea. Naomi was happy as a lark in the sparkle and freshness of the old building renovated into a homey restaurant. She liked to be responsible for something next door to her husband during the day. Not that he needed propping up. If anything, he was a freer spirit than ever. But it was going to be a lot easier to come out of their mess if they could work side-by-side during the daytime and not just be together at the pooped end of the day.

John was back and forth across the lot from the station and somehow, even with Gary, Denise and Vicki needing lots of babysitters, they were finding ways to make it work smoothly. Broke or not, the world around them never saw a hint in their attitudes that a financial disaster had come to the Hail home that day in August.

For sure, Paul Falk didn't notice any disaster in John's expression when he pulled in for gas some weeks later. He smiled at the man holding the fistful of blue paper cleaning towels, rubbing down his windshield. "You got a busy place here," he observed.

"Yeah, we're lucky. People like us. Can I check your oil?" He circled to the front of the hood and took in the plates. "Well, I see you're out of Hoosier-land."

It was a brother of John's who had sparked Falk's interest in coming to Beavercreek. David had talked about Johnny Hail as the world's greatest salesman. He also mentioned that his brother 'had recently experienced some business reverses.' That could be exactly the man Paul was looking for. He climbed out of the aging Cadillac and walked around the tires, kicking at them speculatively while his target was studying the dipstick.

"Down about a quart-and-a-half," reported John. "Looks a little dark, too. Run you through an oil change in about half-an-hour, if you have the time."

"Thanks. Tell you what I'd rather do right now is get you to check my tires...that front right looks low. I'm staying overnight. How about taking me in then the first thing tomorrow?"

John was crouched by the front right wheel. "Be fine. You're low about ten pounds. Just pull 'er over there to the air. We'll get 'er leveled off."

It was just an inconsequential little courtesy performed by John at least a dozen times a day — kneeling, removing the valve cap, adding the few pounds of air to a soft tire. But how many service station owners got their hands dirty so willingly? It had a powerful symbolism to the newcomer in town. "I appreciate that," he murmured as he watched John replace the cap. "Listen, you're busier than a one-armed-paper-hanger, but let me stick a question in your mind. How'd you like to at least double your income within the next thirty days?"

John straightened from his crouch and was silently tucking the pressure gauge into his shirt pocket, eyeing the man's expression carefully to detect signs of the stand-up comedian. Finding none, he let a hint of a crooked smile toy the left corner of his mouth. "You just got my attention," he said soberly. "So why don't you bring your car over to that bay for an oil change right now and you and me'll go grab a cup o' coffee? What's this big opportunity?"

It wasn't the first route to riches John had heard and this was probably another yawner. Still, there was something different in this fellow from Indiana and when someone is selling that hard, John would always listen. Selling was in his blood and how other people pitched was always interesting. At the least, he never failed to get some new idea or technique on how to market and how not to market.

Paul's hand was out and John gripped it as the stranger in town rainchecked the coffee. "I'd really like to do that right now, but I've got another appointment and this is too important an opportunity for you to consider on the run. Could we stay with tomorrow, maybe about ten?"

Next morning they met in The Family Room and while John stirred sugar into his coffee, Paul fingered a business card from his lapel pocket. John grinned at its declaration that Paul Falk was President of Liberty American Life Insurance Company. "You got the wrong man," he chuckled. "I don't know the first derned thing about the insurance game. Only connection I've had with it is the credit life we wrote selling furniture."

"Well, you know something, if you know that much." He had seen the closed and padlocked doors on the store a block away. The long, empty glass front across what had been Johnny Hail's Home Furnishings, according to its sign, made this man across the table all the more intriguing. This was no loser; not with his attitude. There was no fake about it. No tension in that smile. Completely at ease, he was enjoying himself, in spite of whatever it was that happened.

Paul watched the petite, thirtyish blonde move from the counter toward them with the coffee carafe.

"Want you to meet my wife, Naomi. Honey, say hello to Paul here. He's a real live insurance salesman out of Indiana."

"Nice to meet you, Paul." She filled their cups. "Can I get you both some breakfast?"

"Up to Paul." John glanced across the table.

"I'll pass for now, but thanks much, Naomi."

"Just call me." She turned back to the kitchen.

"This is your place, too then, John?"

"Yeah, we just opened it. Not doin' bad at all." He waved to a foursome across the room. "In fact, that woman o' mine is insisting we're gonna start serving dinners, too, in about a week."

"You two have any children?"

"You know it. Three of the greatest."

"It looks to me like the way you've got your troops running over there, your service station can almost handle itself. I suppose you put in some time over here, too, don't you?"

"You better believe it. Just as much as I can. She says she's havin' a ball, but I don't want her doin' this any longer than we need to." John looked out across at the busy station. "You were talkin' about my troops over there. I can trust every one of 'em, too. Most of 'em been with me for years...But tell me what you've got here."

"Well, Liberty Life is just about to start doing business. We're not licensed yet." Paul went on to describe his unformed company. It was in the process of becoming one. Licensing, approval by the insurance commissioner, certificates of authorization still were needed Meanwhile, to build his sales force, he was out recruiting. "Your brother told me about your sales ability, John, and I'm out hand-picking a few good men for a ground-floor opportunity."

John glanced toward the kitchen where Naomi was hurrying breakfast orders at the range. *His wife could probably expound on that ground-floor opportunity stuff!* He listened in silence as Paul described how his recruits would work for an insurance company called Laymen Life, out of Anderson, Indiana, then switch to Liberty when it was set to do business. "Won't Laymen raise hell when you walk off with the sales team you've recruited?"

Paul shook his head. "They're pleased to get the salesmen on their force for however long. And I get the chance to train my men." He went on to tell of the potential in insurance sales and slowly but surely John began to feel the magnetism of this profession begin to grab.

The cup of coffee became two, then three. The cigarettes went from one to half-a-pack and all at once Naomi was at his elbow, her purse under her arm. "Will you close, Johnny? I've got to go relieve the sitter before Gary and Denise get home."

"Sure, hon. See you in a little bit. Hey, I haven't helped you at all!"

"Don't worry. Pat came by to help or I'd have screamed. You didn't even notice her? I must say, Paul, you have had my husband's attention!"

"Now, if I can just keep it. But I apologize. John was saying he tries to get over here to help you and we talked right through your busy time. I'm sorry."

"She's been puttin' up with this sort o' thing for ten years. You'll be interested in this," he said to Naomi. "Paul's gonna let me keep some o' this stuff, so we can talk it over together. But you run. I'll see you tonight."

She bent to kiss Johnny's cheek and was gone.

Paul smiled across the table. "You're a lucky man. I'm not going to kid you about insurance sales though. If you go for it — and I sure hope you will — you are going to see a lot less of Naomi. Anybody tells you it's any other way, is lying. It's the price that goes with success."

Six months had passed and John had come to understand something of the price of success. He had Naomi's blessing to go for the new success and at first he mixed three careers again.

Early morning would see him in work clothes at Knollwood Sohio for two or three hours, opening the station and scheduling the work. Then he'd hurry home to shower and change into business suit and be off to prospect appointments. If there was any way to work it out in the appointment schedule, he'd come by The Family Room midday, peel his jacket, eat and then help Naomi while he told her any news of the day. Late at night he'd come back from his last appointment to check the gas station's day balance and handle any problems, usually still in his suit at that hour, with the tie akimbo.

But the morning never started with opening the station, either. It had long been clear to John that his most valuable hour of his day was before anybody else was up and about. He used it. In the darkness of the living room, he mulled the priorities of that one day. Every day. Not to think about tomorrow and not the distant future, and never yesterday. It was today that he had to use the day well and this was the hour to plan it. If anything cost him that valuable hour of silence and meditation, it was a costly loss.

He had found a new profession in which he was a gifted natural. Nothing else could explain it; he had a gift. A combination of all his past had come together to make John Hail a remarkable insurance salesman. His keen perception of the person he was with, listening or talking, was of course partly an accrual of all the watching and listening and talking of his first thirty-three years. Sure, he'd learned in parsonage and school and athletics. And he'd learned in the Air Force and at Knollwood Sohio, in Johnny Hail's Home Furnishings and Huber Heights Hardware and everywhere. He'd learned on boats, in the air and at home and now it all combined to help him. But when all the learning of the previous experience of his life was wrapped and bundled together, it still left unexplained the talents of John. He was simply a gifted marketer and an even more compelling motivator and those gifts surfaced at once.

Within a few months he was producing 75% of all the personal sales of little Laymen Life. Top salesman for the company in the very first weeks, he had opened a family cash flow that would help him repay debts from his recent disaster. And every weekend he would drive Naomi and the children from Ohio into Indiana to Anderson to personally deliver his sales report of the week, bringing contracts and checks to the home of the Chief Executive Officer. In exchange, he took home a check with his commissions and bonuses for sales performance. John woke quickly to the fact that while he was toting to Indiana the top volume sales report and checks that paid the CEO's salary and kept that one in the life style to which he was accustomed, he, John, was taking back to Ohio a far smaller piece of the pie.

It would be great when the day arrived that would find him at the top of a company. From the first he had absolutely no doubt that he would reach the top, but never far from his thoughts was an irreverent "Top of what? President of peanut Laymen Life or non-existent-yet Liberty?" President is as President does and what he does to apply his skills to make the company successful for *other* people is what John knew would eventually make his company a towering one or a toppled one and him a good or bad president.

John at Laymen Life

And the money wouldn't be hard to take. Eager and aggressive, needled by the experience of the total shattering of security and the collapse of the material comfort he had been building for his family, he was determined now as never before to make it to the high places.

Number One priority, next to sales production, if he was to reach those dizzying heights, was to learn the business. Learn every part of it. How is a life insurance policy put together? What's it really worth? What makes an actuarial table? How is the business regulated state by state? On and on went the insatiable curiosity, driving home.

The price of the learning and the selling was how much home time he was willing to sacrifice. Within months he burned one bridge, turning the service station over to Sohio. He had to have singlemindedness of purpose. There was no longer time for using early morning hours to start the day for someone else. Next came the decision to close The Family Room. Naomi agreed reluctantly, for she had really loved the daily mixing with people. But there was no way Johnny could have a clear mind on the road, knowing she was somewhere between the restaurant and home or having problems alone without him.

"What will happen to Carl?" she asked the night they decided. "He's loved it so, too."

John shrugged, sharing the disappointment he knew Carl would feel. It was the way they had to go, even though both could feel the doors slowly closing on their lives in Beavercreek.

"Tom's going to open his own station, he says." *Why was there always pain to the ending of a chapter? Had it really been twelve years?* "Most all the rest o' the guys there are placed...Say, get a sitter. We're going to Bedford, Pennsylvania in two weeks."

"Bedford? Who would want to go there?"

"You will, Mrs. Hail, when you hear why. I want you to know your husband is the Number One salesman for Laymen and I didn't even get started in this contest till it was three-quarters over. So we won first prize and we get a weekend o' golf and swimming and meeting other people who are makin' it work big."

That little convention at Bedford Springs, nestled in the scenic Alleghenies off the Pennsylvania Turnpike, was to be a critical meeting that would turn John's life around.

"Hail, how does a guy with a golf game like yours manage to sell insurance the way you do? You sell it all

Golf at Bedford Springs

77

while you're out playing golf or maybe at the Nineteenth Hole?" The smile as he tilted the beer to his lips made it obvious he was kidding.

John assessed the man across the clubroom table as he shoved the bills into his sport shirt pocket and grinned back. Tom Hill had a way about him that was a mix of blow-hard and friendliness. He had just been taken for about fifty dollars in sixteen out of eighteen holes by the hotshot of Laymen Life. John was guessing that this guest speaker at the convention was trying to find a needle to take away the sting of losing.

"Matter of fact, I do sell some at the club. Not much though. It doesn't help a sale to beat a guy and pitch him insurance at the same time and I haven't got time to lose any sales. I sure haven't the guts to play under my game."

Tom pulled open the door to the locker room and followed behind as John dropped his golf bag into a corner. "Let me be sure I got you right, John. I'd swear I heard you say you would hate to lose a sale?"

John nodded. "I haven't got time for losing. I listened to a whole bellyful of training about measuring up to rejection and all that claptrap. I get a 'No' from somebody and I'm just gettin' started on the sale. Most important thing I do 'fore I start any serious pitch, is to qualify my prospect. If he doesn't impress me that he's able to buy if he wants to, then I'm gone, man...I'm gone. Life's too short. How about yourself? You been in this a lot longer than any of us. Where do you sell best...home, office... maybe the golf course?"

Tom chuckled. "You mean I lose pretty easy, so I might as well be making a few bucks while I'm replacing the divots I'm ripping up? Naw, to tell you the truth, John, I don't sell one-on-one any more. I'm a consultant. I do things like you see me doing here. I'm what they call 'a motivational expert' and you know what that is. He's an 'ex,' which means out of his territory. And he's a 'spurt,' which means he's a little drip. That's me. I'm a little drip out of my own territory — an expert. You're an expert, too, but for real. I been listening and I'll tell you, you may just have enough to qualify for my organization."

The conversation had suddenly bent in an unexpected way. John had just notified Laymen Life he would be switching allegiance to Liberty American, now that it had its Certificate of Authorization, and they were giving him a send-off this very night. In one short year he had built an incredible sales record and recruited a passle of new agents. He remembered the dilemma he felt when Laymen had asked him to leave behind at least some of the sales force he'd developed. He had agreed to let the President of Laymen put it to every man John had recruited and he wouldn't try to sway the agent from staying. It had not surprised him that every one of them had opted to go along with him to the new firm. He hadn't just recruited them; he'd led them every step of their development and some were already emerging with high earning power. Why would they leave the winner who coached them?

"...So what do you think? Would you be interested in exploring possibilities with me?"

The question jolted him back to the conversation at hand. He was impressed with the idea of consultant. The very name had a kind of classy, above-it-all dignity. And, if the pay was as classy as the name, some day...maybe. "Tell you the truth, Tom, I owe it to Liberty to go with them. I promised Paul Falk I'd come aboard when he got licensed and he's tellin' everyone I'm Liberty's first agent. He's really promoting that thing. Don't ask me why. I promised, so I'm gonna honor that."

"Respect you for it." Tom tossed a damp towel into the hamper and began to dress. "So clue me on how you do your business so well. Give me something to share tonight with these guys, 'sides the fact that they better bring their billfold, if they're playing golf with John Hail. How do you do your sales so successfully?"

"If you really want to know, I do it exactly the way I ran a service station for twelve years. There's nothin' different. I'm not sure I agree with some of the stuff I been reading on how to approach and how to close and settin' goals and all that. I do it person-to-person. I qualify my prospect and there's nothin' fancy about that. Some guy pulls into your station in a heap, has a slick lip and wants a tank of gas, you fill him up and 99%-plus are gonna have the money. If slick lip wants a valve job or a transmission replaced, you qualify him 'fore you do it, to be sure you're not about to be screwed for the bill. Y'ain't got the time to get jerked around. That's the start of it.

"My station sold more Sohio than any place East of the Mississippi, but it wasn't supposed to do better than about 1,000 gallons a week. You believe that? They bet I couldn't bring ten customers a day into my station, and Mr. Sparr promised to shut me down just as soon as I proved his engineers were right. So I busted my buns sixteen hours a day, just like I'm doin' selling insurance. I run my insurance like I ran my station. Not one damn thing different! And the big thing is total honesty. Mess with that, you're dead."

"Listen, John, would you tell the people here some of this tonight? I mean, give 'em maybe five minutes about how one new kid on the block does his business?...Be an inspiration. I know *I'd* sure like to hear more."

"Naw. Listen, I'm a newcomer. Let me hang around awhile and see if I got something to say. Maybe next year. I came to learn, not to shoot off my mouth."

"Ha! I thought so! You give me all that noble garbage about honesty and then you go sneaking off and keep it to yourself. Man, I don't give a damn if you're brand new! These guys deserve to know 'what makes Johnny run.' I mean, you're dumping out on Laymen and you're going to Liberty ..." He cut short as he saw by John's expression he had struck a nerve.

"I'm dumpin' out on nobody! I'm doin' just what I promised Paul Falk and told Liberty I'd be doin' when I came in a year ago! Sure, you think I've got something to say to help you, I'll be glad to speak."

Hill, who was tilting back against the lounge wall, slapped his knee. "Capital! I knew you would! Just give them what makes it work for you."

• • •

That night Tom Hill was pleased to introduce the Chief Executive Officer of Liberty Life, who would present a surprise guest appearance from among the delegates to 'this beautiful Bedford bash.' Hal Lorain, CEO, wasted very little time on small talk. He thanked Laymen Life for its welcome to himself and the recruits brought in by his man, Paul Falk, for training during the birthing months of this new company.

Lorain's mood moved into high gear as he observed that Liberty's biggest debt of gratitude to Laymen was that it weaned and nurtured a budding superstar named John Hail, bringing him from fledgling insurance salesman to the premier position as top volume producer for Laymen in the year that Hail was on loan to them.

"I want you to know, ladies and gentlemen, you are about to enjoy hearing one of the stellar performers in the entire insurance profession today." His voice rose two decibels. "Here's a man who chose our profession at the very height of his career, with his empire spread out before him in major markets of the sovereign State of Ohio...An empire that included well known furniture stores, hardware stores and even a chain of full service gas stations stretching from Cleveland to Cincinnati!"

Bullshit! It was the only word an embarrassed John Hail could think, as he squirmed uncomfortably at his table in the ballroom auditorium. *This guy was going to turn the audience from his peers in insurance to a JURY of his peers! He should have told Hill to stick it in his ear back in the club house. Lorain was making it sound like John Hail was the Second Coming. And to make it really rough, this character was #1 man in the company he was now pledged to work for.*

His hand crept under the table to find and squeeze Naomi's. The returned squeeze helped. She was suffering with him.

"I am honored to introduce to you, the first salesman for Liberty Life Insurance Company, the astonishing John Wesley Hail! Come on up here, John!"

At the podium, he felt suddenly and completely at ease. He knew what he had to do. He knew how to do it and it hadn't taken a Trevecca College education or a Korean police action or any of the stuffed shirt formalism of the mediocre and the non-producers he'd watched so far in this insurance industry, to teach him. Like this phoney-baloney head of his new company. *Time to puncture a balloon and win back his audience...*

"What he forgot to mention was that I'm also one helluva grease monkey." A roar went up from the delegates. "Any of you fellas want your brake fluid checked 'fore you head back down these mountains, you come see me." The explosive response told the speaker his audience was with him and be damned to the lies just told. "I'm not even gonna try to pick out fact from fiction, but if you believe what was just said about me, I got this bridge in Brooklyn I wanna talk to you about.

"Naomi, stand up, would you? Ladies an' gentlemen, I want to introduce the real reason for my bein' up here." The applause rolled for the diminutive blonde in the bright blue dress and the dancing smile who waved from their table as the spotlight caught her and then moved back to center stage. "This woman has had the questionable distinction of being the king's queen while most of his empire went down the tubes. And, since she was also the Chancellor of his Exchequer, you better believe that hurt! All I can wish for all of you is to have an all-weather queen like Naomi!

"I wanna tell you a fact of life that many of you already know, if you've had anything to do with cattle. Out on the great range country of the United States, when the big winter storms and snows come, most of the cattle turn their backs to the wind and take the easy way, following the others of the herd till they come upon a fence that stops their movement. There they stay till they die of hunger and cold.

"There's one breed of cattle, however, that refuses to be followers — the White Hereford. They put their heads into the wind an' band together till they find shelter and food. Because they refuse to turn their back to their enemy and put their heads an' shoulders to the task before them, they survive and succeed.

"I'm not here t' tell you anything about how to run your business. What do I know? What I *do* know something about, is what to do when your business is about to run you right out o' town. Don't turn your back to the wind — face it head on!" He smiled over his shoulder at his new Liberty boss. "Mr. Lorain, my personnel file must say them great things about me and my empire an' I just want you to leave all that stuff in there. I'll never deny it. Paul Falk's to blame for all those lies. He even had me thinkin' if I busted my butt for Laymen this year, there could be a chairman's job open. Now, meeting you, I know I gotta go back to work with these other peons. So, for what it's worth, here's how I do my business in insurance..."

•   •   •

Later that evening Tom Hill came by to say good-night to the Hails in the lounge. "John, you were a hard act to follow! Believe me, you could walk about three hundred agents into Liberty with you, with or without the Chairman's job."

John motioned to a chair. "Sit down. You got a minute? Tell my wife what you were sayin' 'bout your work. Tom's head of an outfit called Guardian Advisors. Said he might could use my services someday. Go ahead, Tom, tell 'er about consultants."

"We're motivational counselors, Naomi. I'd like to talk your man into coming with us right now and since he halfway put down his boss tonight, maybe he's looking for a job."

"Naw," John laughed. "Lorain was just trying to make me look good...Heck, a bunch o' those guys knew the truth about my furniture stores."

"Well, I watched a motivational expert tonight and I'll be coming back at you. Here's what we do, Naomi..."

John's career with Liberty American Life was a dramatic extension of what he had begun with Laymen. It was over two years later before he talked again with Tom Hill about becoming a consultant with Guardian. This time Hill was not about to let his quarry escape.

In the two years since he saw him last, Tom had kept track of him. John had held every field position for Liberty from agent to regional agency director. He had claimed national attention when, in the past year, he and the 85 new agents he recruited and trained were responsible for 90% of the company's production. Shades of Laymen Life!

In that time, he also had taken on another job — that of Interim Executive Secretary for American Life Underwriters, traveling everywhere they needed him to go around the country. Their program aimed to build protection into the careers of independent insurance men. Typical of John, he drove in to help this new program get going because he believed in it and knew it, too, needed what he had to give in leadership, if it was to grow.

When John did agree to Hill's coming back to Beavercreek, he shared his feelings candidly with Naomi about their future in the insurance industry. As a consultant with

Guardian, he would have an opportunity for high visibility in insurance firms all around America. Here was a way not only to help his fellow insurance salesmen, but also to test his ability as teacher and motivator in the seminar rooms of *other* companies.

It was proven there was little chance to move to the top, if he remained with Liberty. They loved him and loved even more his own army of salesmen. They were not about to take him off the field into executive rank.

He remembered those weekend runs he'd made from Dayton to Anderson, taking along his earnings which were happily received by the top man on the totem pole, who then sent his indian back to do it all over again the next week, etc. etc. There was little doubt about his ability now to teach and to motivate and to become a superior addition to the consultant field force. He was probably the most motivated of salesmen, and sometimes the hardest to understand, even by his wife. "Naomi, I'd like to go with Guardian. I believe I can do them good and us good, too, if I do."

She smiled at the earnestness in his face. John had a sense of destiny and a definite game plan for achieving it. She was absolutely sure. He wasn't deceived by the promises from Tom Hill that 'as much as a thousand dollars a day could be made' as a consultant. She also knew with his special magnetism for people and his track record as a salesman, her husband would have superior desirability as a motivator. He was no self-appointed expert, filled with hot air and theory. He had worked the trenches.

John in <u>Death of a Salesman</u>

"Go for it, if it feels right to you, John. You know we're all behind you. But would you please tell me how in the world, with all this, that you also are going to handle the lead in <u>Death Of A Salesman</u>?"

"You heard about that, huh? Hey, it's just a little thing. The company asked me to help out for the big convention this Fall."

Her expression had storm warnings. They were too unusual for John to miss. "I'm worried that you're doing just too much. I know every bit is for us, but I'm worried for you. I'm worried for the children. Gary's getting almost into adolescence without you and Denise is maturing so fast...They'll be needing more of their Daddy than you've been able to give and it may be real soon. I'm so afraid you'll break your health at this pace."

He studied her from across the room as she busied herself at the sewing machine, not looking up as she spoke.

"I don't want to be a nag, John, but we've seen a lot of friends who haven't driven themselves anywhere as hard as you do, who've been cut right down with a coronary. We need you around us, Mr. Hail. You know you're what it's all about for four little Hails."

"Ohmigosh...you expectin' again!" He ducked as the pillow sailed across the room. "So, okay, you aren't all that big either. But you sure throw a mean pillow, for four-eleven ...and-a-half! C'mon, level. Are you gettin' problems with Gary that you're hiding from me? Or is it Denise?"

Vicki and Denise

"Both, I guess. It isn't exactly trouble. Oh, I don't know, maybe they're just typical. Gary is so far from being trouble, I just don't know how to describe it. He's loveable and agreeable and he comes down real hard on Denise when you're away, but sometimes I think he's getting old before his adolescent years really begin. He's so meditative about everything...and maybe I'm just imagining it."

"Does Denise bug him?"

"She can be a holy terror, when she wants, but it's just the mischief in her, I keep telling myself. I just wish...oh, I wish I hadn't brought it up now! But I just *wish* there was a way to have you here more. That's why I got upset about your lead in the play now."

"Listen, honey, let me tell you one reason I let them cast me for the lead. And, hey, I'll give it up, if things aren't right with the kids...Maybe I'm bein' selfish, but you know the story in <u>Death Of A Salesman</u>?"

Naomi nodded. "And you're telling me you don't intend to live out your life as an insurance man who slowly becomes like that one. Is that it?"

Gary in baseball uniform

"That's exactly right. I'm absolutely certain I can take us to a different level in this business. I'm gonna make it happen! Can you trust me through one more step?"

"Of course." Subject closed.

She held up the gown for him to see what she was stitching. "It's the costume for Denise. Don't tell me you forgot! You know we're having a Fourth of July party for all eighty-five agents you recruited, remember? *and* their families! I'm reminding you, so's you'll be sure to save the 3rd all day to be making ice cream."

He groaned. "I forgot. We're having our first rehearsal on the third." He saw her face stiffen. "No problem! I'll get it done, don't worry." He did a flippant soft-shoe across the room, humming "No-business-like-show-business...So what is Denise gonna be in that costume?"

"The Statue of Liberty, what else? No one any better for that part! Here's the banner we're going to sew across her top." He stood behind her, reading the sewn-on letters. "A Fire-Cracker Splash-In Fourth...Liberty-For-All. You sure cast the right kid for that," he chuckled.

He was in Baton Rouge, the seminar presenter for Guardian Advisors before a regional credit life insurance company's field and home staff. His job: motivate company! — Stalemated after sixteen years.

He reached to pull the sheet over his head as his partner's shower baritone echoed in from the bath. No way to get it to go away, so he rolled over and pushed wearily to a sitting position at the edge of the bed. "Say, Bill, tell me again what kind o' fun we're havin', would you? I mean, I like to hear myself talk, but you got me goin' solo darn near twelve hours a day!" He tested one foot and groaned when he put pressure on the ankle, then stood slowly and hobbled into the bathroom.

"Gotta watch those ankles, John. You got 'em really swollen."

"Yeah. Well, with a little *help* motivating and teaching, I wouldn't have to be on 'em all day."

"Like I told you, pal, I'm out drummin' up new recruits for this guy, Collette. Look, this outfit is in need of a lot more than just motivating. Man, Tom told us we were coming to a well established operation, but this United Companies is just makin' it. They need help!"

"Well, Mr. Collette seems to think we're giving it to them. He's sitting out there every day takin' in everything that goes on." John eyed his partner who was already filling his briefcase, about to hit the street. "Listen, you've been with Guardian longer than I have, but this is the first time I've worked with you and you oughta know Mr. Collette was really pushin' me yesterday. He really wants to know why *you* aren't sharing the teaching job. I told him you felt you could be more help out there recruitin'. You know what he said?"

Bill paused, hand on the door. "Yeah, like 'where are the agents' I'm out recruiting? Tell him to keep his shirt on! I'm workin' at a surprise for him." The door slammed behind him.

• • •

It was the last day of his seminar at United Companies and Lloyd Collette had opened the morning session. "John Hail, we're mighty grateful to you for these last two weeks. We'd, by golly, like to keep you here in *Loos*iana. I hear you've become a lover of Creole Gumbo and Treat's Black Coffee. Don't know what that Gumbo has done for you, except tear up your stomach lining. But I'll bet you Treat's is how you been able to get here every morning bright-eyed and bushy-tailed. I don't know about the rest of you folks, but I haven't had more motivation to get on with the job here at United in the sixteen years since I started this company."

As John walked through the shower of applause to the podium to begin the final session of the best seminar he'd had in his year-and-a-half on the road for Guardian Advisors, he thought about that half-invitation.

"Y'know, I come from a poor preacher's family of fourteen kids, Mr. Collette. We always got ourselves into parsonages with three bedrooms and, to tell you the truth, I didn't know what it meant to sleep alone, until I was married!" The class roared. "Now, with all this fun I'm havin' tracking across America so's my boss can sleep late back in Chicago, I'm just about to take you up on that offer. I figure I'm gettin' a king-size bed every night all to myself, but sure as heck, if I came to Baton Rouge, I'd have the little woman and our three kids wantin' to come on down from Beavercreek, Ohio. And five in bed is more fun than one, I guarantee you."

That would be hard to take, he thought, as he rifled his sheathe of papers and surveyed the laughter of the sales

Lloyd Collette

force, many of whom knew every bit of the loneliness of the road that he had found in the five years since he entered insurance. It had to be one of the most underrated professions in the world. Any one of these people before him who became wealthy, really earned it. And the guy who stood before them had something to share and something they wanted to hear, or they wouldn't be involved with what he was trying to put across. Mr. Collette was there, so they had to be in attendance, but, after ten, twelve to fifteen hours in cram sessions for two weeks, they had to be getting something worthwhile to make them that *up* on the final day.

"You know, there's one thing I learned real quick in the insurance business," he began. "And I've tried and tried and tried with every agent I bring into the business, to get him to do it. I cannot ever recall makin' a sales presentation and *not* makin' a sale. Sound like a boast? Well, it isn't. It's just a statement of fact. And to make it happen, I follow a couple o' very simple rules. So, first of all, as we discussed yesterday, I qualify my prospects and don't horse around with somebody who can't afford my product.

"More important, the one thing that people need to learn in this business, or in any business, is if you're training someone or doing it alone, do it by the book — or, count on it, you'll get off track.

"The worst thing sales people do is they get tired of sayin', 'Mary had a little lamb. Its fleece was white as snow.' So they start sayin', 'Mary had a little white; It's fleece was blue as rain'...or something. They don't realize they've changed, but because they get tired of the same old routine, they try to re-invent the wheel. They forget they're talkin' to a parade. They're *not* talkin' to the same people. That's a parade goin' down the street and every sales encounter is different people who are part of that parade you're talkin' to."

Lloyd Collette studied the corp of his sales force, listening to his youthful seminar preceptor with as much attention and more than they would have given someone with a half-century in the business. Hail communicated that rare commodity of making the listener believe in himself...or in herself. (He was proud that he was a pioneer of sorts in letting women become a part of the sales force of what was once totally a man's world.)

"And here's another side of guaranteeing your sales ability," John continued. "I *never* go out on sales calls by myself. I take somebody with me, 'cause I figure the only way I'm ever gonna get any place, is to train people from day one. They aren't my people just because I recruited them. But they came in because of things I promised and things I said, so I owe them.

"I never have gone out on a sales call by myself. Not in my whole life. Now, lemme tell you, a lot of people do go alone because of fear. I *didn't* do it because of fear! I thought the only way I would sell — and I was right — was to have the side effect of another agent listening. That is going to make me stay on track and say, 'Mary had a little lamb' and not 'A lamb fleeced little Mary.' You're going to stay on track and not mess with success in your presentation. You're not gonna play around when you know somebody's sittin' there watching you, getting ready to go out and imitate just what they see you do. So, you go right by the book and if you do, you'll sell everybody."

• • •

It was the tired end of the day and John had just dropped into bed to watch the sign-off news. He groaned as the phone rang and glanced at his wrist watch. Who could it be at midnight? He'd already made his regular call to Naomi when he was done at the seminar, so it couldn't be her... Unless there was an emergency! And where was Bill? He was always in the sack when John returned at night.

"John? This is Lloyd Collette. You in bed yet? Come on over to the office for a few minutes, will you? I've got some bad news and some good news I want you to hear."

"You bet. Be right there, Mr. Collette. Jus' give me ten."

"Your buddy there?"

"Bill? No, I was wondering about him..."

"Okay, then I'll give the bad news over the phone. I've been suspicious of that character ever since he's been disappearing from our seminars. I pay a firm a price for *two* men, I expect to see two men. Lucky for his ass you been doing the job of better-than-two.

"But I had that turkey, Marshall, tailed this morning. You don't know it, I'm sure, but I wanted to tell you before you heard it from him. I've just kicked him out of town.

He's been going right down the street to another motel and checking in with a broad for the day. Letting you do the motivating, while he's doing the fornicating! Whattaya think of them onions? Anyhow, if it wasn't for you, I'd sure see that Guardian would be finished in the industry. So come on over. Got something else I want to talk to you about."

"I'm on my way." John carefully replaced the phone on its cradle. The world suddenly felt like a different place. So much for Bill! The sonofabitch!

He should have figured that out for himself when Bill hadn't given evidence of generating a single recruit in the weeks in Baton Rouge. What did Mr. Collette have on his mind? Maybe he was just softening him up for the real boom-lowering on Guardian. Maybe he really hadn't done all that great a job himself. And that was a crock! He knew from the packed roomful of agents he'd taught morning, afternoon and evening, that he must have put it across.

He turned into the driveway and took the space closest to the front door with the black letters printed on the curb, 'President, United Companies.'

"Maybe you ought to just leave your car there, John." The door swung to admit his midnight guest. "You do a better job than a lot of presidents I know. Grab a seat." Lloyd Collette, a tall, ruggedly handsome John Wayne type, aimed a finger at the chair facing his desk. "I don't even want to waste a minute on that character who obviously enjoyed ripping off both of us. And in a way, I'm grateful to the s.o.b. He brought to a head my opinion of you."

John waited silently, tilting a quizzical eyebrow toward this man who had earned his respect. Mr. Collette cared enough about his United Companies team that he sat through almost every minute of John's seminars — or was it to be sure he was getting his money's worth from Guardian's consultant team?

"I'll come right to the point, John. I want you to join us here at United Companies. We'd like to have you take charge of our marketing program. Will you do it?"

It was not what he had been prepared to hear. As he drove over, whether from fatigue or depression over Mr. Collette's news, he had really expected a tongue lashing for Guardian, with maybe the good news being that he had done a good job personally and Tom Hill was going to be so advised. But a position with United as Director of Marketing? He had just been offered, for the first time in his career, a vice-presidency.

"I'm very grateful, Mr. Collette. There is no one I know in the industry I'd rather work for. Let me ask you, do you expect that you'll always keep United as a credit life corporation?"

Typically John Hail, thought Lloyd Collette. Just as tight on words as I am when it deals with his own affairs. But two weeks of watching this tireless young man with the energy level to sustain him through a day beginning at six-thirty and never ending before midnight, had him convinced that John Hail was extraordinary and just what United Companies needed. He reminded him of himself in many ways. Innovative and unafraid to try the new. John hadn't wasted too much of his life in formal education and that made him attractive to Collette, because he was not the least intimidated by the formally educated. He suspected Thomas Edison would see in John Hail a prime example of his addage, 'A little education won't hurt you, if you don't take it seriously.' And for one who dropped out of public schooling at third grade, he spoke with authority. So did John Hail.

In the twenty-two years since he created United Companies, Lloyd Collette had been watching for an innovative mind like his own. He recalled how he had developed, even copyrighted a lending program that got him a virtual corner on FHA lending in Louisiana after World War II. He had almost caught the corner as the largest lender in the nation. And then came another brilliant Collette innovation, years before its time. It was his concept that people had equity in lots of things, like their homes. Why not use that house equity to finance buying a car? He made it work and again spearheaded a whole new life for United Companies. But progress was stalled. There weren't the minds he needed from the ranks of his sales force to open a new United front. Something told him that this aggressive, open-hearted guy from Ohio with the Pied Piper magnetism to him, was just what United needed.

"May I tell you what I'd really like to do, Mr. Collette?"

"I'm waiting."

"I'd like to join United Companies and I'd like to do it tonight. I'm ready to go. I respect you. I think I can do a lot for you. But I want more reputation than just the mouth at a seminar when you bring me down here to Baton Rouge. I've got an idea for a new kind of way to go at life insurance and that's why I asked if you were sticking with credit life only."

"We're always open to new ideas, John. You got one to give us, we're listening."

"It's not ready yet. Here's what I'd like to have your permission to do. How about making me Director of Marketing for the State of Ohio? I don't care about rank or any o' that stuff, except as it helps me get through doors that open easier to vice-presidents. So just give me the territory of Ohio and let me start from scratch and let's see what happens."

"You got it. We aren't even there yet, as you know, but you go stick a flag in the State of Ohio and claim it for United. Let me see what you can do."

"Thank you, sir." John thrust out his hand and stood to go. "Guess I'll go grab forty winks, then head for that family o' mine. Naomi's gonna be hard to convince that I'm really stayin' in one state, after the last few years."

"Good luck, John. And by the way, consider yourself a member of the Board of Directors back here, as of right now."

"That's great! I'm honored, Mr. Collette."

A tall and stately Lloyd Collette clapped an affectionate arm around John's shoulder as he walked him to the door. "I'm sure that works both ways. United is honored to have you aboard."

He was home again. He was with Naomi again. It felt as if he had been gone for centuries from the love of his life and from their wonderful children. Lordy, how the children had sprouted! How much of their lives had he missed? The off-again, on-again, home-some-weekends, home-next-month routine of his work with Guardian as trainer and motivator had given wings to his kids' growth in many directions.

Time was now to rebuild the father role, if he was to have children who were close to him in a few years when they had left the nest for lives of their own. It was always on his mind in his months away when a fragile telephone line seemed like the only connection to a family of four that was looking to him as father and husband.

But his excellence as leader and motivator of others was forcing him toward a pinnacle of career achievement. He knew it was coming. He accepted his gift of leadership for two purposes and he never let them get out of sight. His successes meant nothing at all to him unless they served the finding of success and happiness for others, as well as for himself. It was a compulsion with him. It was the only real purpose of money. And others' success was the only real sense to his holding high position, too. He never thought of it as a mission or a ministry. That was far too lofty and often too pious a role in those he'd watched, who carried that tag. But, like it or not, John had the mission burning inside which drove him to help others find their own success and happiness. And those closest to his heart and his hunger for those things were Naomi, Gary, Denise and Vicki.

"So, I'm back on Square One," he announced to Naomi. "I'm just where I was five years ago when I went with Laymen. But big things are about to happen." The kids were tuned in to the conversation. He told them they were about to see a lot more of him, on every weekend, at least. A company in Louisiana had made him an officer and let him come back home to begin their company in Ohio. Impulsively he grabbed for Denise and circled an arm around Vicki and pointed an accusing finger at Gary. "Would you believe this guy is gonna be fifteen in less than a week?"

"I'd believe it!" snipped Denise. "He sat on me yesterday and he weighs a ton!"

"Yeah, well, you asked for it! Mom told you to put the dishes in the washer and you made Vicki do it while you ditched out. Dad, she's nuts. She tried to drive the car and I told her it was against the law for eleven-year..." He broke off as his father wig-waggled his hands for silence.

"Okay, okay. Now listen. Dad's home. We're a whole team and we all need each other. Right?" Heads nodded. "Okay, then. Now I'm back home but I'm gonna have to build this company and you're all gonna have to help me and your mother make this work. And we get our weekends together. Okay? Vicki, I want you and Denise to get to be the champion baton twirlers in Ohio in no time, and Denise is gonna be driving a car in a few years — if she doesn't do it anymore *now*. Right, Denise?"

"I guess so." She stabbed a petulant tongue in the direction of her brother.

"Say, how about this play I hear you wrote, Denise? When do we get to see the latest? And what's it called?"

"Mom, you tell him."

"It's called Palace Happenings and it's tonight at poolside in the outdoor ballroom of the Hail residence of Beavercreek, Ohio. It's quite elegant."

"Palace Happenings" was both a treat and a terror to John. It was impossible to avoid the messages of playwright Denise, eleven-plus, going-on-twenty, and probably the strongest willed of his brood. He shivered privately when he heard her have the king say, "Oh dear, tomorrow is that conference. I must get to bed." And the Queen responded, "Dear, how long must you be gone *this* time?"

It was a jolt. It wasn't news. But in his heart John felt a tremor of discomfort. Absentee dad was the last thing he wanted to be. *Was he rationalizing, thinking that charging for the top as hard as he was, was really for these precious people?* 'How long must you be gone...?' It wasn't the Queen asking the question; it was the playwright. And *when he made the top, would they still be his family?* The hundreds of times his Queen had asked, 'How long must you be gone?' as he left for a Liberty American sales campaign...a Laymen training conference...a Guardian Advisors extended motivational seminar with him in charge...and now back to Ohio with United ...and here we go again! *Would it one day be too late to be a Dad?* He shuddered privately and nobody noticed.

Hugs and kisses all around for another Academy Award worthy play by Denise Hail and performances by his kids with Amy Herzog, too. "I hate to make like the king, but would you believe Dad's tired and I must go to work tomorrow?"

"Not another conference," groaned Gary in mock dismay.

As he headed for their bedroom, John cupped an arm around the small of Naomi's back. "I'll tell you one thing, we're gonna have you with lots more husband and father very soon. I think the breakthrough is a lot closer than either one of us thinks."

"That'll be wonderful! John, if you believe it's going to happen, I don't care what it is, it's going to happen! You're doing it for us and I believe in you."

"I know one thing — that none of what's coming could ever have happened without you." His fingers tightened at her waist.

"And I know something else," she replied. "You've kept telling me on the phone what Guardian has you do in motivation lectures — to 'brainwash 'em.' I'm the *best* at that. So I better start pulling my weight. I have an idea..."

"Heck, I knew all the time you were doin' a number on me. What's your idea?"

"It's really simple. I should have thought of it way back when you started selling insurance, but I didn't know anything then. Now I know what's going to happen here in Ohio the minute you start. You're going to have a lot of eager young salesmen recruited and wanting to do it John Hail's way and I bet you anything we lose some of the best just because their wives can't take their long hours and their days away from home."

"Yeah." He was peeling his tie as he scanned his wardrobe for tomorrow's wear. "Sure lose some. What can we do?"

"How about if I go to work on helping the wives understand this business, too? You know, get the women in here every week, or go where they are, and just talk to them about how this work challenges their home and family life. I could do it well," she laughed.

"You'd do that?" He caught her in his arms. "I think that would be fantastic! Listen, you could just turn the whole scene around for a bunch of them who don't have the slightest idea how to cope. Do it! I love you for wanting to."

"Sure you do. You just want the play written over so's the King gets to ask the Queen. 'How long must you be gone?' By the way, I saw your face. That kind of shook you, didn't it?"

"Yeah, it did." He pulled the beige and brown checked jacket from the rack. "I guess I just heard a pretty good warning from my kids...and...well..."

"And they love you terribly. Each of them."

❖   ❖   ❖

In four short months John had produced a miracle for United Life in Ohio. He had recruited and trained eighty-one new agents who now were producing from five to six million dollars new income for the company every month. Baton Rouge headquarters was thrilled with the miracle to the North.

He had developed a plan for a life insurance program unique and so different from others that Mr. Collette was completely sold on his proposed new way and went to Ohio personally to bring him back to Louisiana. He wanted John in a key role. This time it was not to motivate his United sales force and teach them technique. It was to be Director of Sales for the whole scene of United. Time to burst from the cocoon of a small regional credit life company to a full-blown national power. John, with his original thinking, his driving energy, his persuasive power with others, his absolute genius for putting his finger on dynamic marketing ways, was the key to that future.

Gary, Denise and Vicki

John was ready. He had proven to himself he could work as a leader with a United sales force, marketing the United product as no one else could. Now he could help Mr. Collette break from the local bonds of a Louisiana-bound firm and go for national spread. If his climb seemed meteor-like to some, it was at a pace to be expected to those who had watched him closely. There was magic to the touch he brought and because of him and his program, the company name fast became well known. John appeared in states where he had served as a Guardian lecturer and was back now seeking a Certificate of Authority for United to do business there. And from three states the company grew to thirteen.

Naomi's brainstorm to help wives understand and help their husband's new career had blossomed to a company-wide effort and she was as much in demand as John on the platform, sharing her ways for dealing with the frequent one-parent home life.

For both John and Naomi there was a special kind of satisfaction, too, that came with the presence of so many of their own family in the company work — Hails together with Morgans, now in the midst of their own careers with United. There was Fred Morgan and Bob Morgan and Don. There was Lloyd Hail and John Shultz and there was Norman Hail and there were others, including Don Herzog. Still in his own business, he was put on the Board of Directors of United in Baton Rouge because, like all the others, he too, was attracted to this company that had John now nearing the dramatic pinnacle of leadership.

Some were surprised when the simple, unpretentious note from John and Naomi reached their homes in 1970. It wasn't

We wish to express our sincere appreciation for your support in helping us realize our "Impossible Dream."

In our new position as President of United Companies Life Insurance Company, we pledge to do all we can to keep this the Company where you may realize your dreams.

John & Naomi

an embossed and gilded corporate announcement. It was a simple photo of a husband and wife, grateful to the thousands who had helped them. It was a pledge to his friends, so completely typical of John's personal concept of the place of honor.

❖ ❖ ❖

Seven hundred miles away in Oklahoma City, another Chairman of a life insurance company took note of John's ascendancy to President of United Life in Baton Rouge. Nick Pope wasn't the least surprised. He had watched John at work in committees they shared. He prided himself in knowing the best and the worst in the insurance industry. Of the many outstanding marketing people, none held a candle to John Hail.

He was plainly and simply the best in the whole United States. Pope should know. He chaired a national committee that saw every level of performance by the leaders of the industry. John Hail was brilliant and Nick Pope privately resolved that one day he would lure him from Louisiana to head National Foundation Life in Oklahoma City.

The spectacular record John had made before he came to United as its President, gave everyone good reason to hope there would be a turn-around in the affairs of the company. No misplaced optimism there. After twelve years in existence, United Companies had a total ordinary insurance in force of $31,000,000. Bottom lines are clues to what happened in the five years he was in the leadership role with the firm. In the last year of his presidency, the company wrote $290 million in new business. They had expanded to a nationally respected company and the force he had recruited over the short few years numbered more than five thousand sales agents.

It was still John's fundamental thrust in working with his people that they were *his* people. Not just one of five thousand digits. His office, even when he reached the pinnacle as President, had an open-door policy. The discouraged salesman, the frustrated office employee, the winners and the losers of the moment, never had to fight their way into his office. It was as open to any one of them as his office had been in the gas station in Beavercreek. If they were good enough to be his employees, he believed, they were good enough to be his friends and shouldn't have to claw past a battery of secretaries to have a conversation with the boss, either in person or on the phone.

• • •

John's open phone is the only reason one of his youngest agents became a multi-millionaire. The fledgling agent was East of Lexington, Kentucky on a wintry night, almost out of gas and totally out of morale. He pulled into a gas station and spent the last penny he had for a few gallons to get back to Lexington. Then he remembered John Hail's open phone availability.

J. L. called the Hail residence on an impulse — collect — and told John he just couldn't go on; there had to be something wrong with him...He just wasn't getting the sales...Maybe he was just not the right man for people to take him seriously about insurance...

It would have been easier to brush him off. *Hell of a time to call and anyway, the guy's a quitter. On my nickels!*

That never could be John's way and it wasn't then. He reached for something that had worked for him and said, "J. L., I know where you're coming from. But you've had a bunch of 'No's'...Why not try just one more call 'fore you give it up today? Will you do that? Just one more. It could be the big one!"

It was. J. L. turned down a long country lane where lights were shining in one wing of a house on the hilltop. It was the manager's residence at a large horse breeding farm. J. L. won't forget the surprised look on the man's face as he opened the door to his late-night caller. He welcomed him in, listened and bought. He and his wife offered J. L. late night supper and hospitality overnight and wanted him to talk to others of the farm in the morning.

And the next day J. L. sold more and was on his way to success, because his boss had listened and had shared a reason *why* to do it and hadn't wasted time talking about *how* to do it.

That difference was on John's mind when one of his subordinates was grousing that the company ought to be doing more training. "People who are out there selling, ought to be getting more information on how to do it," he said.

John's answer was cryptic and to the point, in the Hail fashion. "I still believe the one philosophy that's done more for me than anything else in the world — and can do more for anybody — is to really understand that telling people *how* has got nothing to do with nothin'! It's giving them a reason *why* that makes the world go 'round.

"If people have a *reason* to go out and do it, they'll figure out *how*. Who in our company doesn't know how to sponsor? Who doesn't know how to write policies? But so many want to spend all their time telling people how to do it. That's the trouble with a lot of the professionals, the CLUs. I have no objection to all the training in the world, but once a CLU thinks that his designation as a Charter Life Underwriter is going to sell insurance for him, he's done! It won't!"

❖ ❖ ❖

Leon Hooter met John early in the '70s at a Louisiana meeting and was captured by his simple down-to-earth openness. He was first caught by the selflessness of this man who seemed not the least interested in impressing others with his importance as the chief executive officer of a large insurance company; who was far more interested in turning the credit to someone else. As Leon went to work for John, he discovered that often when John bragged on one of his subordinates, it was for something he wished that one would do.

When a program surfaced that likely had its roots in long-ago thinking by John Hail, it was always someone else who got credit for the idea. John saw to it. And the one who had been given the credit, had the inspiration to work harder than ever to make "his" idea work.

It was a lot more than what some describe as charisma that surrounded John. Leon felt the difference from the beginning. "He makes you believe in yourself. He makes you do more than you can do, without ever demanding it. He goes for the beyondness in a person. Part of the magic in his leadership is his handling of whatever expectations he may have of a person. No one ever has been cast in a mold of what John expects of them.

"Never does anyone have to perform to his standard or his goal for them — or else. He always gives away the right to develop at another's own pace. No doubt he privately has expectations for every one of his people, but he never makes a job description on an iron mask into which another must fit and live, if he values his job."

• • •

One of the fascinating things that those working close to John discover, is that he has one total conviction about decision making. It applies not just to his own way of leading, but to those who work for him.

Once when he was with a group of United Companies executives, he put it to them: "I don't know if it works for anybody else, but it works for me. You make the decision and *then* you make it right. You don't make right or wrong decisions. So it never has bothered me to make a decision. The wrong implementation might have made it not work, but then you just make the implementation right. Flexibility is the thing. And you never do it by yourself.

"They try to say that command is a lonely role. I don't look at this as a lonely job at all. Every time you make a decision or a sale as a leader, you should be training somebody else. Never do it by yourself. Make sure you have people around you all the time."

• • •

The very accessible chief executive of United Companies Life Insurance had some real live encouragement to keep it humble from the small fry of his family. Still remembered by many in the audience who were there, was one introduction of John to a large audience of sales agents who had come to Baton Rouge from many other companies. To be sure everyone in the auditorium knew the importance and prestige of their featured speaker, his introducer walked the crowd through a catalogue of John's achievements in sales and recruiting and executive leadership. He left no doubt their guest was one of the most important figures in America's insurance industry. "...and now, ladies and gentlemen, I give you — John Hail!"

As John strode from his seat toward the platform, to the thunderous ovation of the crowd, a quiet voice drifted after him from son Gary, who had been brought along to the meeting. "Big deal...!"

What could be more eloquent for a dad to hear than the caustic teenager evaluation of an introduction? Little wonder that no one in the Hail family, from Dad through daughters, ever has had a problem with ego!

• • •

Not to pretend there weren't problems within this remarkable family. There is no one, but no one, at the creative edge of a top leadership role in any service industry, or in *any* industry, who does not have a tremendous challenge to fulfill the family life he holds in first place in his heart. Everything that came of his and Naomi's love — especially their children — was John's reason for being. It was no different when he reached the top.

Through the years in Baton Rouge, as success topped success, Lloyd Collette and his firm showed their gratitude to John for his leadership. That he was now a wealthy man had no bearing on John's personal opinion of himself. How it helped others was what mattered. He lavished material love on his family.

Sure there were problems, when Dad was forced by his role to be everywhere and Mom was supporting the heavy demand on her husband by being with him most of the time. But out of the problems, there were three remarkable children become teenagers in a home of plenty, moving ahead as they saw the way. It burned home to John and Naomi that they were in the heart of the hurricane years of their children's adolescent development, and in the eye of the same hurricane years of John's acknowledged leadership role in America's largest industry. There were frightening hours.

It's one of the seldom-talked-of sacrifices that goes as part and parcel to great achievement. The achiever has the decision to make of what price he or she is willing to pay from his family time and the chance to be intimate with his children through their years at home.

Nick Pope was the exultant Chairman and Chief Executive Officer of National Foundation Life in Oklahoma City in 1972. The firm he had created and led through two decades of remarkable growth, had stalled. Nothing short of a major leadership change was going to blow it out of the doldrums. Somebody had to turn things around or the prestigious NFL was lost. Common stock had dipped to nearly worthless. The Annual Report did its best to keep a stiff upper lip, but Insurance-In-Force was down; Premium Income was down; Total Income was down and there was no way to be manful about a 30% loss from the year before in total operations. It would take a some-*body*, not a some*thing* to turn things around.

And now he had the somebody. John Hail had just agreed to take the post of President and Director of National Foundation Life Insurance. Nick had good reason to exult. He had the man he considered the best in America as his company's leader. For the past five years he had watched the life insurance program John created and brought to United Companies accrue more than $600,000,000 in sales. He had watched as United's sales force rose to five thousand agents and spread coast-to-coast. He simply had to have this man!

And John listened. National Foundation Life was a smaller company. Their current picture was not promising. Lloyd Collette was his boss and the man he would always respect for his business ethics and honesty. Mr. Collette (John would never think of him as Lloyd) had shoved a signed piece of paper across the desk when John said he was going to leave. "Name your price. We'll meet it."

Nick Pope

That would be one of the greatest compliments he'd ever have. But the opportunity now was with National Foundation and in the end, he chose to go. If there was any one secret to his decision, it was the complete autonomy Nick Pope offered him — to be completely in charge. It never had been an opportunity he had had before. It was too much to resist.

And the magic touch was there from the moment John took office. The firm had done only $200,000 in new business the year before. In his first year in command, sales swelled to $2 million and the next year to $13 million and to $20 million the next. National Foundation Life was out of the woods. John Hail had arrived.

• • •

Where was the magic? Where it was at the gas station. Where it was at United. From a few hundred agents, the sales force grew to more than 1500 in the field. And in that small army, heroes were beginning to appear. People who described John as 'the motivator's motivator.' Numbers of them were moving into the Millionaire's Club. More than once he was asked how many millionaires he had made and his reply always was quick. "I never personally *made* a millionaire. I just give the opportunity to many and some grab it and run with it. And some make millions." His open secret was what had always been his driving conviction: *You give them a reason why.*

• • •

An article in the Beavercreek, Ohio News May 8, 1979 described the state of the Hail family after the first seven years in Oklahoma City had passed. It reads —

"Hail's success story in the insurance business is something that should be put in book form. He landed on his feet with United Companies in the sixties and worked his way up to the president's chair. In 1972 he was lured away from the Louisiana company by officials of National Foundation Life. At present he's President and Chief Executive of National Foundation Life and Vice-President, Treasurer and Director in the parent NFC Corporation. He's also a Director and member of the executive committee of NFC Petroleum, an oil and gas exploration company affiliated with NFC Corporation.

"John Hail and his wife, Naomi, have been married 28 years...Naomi is an accomplished speaker and has been a most active partner in what John regards his most important assignment — the motivation of sales people and their spouses. John and Naomi have three children: Gary, a radio executive in Baton Rouge, and Denise and her husband, Dennis Loney, who also live in Baton Rouge, and Vicki, married and living in Stillwater, Oklahoma, where both she and her husband, Andy Bogert, are students at Oklahoma State University. Vicki recently posted a perfect 4.0 point and made the dean's list. The Hails have four grandchildren.

"John was born in Dayton on November 11, 1930, one of 14 children. His father was a minister and both John and Naomi are active in the Nazarene Church.

"John Hail has become such a tremendous success because he knows how to treat people. He's come a long way since pumping that quarter-a-gallon gasoline just East of the underpass on old Dayton-Xenia Road in Beavercreek and is one of the few in the multi-millionaire class. The Hails have two yachts based in New Orleans, a summer home in Baton Rouge, a condominium in Horseshoe Bay, Texas, next door to LBJ Ranch, and a 43-foot motor home which he makes available to employees and their families for weekend jaunts."

That he was a multi-millionaire was the very last thing on John's mind. It had never been his motivator. It never would be. At the moment, a kid in Louisiana had his attention. John Locke had been written off and fired by one of his managers as too young to sell insurance and one of those 'hippie culture guys' anyway.

"You a hippie, John?"

"No sir, Mr. Hail. I used to be. Long hair and all. But I cleaned up my act. I was a student down at Northwestern in Natchitoches and I've been working with John Anderson. He'll tell you I'm good, even if I'm only twenty-one. Look, Mr. Hail, all I want is a chance. It won't cost you a dime, if I don't make it. I can work part-time at another job and sell insurance in the mornings and evenings."

John listened to the eagerness and the desire to succeed in that voice and knew before he even agreed, that he had a winner. There was no way he ever would walk away from that kind of man or woman.

He sent him to Lafayette, Louisiana for a few months test. Company word had it that everyone in Lafayette spoke Cajun and that's why the last five agents had quit National Foundation. John Locke didn't quit. He soared to Number One in company sales in a few months in Cajun country.

More testing was needed and over three years Locke moved fifteen times as he proved beyond a doubt he was a winner. And within those three years, still in his young twenties when some say a man or woman can't sell insurance, John Locke became a National Life General Agent over Kentucky and North Carolina and eventually, Florida. John Hail was like a father to him, he declares, and how many millions is John Locke worth today? Who counts?

And anyway, John Hail didn't make him a millionaire. He just made very sure that the opportunity was opened for someone as determined as John Locke.

PART TWO

Chapter One

Irvin Carter watched from the dust-smudged window of his office, puzzling at the purposeful stride as Harland hurried down the dirty, rutted street away from school. He turned and smiled at Gladys King, "There goes Mister Determined."

"He'll be a writer..." The English teacher paused at the door and looked across the room at Tupelo's principal. "Or maybe a poet. He writes very well."

"Now if he can just find a practical talent, he can make a living," chuckled Irvin. "Well, I think we both know what the problem is now."

'A family errand,' Harland had told Mrs. King and would they excuse him to go do it during lunch recess? He'd be back promptly at one.

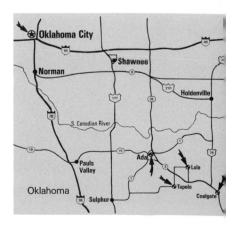

Watching the proud, string bean leanness of the twelve-year-old, dark hair whipped by the wind, trotting as he rounded the corner, Carter wondered. He would like to have pressed him for the purpose of three such 'errands' this week, but that would only have embarrassed the boy. He would have told the truth, because that's the way he was.

There was little doubt anyway just why he had to disappear from school every noon hour. The situation was unhealthy for a growing boy. If only Viola and Allen Stonecipher had a phone, he might be able to help. The retreating figure disappeared behind a stand of blackjack oak trees.

School lunch room, 1950

Irvin shrugged and turned from the window. He was willing to bet Harland had left home in the morning with a lunch bag and it was hidden along the route, rather than have it known that he was the only seventh grader who didn't have twenty cents for lunch in the cafeteria.

It was poorer out in Coal County in 1952 than it was richer. Irvin knew that kids could be just as cruel with looks and attitudes toward anyone different as they were when he was a boy. But Harland was liked by everyone for always being ready to help any of them having learning problems and if he had a kind of seriousness about him, it was not from gloom or self-pity. Just a very deep thinking young man, making up his mind about a lot of things early in life.

Carter sighed and reached for his jacket. It would be failing to do his job, he decided, if he didn't bring this matter to a head with Harland himself. Even though he could guess at what the problem was, the kid *could* be in some other kind of difficulty. With only twenty-eight students in the seventh grade, he'd be a sorry principal if he let any one of them get into trouble without getting involved himself. And this boy was special.

He turned the cardboard hands of the Be-Back-Clock on the outside of his office door and headed across the street toward his car. He had to have a look.

In the patch of scrub oak Harland dropped beside the table-shaped outcropping of sandstone. For a few minutes he rested back against the rock, surveying the flat terrain around him. It felt sometimes when he slipped into this private little hideaway, as though he was an intruder into a foreign land. Not too far away in the Ada area had been the headquarters compound of the Chickasaw Nation of Indians. And not much farther was the infamous Trail of Tears, where the Cherokees had been marched through Winter and death and where the maverick Seminoles from the distant East coast had been brought to a new exile.

Oklahoma wasn't really that many years from the time when Indians held it as their home by birthright. It wasn't even half-a-century ago that this was still Chickasha Country and the settlers were scrapping for statehood recognition in this stepchild region of the Union, where rebellious tribes were sent. And down the road a bit, what was now Hudson's Big Country Store, was a lonely trading post run by some gutzy Hudsons for some even braver settlers heading further into Indian land.

He pulled the Zane Grey anthology from the hip pocket of his overalls, wondering if this was the Fall his parents would buy him some slacks on the harvesting trip to Mc-Alester. That was when they took the money from the peanut crop and repaid the merchants and laid in for Winter. With all the rain they'd had this Summer, not likely that the 30 acres in peanuts would yield that much...or even the return from the whole 170 acres do it, for that matter.

Childhood home until marriage

A grab in his stomach drove his thoughts to the kitchen part of the sharecropper's shack they called home. His parents probably were there right now, in for dinner from the fields. Regular as clockwork. He could see Dad drop tiredly onto the just-as-tired cushions of the front room couch while Mama was at the sink a few feet away.

She was really something else, his mother. Up before dawn with her husband and boy, making breakfast from flour and water and last night's leftovers — if she had any — and if not, she simply made biscuits and gravy. Then off into the dirt of the fields with them for five or six relentless hours in the morning sun. After lunch, with no break for rest, back into the fields for five or six hours more. Their drawn, sun-weathered faces and lean frames testified that the land they farmed for the right to live on it, demanded its price from both Dad and Mama.

He pulled out the magazine advertisement used for a bookmark and lost himself at once in Zane Grey's "Story of a Lion Dog." It was the best way to escape hunger

Harland with Mama and Dad

pangs and when he couldn't totally, he reminded himself that it was his own fault that he was too proud to be the only boy bringing his lunch, advertising that he was even poorer than the rest. Besides, supper wasn't that far away.

Irvin Carter had almost passed the cluster of oaks when he caught a glimpse of a faded blue cotton shirt at the edge of the grove. Harland, legs crossed, chin on the palms of his hands, was there absorbed in a book. For just an instant he thought to pull to the shoulder of the road and deal with this head-on, but then instinct deterred him. There was a kind of purposefulness to the kid, even in self-imposed exile. And certainly at this age he didn't prefer books to food and he wasn't starving to death. It would be interesting to see whether he would show resourcefulness with his problem.

Driving back to the school, Carter couldn't shake him and his pride from his thoughts. As principal, he could authorize a hot lunch free for the youngster, but that would be a bigger slap at him than the government's requirement that a student sign a hardship slip, appealing for free lunch.

Irvin Carter

• • •

A dog's bark penetrated Harland's escape to another world. This time he heard an urgent three snappish barks in rapid fire sequence. A running hound. Did he have a quarry cornered? It was the lure that surpassed all others for him.

He pulled out the torn advertisement from <u>The Hunter's Horn</u>, folded in his shirt pocket, and for silent seconds studied the photograph. Wolf hound pups. He mulled the prices and the impossibility of getting them. *Fifty dollars! Dream stuff! It might as well be a thousand. If there wasn't going to be money for needed clothes and if there wasn't any to have twenty cents a day for lunch at school — less than forty dollars a year,* he figured — *then for sure there wasn't ever going to be any fifty dollars to buy a pair of hounds.*

Just why did it matter anyhow? he wondered, twisting on his butt, then slouching back against the rock, chewing listlessly at a stalk of wheat. The despair penetrated briefly, deep and pointed...*Faced squarely and without pretend, the Stonecipher family was barely surviving...None of the older brothers and sisters, years before him, had even finished high school and he knew why...They probably had to get out and start making a living...There likely wasn't even food enough to feed them...*

The signs of poverty were everywhere. Especially in the metal covered hovel which was barely protection from the elements. No plumbing. His dad had dug two wells to go for water and, worse the luck, the one nearest the house was a salt water one and the other, some distance back, able to yield only a few gallons a day of fresh. (Salt water here in Oklahoma?) The family bathtub was in the back yard and in the morning one of his duties was to fill the old round tub with salt water, pulled up by the bucket on his homemade wrench held on two forked branches, and to let it sit there and warm all day so that at evening, modesty put aside, each of them could bathe away the day's dirt from the peanut patch in lukewarm salt water.

Forked branches of the well

For Harland it was just another painful symbol of their condition. He usually did his own bathing in the cattle pond down at the foot of the hill. And did his reading by their one oil lamp, shared with Mama and Dad. No electric power was in that part of the country and probably wouldn't ever be for the Stoneciphers...not on the few hundred dollars they earned annually from the land.

It wasn't in Harland's young mind to live his life in bitterness, only awareness of the family's lot. *There just had to be something better!* But there wasn't much around to compare their lot with. Well, wrong — there were the Crosses a mile away. They had a little more. But something was terribly wrong — even without comparisons — for his mother and dad to work so hard so constantly and to be so honest and loving, and yet to have nothing. Something was rotten somewhere!

How in the world did his dad find strength to stay so optimistic? To believe in some kind of better future for Harland, his youngest son? But he did. He always said so.

• • •

There was the bark again. He shook his head and pushed the ad into the pages of the book and stood up stretching. He had to have a hound. No, he had to have a *pair* of hounds. Two were all he would settle for. Edgar Cross always hunted with two dogs and he wanted to do like him. And it was ever so much more than being like the neighbors,

111

too. It was *needing* the dogs and the hunt and the victory. He had to take all that belief in himself that his dad had ingrained in him, and score some victories. *Now!* That was what the dogs were all about. It wasn't just escape when he went coyote or coon hunting with Edgar. It was a whole lot more.

"Them other folks, they don't understand," said a sage Edgar. "Either you care 'bout runnin' with the hounds and the thrill o' the hunt, or you don't. It's born in ya. I could tell first time we went out, you was hooked." Harland was hooked.

Abruptly the chance question when he was leaving Wofford Battle's place with Edgar came back. "Edgar, might you be interested in a couple o' good dogs?" Mr. Battles had asked.

"Don't reckon so. Why? You got some comin'?"

"Most likely. Make you a good price, mebbe three, four months."

Harland was suddenly aware of what he had to do. *Why, he'd get out of this condition that made buying his own dogs a hopeless dream. He'd escape from having to hide from classmates who bought their lunches or from wondering if he'd have wearable pants for Winter when they'd begin to wake to cold, crispy mornings and the harvest yield was tallied in dollars and cents — and once again there was not enough.*

He knew what he had to do. It was simple. Make money himself.

He knew his father would give total approval to dogs and school lunches and clothing, if he could find a way to get them for himself and approach him right for the permission.

"Steve!" The name burst from his lips as he trudged the road back to school. Steve was his friend, nearest of the Stonecipher neighbors, not more than part of a mile across to the hilltop to the East. He'd bet *Steve would instantly share his enthusiasm for going after their own money...They could do it as a team.* He had no doubt they could make dollars, if they could team their strength and go to every farmer in the country, ready to do anything, even the most menial chores for the cheapest prices. *It would work...Steve even had transportation, too...A horse ...They could ride together and could definitely make it work...*

• • •

Irvin Carter lived directly across the street from his school. He was about to open his front door to go to Algebra, Junior's Section, from his own lunch when he saw Harland coming up the road. Same hurried, confident stride. Lots of purpose and determination there.

"Nell, come quickly!" he called to his wife. She hurried from the kitchen, her hands covered with soapy dish water. "I want you to see somebody."

Dark-haired, pretty little Nell, his bride of less than a month, peeked through the organdy curtain. "Who is he?"

"A seventh-grader named Harland Stonecipher. He's a different one, I'll tell you."

Harland was carrying his book, brushing his hair back into place as the wind sent it skittering again across his head.

"Nell, there's a winner. I've got a good feeling about him."

"He's tall like you, Irvin. And he's got dark hair. That makes him special already."

He wondered what Harland had been reading. He hoped it was other than Steinbeck. Shadows of Grapes of Wrath seemed to linger everywhere in the Tupelo area and it was hard to find any bright and shiny good reasons for optimism and expectation from the area to which he had brought Nell. He had seen a great number of young Oklahoma boys and girls filled with purpose and determination. Few came from families in worse straits than the Stoneciphers and few, if any, achieved beyond a marginal living.

Harland Stonecipher, 1952

The horrible part was that those in that depth of poverty often were victims of innocent circumstances. Good, honest people teaching their kids those values, but not seeing much more. Caught in a trap not of their making. They were a part of the Oklahoma soil that seduced men to be farmers, then spat on them as they tilled barely profitable, sandy, infertile soil from dawn till dark every day for the rest of their lives.

Soon it was dust to dust and they were gone and their offspring either took over the family homestead back in the pasture, or moved to town, going little further economically than if they had remained sharecroppers. Free not to have to divide their meager earnings with the owner of the land, but not free at all.

Unless Harland, now swinging confidently up the steps of the front door of the school without an apparent worry on his mind, was very different, he was destined to go the route of the rest. But there was something about this boy. Carter knew they would keep an eye on this one. He was someone special to share with Nell.

"Bye, dear. See you in a bit." He hurried across the rutted dirt road that passed for the main street of Tupelo and Nell watched her man go. Speaking of winners, she had married one, she knew, and she loved him for the way he cared for his students. He'd be something special for education, she was sure. Already he was mapping out the way he'd be able to commute to Norman several nights a week to get that coveted PhD. And the youngster they had watched returning for afternoon classes had no notion in the world he had already become someone special to the Carters.

There was visible animation in Harland's face when he talked quickly with Steve Breed as History class was about to convene.

"All right, seats everybody. Who's going to tell us today what the Battle of Yorktown meant to the Colonies? Harland, why don't you start?"

The Battle of Yorktown was the last thing on Harland's mind. His thoughts were loaded with a program to which Steve had just given one hundred percent of his usual enthusiasm. It had nothing to do with an event that happened almost two centuries ago. This was something he had to do for his tomorrow and he wanted to get on with it.

He swallowed and stood by his desk. "Yes, sir. Well, the Yorktown battle was the last of the Revolutionary War and was with the English and was the last fight by the

British soldiers who came to keep us slaves to King George. Gen'l Washington beat 'em real good."

"Very good. Who wants to take it from there?"

Fortunately there were the usual hands jabbing skyward for the chance to show their knowledge and Harland was reprieved. History was definitely not his favorite subject and with good reason. Till the past could show any good impact it had made on the present, it was very hard to get stirred to read by the oil lamp at home about what others who lived by oil lamps and hand plows had to say to a new world living by electric power instead of candlepower, and tractors instead of ox-drawn plows and chrome wheels instead of wagon wheels. This was the need that burned in Harland. It was time to get into the 20th Century and it wasn't happening for him.

There was no way to keep his thoughts from the great decision he had just made with Steve. The two were going to find financial independence. Now they had a plan to do it.

• • •

"Do like I did," Steve told him impatiently. "Jus' tell your ole man you want to make your own money and that's that. Know what my pop said?"

Harland shook his head. It seemed weeks ago since he and Steve had talked about his plan. It had been two full days.

Steve Breed

"He said we could use one o' the horses any time we want to and he said somethin' even better. From now on we get ourselves two cents for every bale o' wheat we roll. How 'bout that?"

A grimace tightened Harland's expression. "Not quite that simple with my dad, the way I see it. You own your farm. Bein' sharecroppers has been hard on my folks. They've always wanted to own, but it just doesn't work out. So, 'bout the only thing my father has right now, is his pride. I sure don't want to stomp on that."

"So, when can you talk to 'im? Time's awastin'! You know we could get agoin' on makin' money this Saturday when everyone's out to your place harvestin'. Can you talk to him 'fore then?"

"Only if I can get to him alone. That's hard. Mama's always there. He always says he's our provider and if I don't ask it just right, it can look like I'm sayin' he's *not* providin' and hurt his feelings in front of Mama. Man to man's the only way. I may get a chance tomorrow though. He's goin' over to McAlester for some stuff for the cotton. He said he was gonna take me with him."

"You got problems with cotton now?"

"Jus' begun. Dad says seems like it might be weevils. You know what they'd do to the crop."

Steve shook his head. "My pa says it's hopeless to grow cotton hereabouts anyways. Ground's too sandy. Your pa sure has tough luck."

"Yeah. Well, he's no quitter."

•　•　•

It was never going to get any easier any time, thought Harland. He drummed his fingers on the window ledge of the eighteen-year-old pick-up and for once he was glad of the snail's pace twenty-miles-an-hour his father drove the rusting old red Chevy. It had been the family automotive transportation since before Harland was born and, to be sure it ran forever — some neighbors teased — Allen Stone-cipher always planted his foot on the accelerator pedal to travel exactly twenty-miles-an-hour. He never varied one mile faster or slower. Always exactly twenty. Not even for corners and some of his right angle turns in town at twenty-miles-an-hour were legend.

Still the weary pick-up rolled on. By Harland's calculations with McAlester still thirty miles away, he had an hour-and-a-half. It was time to broach the subject, but how? He had to bring it up now.

He squirmed in his seat, studying his father's expression out of the corner of his eye. *Was now the right time?* Once again, not knowing how to start, he looked back out the window. They passed a newly set out fence line on the right side of the road and that was his opportunity.

"Say, Dad, Steve and I have been thinking on an idea we'd like to try on some of the farmers hereabouts. See that fence right there?"

"Pretty new, I'd guess." The senior Stonecipher tilted a quizzical expression toward his son. "So, what's on your mind?"

"Well, someone had to put that fence in and right now, with crops to lay by on a spread this big, that took a lot o' figurin' to know where to get the time." Harland saw his father was half-watching the road and half-watching him. He had his attention, so this was it. Heart pounding with excitement, he charged on to his great idea. "Me'n Steve figure to spread the word we're the hardest workin', cheapest labor in Coal County and we'll do any kind of job anywhere that's one too many for a farmer. See what I mean, Dad? First I get done all the chores you need for me to do at home, then I hire out."

The car and the whole world turned very silent as his father mulled what he had just heard. Harland wanted to say more to get his father to agree. Some gut instinct told him to be silent and let him react.

"You're tellin' me you want to start earnin' a living diggin' post holes and plantin' them bois d'arc posts in 'em? Are you forgettin' how tough bois d'arc is?"

"I know!" he enthused. "I got callouses to prove it. We don't care! Even if it's the toughest wood in the whole world, we can do 'er, Dad!" He couldn't hold back his enthusiasm now. "See, we, Steve and I figure if we do tough jobs real cheap and real good, word's goin' to spread and in no time we'll have more'n we can handle." He took a deep breath before going on. This was the hard part. "What I was thinkin' was, that instead of always costin' you, I could earn my own clothes and get the school lunch and anything special I want I'd have to get and if it would help out, I'd be glad to put some into the farm, too, to help pay my way."

Bois d'arc fence posts

Allen Stonecipher thought about that, scratching his chin reflectively. "You can forget that 'pay your way.' I reckon your Mama and I can handle it our own selves... you tend to your affairs."

"I didn't mean nothin' like that, honest!" Harland was instantly miserable, aware he had touched a sensitive chord in his father and done it the wrong way. "It just looks to me like I'm growin' up and I could do more. You know, Dad, with the fire and all, it's about more'n one man can handle."

His father's dry chuckle was the best sound he'd heard all morning and when he reached across from the driver's side to slap him on the knee, even before his dad spoke, Harland knew he had approval.

"You remember that fire, do you, boy? Sure cleaned us out. We came into these parts in two wagons and this old pick-up carrying everything we had. Time that fire got done burnin', we had less than we arrived with. And all the water we coulda used to save the house had already fallen for months on our peanuts and just about ruined that crop. Don't know what we would've done if we hadn't had neighbors who helped winch that ole shack we found onto the flat bed and helped me bring it on out here with pots and pans and clothes to start us up again. Yeah, I might of used some o' your earnings then.

Parents at home

"I figure it this way, son. A man's got to pull his own weight and you got to know I want you to pull yours. And I know you're goin' to. You've got something in you and it's goin' to get a chance, if I have anything to say about it. Your mother and me have had five wonderful children and not one of 'em has even finished their schoolin'. I want one o' my kids to finish high school. Let me tell you, boy, I want to see you go get a *real* education after high school, too, if you want."

"College? Really? You mean like go over to East Central in Ada?" He was dumbfounded. He never had guessed his father thought outside the world of their little farm in Centrahoma.

"Ever think what you might wanta do when you're grown up?"

Harland nodded. "I guess I know already."

"What's that?"

"Reckon I'd like to teach, like Mr. Carter and Mrs. King do. They do a lot o' good and they make a lot o' money, too."

Allen Stonecipher slapped the wheel in unsmiling approval. "So there, you see. You're gonna need a college education to do that. And, Harland, that means money. Well, I believe you can be the best teacher in Oklahoma, if you wanta be. And all I'm takin' out of this ole ground is just about enough to keep us alive and that ain't much. So, boy, you're all right! You're on the right track and yes, your mother and I will agree with you right now. It's okay to go for those jobs and start makin' your own earnings."

It was Saturday. If there was one thing that really pulled the neighbors and families together around Tupelo and Centrahoma, Allen Stonecipher often declared, it was their farming. When it came time to lay the crops by, everyone came from everywhere. Today it was to the Stonecipher farm to work their small peanut crop. It was a special day because Edgar Cross had just purchased — actually bought with cash money — a tractor and thresher.

Harland and Steve swung barefoot on the metal gate at the turnoff from the road into the Stonecipher's, watching the approach of the newest, most advanced equipment for threshing peanut crops in Coal County. It took to the rutted, stony dirt road up the hill like a confident monster.

"Haul yourselves aboard, boys!" Edgar sang out as he swung wide to straddle the deep ruts entering the uphill path. "Gotta watch these turns with this new rig," he hollered over the tractor engine. "Whatcha think of 'er?"

"Hey, this is great!" shrilled Harland, voice breaking in its pre-adolescent switch from boy soprano to semi-bass. He crowded tight to the driver's seat as the tractor accelerated against the climb.

Steve was watching the thresher trail behind them. "Hold on a second!" he sang out.

The tractor shuddered to a halt and both Harland and Steve jumped to the ground.

"Okay, go ahead!" Harland yelled, darting to the front of the machine. "Watch my hands. If I wave, there's a rock needs movin'."

"Don'cha wanta ride?" Edgar tilted his jaunty, worn Western hat forward against the early morning sun and squinted down at this youngster who spent almost as much time at the Cross house as at his own place. "This here's a brand spankin' new Ford. She eats rocks for lunch."

The lanky kid with the dark eyes and the warm smile stood arms akimbo, fists on his hips, feet planted widespread and squarely on the ground. "She'll stay new a lot longer if she doesn't have to. Let us get 'em outta the way for you."

A hundred yards up the hill and two stops for rocks later, Cross was appreciating the eager help.

"Say, Edgar," Steve grabbed the opportunity. "How about a couple o' strong hands to go with this new rig? You know, you're gonna get a whole bunch o' people wantin' help from your Ford. Not just harvest time when everyone's pitchin' in."

"Whatcha got in mind, boy?" As if Edgar didn't have a pretty good idea. He slowed to a stop again as Harland wig-waggled his hands to wait while he pushed a sharp-edged boulder out of the way. The tractor idled quietly.

"Well," Harland picked up the conversation, "me'n Steve are teamin' up for anybody who can use some strong backs and cheap labor. And I sorta figured there are plenty poor folks who could get a lot more cash crop out o' their ground and make a lot more for themselves, if they could get a rig like this to come in regular. What we were thinkin' was, with two hands workin' the ground while you drove, you could do, like...well, my Dad's whole thirty acres o' peanuts or his milo or whatever, in no time."

Edgar Cross eyed the enthusiasm in the twelve-year-old, "Tell me, son, this got anything at all to do with a couple o' running dogs?"

Harland smiled and nodded. "That and some other things, I guess. You know, Mr. Breed is having a hard year and, well, I talked to my Dad about me goin' to work and Steve did his, too, so's, you know, we don't have to ask 'em for money. And my father said 'okay'."

"So, how d'ya see me helpin'?"

"Well, sir, with your tractor and thresher and binder and everything, lotsa people call on you to help 'em, like today at my folks'. Most times we'll be there pitchin' in with the rest, like neighbors, but when we aren't, maybe you could just mention you know some mighty hard-workin' boys, in case any special jobs come up. I was wonderin'... would it be too much trouble to let 'em call you, where you have a 'phone?"

"Son, that sounds like you've got it figured real good. Tell you what...Stella's gonna be the one we want to speak to about the 'phone. No reason I see she can't be the message taker, seein's how I'm out most o' the day."

They were at the top of the Stonecipher hill now and already there were more than twenty husbands and wives and their kids working down the rows, pulling vines and turning the buried peanuts to the sun to cure. Before the day was over they would have worked all the acres and done what would have taken Allen and Viola from sunup to sundown more than two weeks, even with Harland's help after school.

A special camaradarie always pervaded the times when the neighbor farmer families pitched in to help each other. There was almost a party atmosphere which seemed to override everything with good humor, even the merciless, intense heat of the July sun. The self-appointed experts among the men, who could guess the yield of an acre from the first few acres that Allen and his wife had already pulled to test their readiness, said the Stoneciphers were about to have their best-ever yield for any year.

"I'd reckon you to have half-a-ton o' peanuts for the acre," announced J. W. Breed, Steve's dad. "Bringin' 'bout three hundred a ton up in Ada, I hear tell."

"I won't argue with that," replied Allen. "Say now, will you look at Edgar's new rig."

Everything stopped as the tractor towing the thresher made across the field to the peanut acreage. "Come watch the demonstration," he called to the collection of sweating, curious friends. "Want'cha to see what's gonna happen when we put a thresher to work in these fields." He lined up with the rows and set off at a crawl through a swirling cloud of dirt and dust. Fifteen minutes later he was back, grinning at the cluster of watchers. "See that? I just threshed right down four rows. Allen, how long you reckon that would take all these people to shuck?"

"More'n an hour, anyway," Allen shook his head. "You got any more tricks?"

"Got one for you later." Edgar had that little boy smiling twinkle of adventures unlimited as he jerked his thumb back toward his property. "Soon's we get through threshin',

I'm gonna go get my new plow and show you all how this rig can plow out a row and save us all lotsa time pullin' these danged peanut vines."

Harland watched the admiration in his dad's expression as he rode along on the tractor. This was the stuff of the 20th Century that he knew his father longed for as much as he did. The Crosses had started the same way as the Stoneciphers, twenty-five years before on land that wasn't their own. Now, after a series of good crop years, they had managed to buy their property. It wasn't any more acreage, but the ground was lower and richer and it was far likely to bear more with the help of the tools of the present century. He knew Edgar would share his equipment just as much as he possibly could. He knew he would never hear an envious word from his father about the good fortune that seemed to be around the Crosses by comparison with the Stoneciphers.

A little later the families were sharing the meal prepared by Viola and Stella and Steve's mother, Letha Mae. It was simple fare but it felt like a very special meal. No speeches were made to thank everyone. It was like the whole event of 'laying the crops by'...the neighbors just did it to support each other. Everyone was hard-pressed to make this back pasture of America profitable. A dry summer, a wet summer, a fire, an injury and any one of the cluster of fifteen families could be wiped out of farming. It was understood. It was feared. It made for a special bond.

"Got two new businessmen here I wanta tell you 'bout," announced Edgar, smiling at Steve and Harland. "These two young fellows are jus' about the hardest workers I've ever had helpin' me and I'm announcin' they're in the special job business. If you got anything you don't want to do or can't do yourself — don't matter what, they tell me — pullin' cotton, building bois d'arc or blackjack fence lines, cleanin' out stubble, you name it an' these boys come cheap. Lemme tell you just how cheap. They'll help bale hay at a penny a bale and that's dirt cheap. Jus' you call Stella an' she's already told me she'll give Harland an' Steve here the word when you want 'em."

Within two months Harland's great idea for financial independence had brought him twenty-five dollars closer to his goal. Stella Cross, rocking on her front porch, saw the string bean figure of the boy who had long been to her like a second son, running down the hill across the fields.

He was breathless when he hurried through her gate and up to the porch. "Stella, is Edgar home yet?"

"Just now freshenin' up, Harland. Sit a spell. He'll be right out. Is something goin' on? Can't be huntin', 'cause you were out almost all last night. I declare, I..."

"I can buy my own hounds now!" He was flushed with the excitement of his announcement, nervously hitching up the strap of his loose-fitting overalls, then brushing the hair that had tumbled over his forehead in his mile run across from home. "I've got twenty-five dollars for 'em."

"Why, Harland, that's wonderful! I knew from the calls I've been gettin' you had to be makin' some money, but I had no idea it was that much already."

Edgar appeared at the living room door. "What's that I've been hearin'? You in the market for a dog?"

"Two of 'em! You reckon maybe Mr. Battles might have those dogs he was expectin' about this time? Said he would make you a real good price. I've got twenty-five dollars, if you still think he'll sell 'em for that."

"I'll just go find out this minute. By golly, that's a right smart piece o' change!" He headed for his phone and minutes later reappeared, face wreathed in a triumphant smile.

"You jus' bought yourself a pair o' dogs, young feller. Jus' born two weeks ago."

"No way to hold back the exuberant yelp of delight and Harland danced excitedly across the porch.

"You sure you got twenty-five dollars?" Edgar teased.

"Oh, yessir. I've been countin' it every night." It was really happening. It wasn't a dream. At last he was buying something for his very own with money he had earned by his own sweat. "When do you suppose we could go for the them?"

Edgar chuckled quietly. "Well, if we don't just sit around here till it's Monday, we jus' might be able to make it over to Coalgate and back 'fore dark!"

Chapter Two

Something wonderful happened inside Harland when he walked up to Wofford Battles and said, "Sir, I'd like to buy those two runnin' hounds I hear you're going to sell. I've got twenty-five dollars for 'em."

And Wofford, briefed by Edgar on the enterprise of two youngsters going anywhere in Coal County to do whatever needed doing, measured up to the moment. "I'd be honored to take your money, son. My friend Edgar here tells me you really worked to earn these hounds. You must be hooked like the rest of us on chasin' critters."

"Jus' for the sport of it, sir. I don't really care about killin' foxes and coyotes, even if some of 'em could sure use killin'. One got a dozen of my dad's best layers last month. But I just like to listen to the dogs runnin'. Edgar here is teachin' me how to train 'em."

Mr. Battles collected the two tiny puppies from their mother and presented them to their new owner. Cupping them in the palms of his hands, Harland bent to reassure a parent who seemed to accept the coming separation, even as her eyes mourned what she sensed was coming. "I'll take good care of your boys, mama." He fingered affectionately under her ear and the pups' mama nestled chin between paws to watch quietly the last minutes with her offspring.

The dream had really come true. These were no longer an advertisement in a magazine. Harland looked at the pair as they cuddled close together in the box nest he had built at the corner of the house beside his room. Lake and Drive were symbols. From the very outset there was the love of a boy for his dogs and dogs for their master. If Allen Stonecipher didn't feel the lure of the hunt, he did see plainly what was happening inside his son as he moved to a new plane of independence. And he liked what he saw.

Very patiently Harland trained the pups, never giving too much love or too much discipline. They responded quickly to his leading and seemed to reach to achieve for him. He devoured the monthly Hunter's Horn and Red Ranger on what and when to feed them and with Edgar and other neighbor farmers, he was soon mastering the arts of the hunt.

Edgar Cross worked a whirlwind day every day all day till dark and often beyond. At noon Stella would seek out her handsome, lithe-bodied man, bringing his major meal of the day to him wherever he was working. After twenty-five years of marriage and hard work, he still packed what seemed boundless energy into his five-foot-seven frame. He was incredibly strong and confident and there was no tiring the man and no exhausting his humor. With a good break in the amount and timing of rainfall that fell on his fields and a clawing determination, he had moved through the years from sharecropper to owner.

After a full day in the fields working his own crops or helping a neighbor, when it was the night of a hunt he was always visibly super-charged for the chase. Stella was privately sure the event, which came as regularly as clockwork twice a week and always on Saturday nights, was more social than sporting. She kept her thoughts to herself.

It was a special kind of patience that helped her encourage her man to enjoy his love of dogs and hunting. Packing food and the making for a fire and coffee for when the hunters stopped to wait and listen for their dogs, she always had the fixin's ready about sunset of the appointed night. Shortly a boy and his dogs would appear at the crest of the Stonecipher Hill and move quickly across the fields and over the fences toward the Cross farm.

The hunt had one special beauty for Harland, that was neither social nor sporting. The hunt gave him think time; the time to reflect on directions. Evenings at home in the tiny living area of the cabin, huddled by the oil lamp to read, were not the time nor place conductive to opening horizons for his thoughts. His dad, dog-tired from the day, most often would be dozing there on the davenport. His mother would tidy the kitchen part of the room, then sink to the couch beside her husband, watch Harland at his doings and gradually succumb to the exhausting hours of her day as the heat, still radiating from the unforgiving tin roof, gradually anesthetized each of them in the room.

Tonight was one of those nights to stay at home; a night when he had to be honest with himself. His English teacher wanted everyone in her class to express in a short essay just what growing up in Oklahoma was meaning to each of them. Harland had thought about the assignment for several days, even tried to put it into verse, since Mrs. King had praised the few poems he had written before. But there was no way he could make anything poetic out of life as he knew it now at fifteen or through the past growing up years. *And how to tell it like it was? Well, he would just have to write honestly.* Everyone knew that he and Steve were from exceptionally poor families, but he finally had grown past the fear of ridicule. As he got older, it seemed unnecessary that he had gone for two years without lunches just so he wouldn't be embarrassed at school.

His working together with Steve most every afternoon was well known now and envied by his classmates. Pulling stubble from fence lines, plucking cotton, milking, plowing, cultivating, clearing rocks from acre after acre and always the bois d'arc cutting. It had to be the toughest wood in the West, but it made them their most money, post holing, cutting the posts — sometimes as many as hundreds a day — hammering in the barbed wire. It was unusual when the day was over and they were walking home, if each would not have at least a dollar for the four hours' work.

"Almost able to buy Dad's pickup for myself," he had told Steve the day before. "It's so old but maybe I could get it and trade it in on something newer."

He sat at the table alone with his thoughts and wrote straight from his heart...

"Growing up poor does something for you. It makes you *afraid* of poverty. Some people fear dreaded diseases. Others fear what poverty does to you. If you haven't been there, you can't appreciate the feeling.

Harland's room

"From the above you can appreciate that my father didn't give me status or money. He does give me integrity and belief in myself. He causes me to believe that I am special and can do anything I want to. As I look back now, I realize I am not anything special and don't have any more ability than anyone else, but Dad believes I do and as a result, I believe I do. Believing gives you strength to overcome.

"A couple of teachers make me believe that being born poor is not a problem that cannot be overcome. They reinforce the seed my Dad has planted in my mind — 'You can do anything you really want to.' I believe them and my Dad. This has caused me to know how important it is to help people to believe in themselves. Each of us needs to know that someone else believes in us. By letting other people know we believe in them, we can help them believe in themselves.

"I dream as I chop with the hoe at the weeds that are mixed with the peanuts. The temperature is over 100 degrees. I feel heat waves along the rows and my bare feet burn and I dream of cool places and a better way of life. At times I find myself hating my parents because we have to work in the heat and the cold and never have enough of anything. Even though that feeling never lasts long, I don't ever want a family of mine to feel that way toward me. I have a fear of that.

"Mother has breakfast ready at 5:30. She cooks our noon meal when she cooks breakfast. By 7:00 a.m. all of us, my mother, dad and my sister (till she left home), are in the field. From 7:00 to 12 noon is a long time. At 12 noon we walk from the field to the house. Each of us, other than mother, has a few minutes to rest. Mother begins putting our dinner on the table. When we are finished eating she washes and dries the dishes and is ready to go back to the field at 1:00 p.m. I never have missed a meal unless it was my own fault and I never go to bed in an unmade bed.

"When I was in grade school, I carried my lunch in a paper bag. A lot of us did. By the time I was a freshman in high school, I was the only one. Everyone else ate in the school cafeteria. I was too embarrassed to be the only one carrying my lunch and so now I am a junior in high school and I am completely self-supporting and eat lunch each day in the school cafeteria."

Harland Stonecipher

A few days later Mrs. King sat quietly at her desk in the empty classroom reading again what one of her favorite students had written. She dabbed at the tear forming in the corner of her eye. It was a very private communication and not a classroom essay. But she really had to share it with Irvin Carter.

This night was a different night and Stella wished Edgar and Harland would shift their plans for hunting till tomorrow. There was a problem with eggs. They badly needed incubating and the nearest incubator was in Ardmore, sixty miles to the South.

It was in the wee hours of the morning that she knew Edgar had forgotten time. The problem to save the hatchers was fast approaching crisis. Where to find her man was a question as big as all Coal County as she began the search. Across county roads and secondary roads, up dirt trails and down long, dark drives she hunted. Finally, toward dawn, she found them — Edgar, Harland and five others — below Coalgate, over ten miles from home, whooping it up as if it was the end of the war.

Stella and Edgar

Stella for once was more than provoked and she ignored her husband's enthusiastic greeting. "Edgar, will you please tell me how I'm to get all those eggs to Ardmore with you sittin' here?" After her own three hour hunt, there was something that looked absolutely ridiculous about half-a-dozen grown men and a boy crouched around a fire in the middle of the road at five a.m., celebrating their fox hunt with ersatz coffee, biscuits and eggs.

"Arnold Pinder, meet my wife, Stella." Edgar ignored the egg crisis and her mad was back. "Arnold has that farm over yonder and would you believe this ole boy came out to greet us and our hounds with a genuine thirty-thirty? Wanted to know what we thought we was adoin' on his property at two a.m.

"Well, when I 'splained to him that our dogs had a coyote or something under his barn, he was just more'n glad to welcome us."

"Nice to meet you, m'am." Pinder tipped his cap. "I'm right grateful to these fellers. They got rid of a right dangerous varmint for me tonight. Y'know, I got young uns and this Edgar of your'n and his friends done trapped them an' honest-to-God lobo 'neath my barn. That's some passle o' dogs, I'll tell you." He motioned toward the pack lying quietly now around the lifeless white carcass.

Stella knew about the lobo wolf. Her father had told her how in the '90's the 'silent killer' of the plains had decimated livestock and cattle and when cornered, would attack and kill anything in his way. The rancher and farmer fear of the lobo finally grew so great that as much as a thousand dollar bounty was paid till at last most of the lobos had been exterminated. Lover of all animals, Stella felt a sad grab for this creature, who must have weighed seventy-five pounds or more, lying dead at the roadside. He was only living the life nature had condemned him to live.

"How did you catch him?" she asked Edgar, her temper quieting.

"Better I tell," interrupted one of the neighbors. "Edgar here will just wantcha to believe he wrung that ole boy's neck with his bare hands."

"Harland, you tell Stella," directed Edgar. "You was nearest in under the barn and it was your Lake who had that ole wolf cornered. We got to teach your dog when it's time to be scared."

"Yeah, he really was right close to that wolf, Stella. And Edgar here went around behind the barn and he peeled a slat off the siding and hit that varmint right over the eyes. Addled his head enough for Mr. Pinder to get him with the gun."

Harland's parents were not the self-pitying kind of people who found life had laid a cruel trap and forced them to a below poverty margin in a country that advertised itself as a land of opportunity. The gross income they could take from their share of the crops never got above fifty dollars a month, but there was no sour note in Allen Stonecipher's exchanges with his son. A smile was a rare commodity with him, but still he showed no bitterness and always there was absolute, impeccable honesty from him. When he owed, he paid. When he promised, he performed. Integrity was a priority in life that he found an absolute, an undiscussable imperative and a must to pass on to his young son.

The humble dwelling that became the Stonecipher home after a fire destroyed everything that had been before, was only a shack...a beast through the summer months which made the cold, windy, winter ones almost a relief. The metal of the roof and siding would never cool till about three a.m. for the inhabitants to rest and five was the rising hour, if the day's work was to be finished.

Through it all, the mother named Viola was destined to sixty years wedded to the uncertainty they would be able to survive another year farming an unforgiving back acre of God's earth. Whatever her inner anxiety, Harland and his friends saw only an exterior of love. Viola had a curious stammer that went with her through her life, but there never was a stammer or a falter in the affection Harland and his friends Steve and Steve's older brother Weldon knew from her. Wide-opened arms, affectionate squeezes belied she had just returned from exhausting hours in the sun coaxing reluctant seeds to grow in sandy soil, guiding the plow, cultivating, plucking, piling and bailing...and never, within the hearing of her son, complaining at her lot.

The confidence which parents in such a downright miserable condition conveyed to their youngest, began to surface in Harland's desire to write. He came across a magazine that offered money for any reader's work which they would publish. Harland worked at it privately at night, then quietly submitted his first effort — a few paragraphs on dogs. There was no way to contain the enthusiasm of the teenager when the seven dollar honorarium came back from the publication. It was little, but it was a whole lot. Another world had just sent signals to the kid living in the back pasture that it was listening; that it was receptive to what he had to say.

Irvin Carter, still watching carefully as this young man moved through high school, felt the growing determination inside the boy. He noticed how quickly Harland grew to another new level of self-assurance after he and Steve declared themselves in business to do anything and everything, anywhere. First he quickly became part of the school lunch program. Then there appeared a distinct new difference in his way of dressing. He was visibly taking special pride in what he wore to school. There was a new bearing not seen earlier in his appearance before the whole school in special programs.

Irvin shared his delight with Nell. "It is sure satisfying to watch something special start to come out of someone who should be ordinary. I guess that's what teaching's all about, but it doesn't come from our classroom, Nell. It must just be there in a boy like Harland. We only give it a chance to appear."

With each passing month through his adolescent years Harland was more certain of himself. His earnings increased and there was more play time, not just running with the dogs, but riding and roping and giving vent to being young. Notions that he could be something special were, for the moment, limited to the world around him. But he was almost fearless in his demonstrations of how he could handle himself. He even persuaded Steve, when they were together in Breed's corral behind the barn, that he had been practicing long and hard at home with the lariat and could work in a full-fledged rodeo, he bet. He was even ready to show the world — or at least Steve — how he could handle the old bull in the Breed barnyard.

Harland with hound

Steve was skeptical. "You mean that Black Angus here? Reckon that's gotta be the meanest ole bull in the world. Well, let's get you a mount t' go with your mouth, 'cause this one's gonna be tough. You're goin' to have to put a rope around that bull's neck and show him who's boss."

Harland's cockiness was convincing. Steve almost believed him. "You better saddle up for this one anyhow," he warned. It was a rare treat to use a saddle. The only one available belonged to Steve's dad. This was far and away too urgent a challenge to wait on Mr. Breed's return from town for any niceties of asking permission to use it.

"Cinch her real tight," Steve warned as he snugged the saddle strap. "I'll go down and turn the bull loose, but I think you're nuts, Harland. You ain't never tried nothin' bigger than a persimmon bush 'fore this...and you fell then, remember? Broke your arm real good that time!"

"I'm tellin' you, I can do it! You just get up on that fence and watch me. I'm comin' out smoking!"

Minutes later horse and rider faced a docile Black Angus from opposite ends of the corral. "Thought you said this was a mean one!" Harland loped his mount toward the motionless bull.

"You jus' get close and you'll see mean," yelled Steve from his perch on the top rail. "An' get your rope off'n that saddle horn!"

Magnificently the bull stirred. Pawing and snorting, he tossed his head at the horse and rider intruding his space. Nonchalantly, Harland hefted the lariat as he passed and casually slapped the bull across its left flank. "That oughta get his attention," he yelled as he trotted to the far end of the corral to set up his demonstration. The thunder of hooves and the yelp from his buddy caught him as he was turning and suddenly the race was on.

Adrenalin pumping, the best action of the heroes of fiction racing with his blood, Harland spurred his horse for the opposite end of the corral, watching over his shoulder to see if the bull was still charging. The animal had stopped mid-way and stood watching the retreat of man and mount with red-eyed satisfaction.

It was now or never, if he was to regain any respect from Steve. "Yeah...HAY!" His horse wheeling to the attack, lariat circling his head, Harland bore down on the motionless bull, sweeping by at full gallop and turning just as the bull moved. Horse and rider careened toward their target as the black tonnage of an outraged bull roared its fury at being harassed and trotted straight for his tormentor. "Okay, Steve-boy! Here we GO•O•O•O!" Half-standing in the stirrups, the lariat curling in brazen eagerness to bring down the beast, Harland threw the rope with cool precision, guiding his horse in a last second veer-away, even as he watched the lariat circle the bull's massive neck.

"The hornnnnn! Harland, the rope's around the...OH, WOW!"

Too late Steve's cry reached the rider as suddenly the slack was out of the lasso. The saddle was jerked savagely from the horse, spewing rider — arms, legs and pride going in opposite directions — all heading for dust and disgrace in the corral dirt.

"Git you outta there, Harland!" screamed Steve as the bull thundered to a last second stop against the rail fencing forty yards from him.

For a stunned instant a disoriented Harland stared from the prone, then pushed to his knees and lurched to a stumbling run as his adversary grumbled in low key warning less than fifty feet away.

"Forgit the saddle...git clear of 'im! Shag it outta there!"

"Get the gate!" panted Harland, dashing back for the saddle. "Hurry up!"

"Judas! Will ya forget that stuff...he'll come fer you!"

"Can't..." gasped the would-be rodeo champ. He was grabbing for the dangling reins as his mount pranced nervously nearby and seconds later the dethroned rider, guiding his horse to safety and carrying his gear by the lethal saddle horn, reeled through the gate.

"Well, you sure got spunk! I'll hand that to ya!" praised Steve. "No brains, but lotsa spunk." Harland looked more than the worse for wear. "Let's go swimmin' in the tank. I saw Weldon headin' down there just 'fore your big show."

"Maybe we oughta go see if Stella has us any jobs first." Harland was limping down the hill toward the cattle pond. The extra long toe on his left foot had always been vulnerable to their barefoot play and he'd torn off the nail again from what Steve called his 'cultivator toe.'

"You got more hunger for workin' than anybody I ever heard tell of!" groaned Steve. "You most get torn up by a bull and you still think about workin'. Y'oughta be glad you're alive! So first we swim and then...hey, howza water?"

"Great...cool," Weldon called back. "What was all that caterwaulin' I heard up by the barn?"

"Ask Steve." Harland was stripping to the buff and sliding from the pond edge into the muddy looking summeriness of the water. "I don't wanta talk about it."

Steve regaled his audience of one with the collision of Harland and the bull.

"You know what you have to do, don'tcha?" Weldon declared as they sat on the bank later. "You gotta go pick on someone your own size."

"What's that 'sposed to mean?" growled Harland, tiring of the enjoyment of his encounter.

"Well, there's a goat ropin' contest in Lula this weekend. You get back from huntin' in time and you're as good as Steve thinks with the ropin', well, why not go win you some money?"

"You think your dad would let me use the horse? I'd sure like to try it. If I win anything, I'll split with him."

"After today, I think you oughta split with the horse. Hey, let's have us a party an' celebrate your survivin' the bull fight. Mama had some leftovers this mornin' and we can get some grape juice from the cellar again..."

"Too much like work," Weldon groaned, sinking to his back in the sun.

Harland turned to gauge whether the walk to the root cellar was worth it, then slipped into the water and said calmly to Steve, "You-mean-that-cellar-out-in-your-backyard-that's-all-underground-with-a-fireplace-and-sleepin'-places, in-case-o'-tornadoes-and-all-that-stuff?"

"The only one we got! What's wrong with you?"

"You mean that one," he went on very quietly, "with the cover roof right down at ground level that kind o' slants thisa way an' has your sister dancin' on top of it while she watches us bare-naked down here?"

"Ohmigosh!" Weldon looked over his shoulder at the five-year-old watching the three boys skinny dipping. Jill had been told she couldn't swim that way with them, but no one said she couldn't watch. "Hey, runt, beat it!" yelled Steve, joining the others back in the water. It may have been poor outside, but family life in what was still pioneer West, had a fierce adherence to lines of cover-up and behavior.

A short time later, with Jill in tow, the four were out by the stream in the corner of the property. A fire burned over the buried potatoes and a few pieces of sausage and biscuits were warming above the flame. "Here's to the goat roping champ of the town of Lula!" Weldon raised the tin cup in salute of their fearless friend. "And if this stuff gets any stronger, we might send him over there drunk." He poured himself more of the juice. "Know why they call this possum juice, don'tcha?"

"Tell me," said Harland, nursing a bruised elbow.

"'Cause it's got the old paaaa-zoommmhh! You'll be a tiger with them goats, if you get a load o' this in ya!"

It was an old routine of fun between the boys but it was the first time for Jill, who never had been allowed along to their sanctuary at the end of the woods. The talk of Mama's grape juice making anybody drunk was more than she could grasp. She could trust Steve, even if he was the biggest tease. "Will I get drunk, too?" she asked him.

"Naw, kid. Not a chance."

Steve studied the anxious little face beside him and decided she was too young for the game the three boys had played for years. And *they* were getting too old for it. It had been great to escape by 'camping out.' Packing a sack of anything they could find to eat and a jar of juice from the storm cellar, the trio could disappear from the real world of work and worried conversation of grownups talking about being 'starved out.' And it was easy to convert the possum grape juice that Mama had standing 'till it was right' into moonshine in their minds.

Steve looked from Jill to Weldon to Harland. "Time's a-changing," he said. "Did y'hear they're gonna close Lula school and all those kids are comin' over to us?"

"To Tupelo?"

"Straightaway. They's not enough kids in that town to keep the school goin', so they're gonna bus 'em over here."

"Sure gonna make a bunch of us! Kinda glad I'm finishin' up next summer," Harland said.

"So what you all gonna do when you get done with school?" asked the older boy who had already passed that decision.

"I'm going to college," declared Harland.

"Yeah. Me, too," echoed Steve.

"You know what it costs to go to that teacher's college in Ada?" Weldon pushed some of the embers out of the way and probed for the buried potatoes.

"Yeah. Costs a lot. I just know I'm going to do it."

"Good luck. Sure is expensive. Maybe I'll go, too." Weldon broke off the conversation. No way would he dampen their determination, but there also was no way cutting fence posts or pushing rocks around was ever going to pay college tuition. "Got us some done potatoes," he observed. "Jill, don't you touch 'em yet! They'll be red hot."

A thousand miles from Oklahoma a girl was weeping. She had had just about enough of moving from farm to farm as her parents followed the crops, working in Arizona and California and Western Oklahoma and now in New Mexico. Shirley Thompson, as American as apple pie in pony tail and ankle socks, looked around the dusty, country classroom. Not a single one of the others in her class even looked American. They all were strangers and her classmates for a couple of months this time before she and her family moved on to another place or back to Oklahoma.

For a short time in the summer her hopes were high that they had at last settled down. Her parents found a little house in Lula, Oklahoma and talked about how they wanted to move in and make it permanent, if Dad could find work. He was sure he could.

That had raised her hopes that life was going to change and become like other people's. She had met two girls in Lula who would be her friends at school and they all were so excited. Lula school was going to be closed up and they were going to go for classes every day to a place called Tupelo, seven miles away by bus. It would be wonderful. Lots more boys were there. And there were churches and stores and a movie house in the town of Tupelo. For the very first time since Shirley could ever remember, the Thompsons had plans to stay in one place to live.

Her two new friends had had her undo the pony tail and let her thick, waist length hair tumble free and loose and it was a symbol to Shirley. They told her she was beautiful, just as her mother always had. But to be told that by other girls was different. Life was opening for the fifteen-year-old.

That first month she was in Lula she had so much fun. The girls introduced her to many new games and to one of their favorite entertainments — the traveling revival. That religious event made its regular trek through Lula where there were a hundred or so residents scattered nearby. For the young girls it was a brand of frightening adventure and impending destruction that terrified and lured at the same instant and Shirley joined the others in their annual trip down the sawdust trail to salvation. It made their walk home in the dark of the night ever so much safer, in view of the 'dark days coming'.

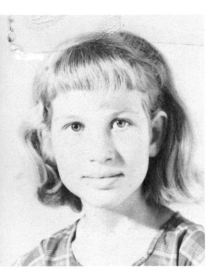

Shirley, age 11

She thought of that experience now in the loneliness of the New Mexico classroom. No friends were here at all to do anything with — only all of these unpleasant looking strangers. When her dad had not found work in Oklahoma by the summer's end, there was nothing for Marvin and Sally Thompson to do but to pack the still-at-home children, John and Shirley and the three younger ones from their family of nine, into the old truck and head West again for a few months. They could always go pull cotton. At least it was a way of survival. With the six all working, they could bring back enough dollars to carry them through another winter.

A Fall frost had made the pulling easier and the barbs of the cotton boll rarely got to her fingers, once the cold came. For all its monotony and dustiness and lugging of the bag weight, Shirley would far rather be in the field with her family than in this classroom with these hostile looking boys and girls from South of the border. *It was no wonder her father made her keep away from other migrants like these working the same crops,* she thought. *They were not to be trusted,* she was sure. *Probably not a one of them even belonged in the United States.*

The teacher of the two-room school had been especially friendly to Shirley when she arrived the first day. She understood perfectly that this girl would be a short term student before the family had to move on. Shirley was most welcome and school was over early enough in the day so she could get back to work in the fields.

"Let's stand and repeat the Pledge of Allegiance to our country, class, and then we'll all recite the Lord's Prayer," the teacher announced promptly at eight.

It was that that had opened the floodgates for Shirley. It seemed there was no way she would ever have a semblance of some place to call her home and a school where she really belonged. She looked at the dark-haired, noisy, strange children saying dutifully, "I pledge allegiance to the flag of the United States..." A moment later, in concert with the others, she heard herself praying, "Our Father, who art in heaven..." At least some of them knew *that* much English, she thought. The rest was that excited sounding language from their homeland which they all spoke at full voice.

Somehow she survived the first morning and then it was noon meal time. She stared at the strange concoction dipped from the deep soup tureen for each of the students. It looked like rice, but it was loaded with colors other than white. There were red, black and even yellow spots in it and it was so runny — *it was sickening!* Shirley hugged her pink jacket around her and tried a tentative taste. The lettering on the sign above the serving counter read 'Spanish rice.' There was no charge for noon dinner at this school, but it was certainly expected that you eat it, she knew.

Nobody was paying the least bit of attention to her and her thoughts. Everyone else was wolfing the rice down as if it was the last meal they would ever have and those who had finished, were already babbling again at each other in those fast foreign words. Waiting till she was sure no one was watching, she fingered the rice from her plate into the side pocket of her jacket. It was warm and yucky against her thigh, but at least it wasn't in her stomach. She'd throw it outside later. Wait till evening. Then there would be food she was used to. She lost herself in her quiet corner in the classroom, thinking about her mother. *Somehow, no matter what the family circumstances, Sally Thompson, like her husband, always kept the care of her family first. She was a wonderful cook and could make anything taste good* so Shirley knew that her stomach pangs would be changed by nightfall, once she was with her family. Her favorite food of anything was a piece of fresh fruit, just any kind, but of course that was a special Christmas treat or for a birthday celebration.

The thought of all the afternoon hours in the cotton field struck uncomfortably. She looked around the room. Everyone else here would be doing the same thing after school. The bus would drop them by whatever field was being worked. She would place her school books and her shoes carefully in their pick-up truck and go to the field wagon for a cotton sack. Then it was out to find her place in the field where her family was and begin the tedious work of pulling cotton from the bolls.

Slung over her shoulder, the sack was long enough to hold a hundred pounds of cotton, dragging behind her as she worked. In the next row was her father and beyond him were John and Nova and then her mother. The two youngest, Jerry and Virginia, usually waited back at the wagon to help them unload the sacks. When Shirley's mood was down — and it never had been lower than this day — there was something special in being able to see that Mama and Daddy were always there, too, doing just what they told her to do. She kept reminding herself that she was helping them all get back to Lula, Oklahoma with every heavy sack she dragged along the ground.

The cotton they picked paid three dollars for a hundred pounds. Shirley would tug the sack behind her till it was at least half full. Then she'd drag it back to the wagon and Jerry and Virginia would help her haul it up and dump it with all the rest. *Picked* cotton was worth a dollar more a hundred pounds than *pulled* cotton was, and it should be, she thought, wincing as a barb in the boll nipped at her finger. The after-frost cotton was pulled easily and even though it paid a dollar less, they could pull faster.

Finally another afternoon was done. The Thompson family headed back to one of the little unpainted houses the farmer always held for migrants to return each Fall. They carted along with them as many utensils and possessions as they could, travelling to each work location, so it seemed like something familiar was there. An hour after supper, when fatigue overwhelmed any need to do schoolwork, Shirley would follow the rest of the family to bed.

It was going to change someday. Daddy said it all was going to be different for them. And Sally Thompson, too, believed her husband, so it must be so.

Harland was in Mr. Carter's office. It seemed impossible that this might be the last time he would stand here in front of the principal's desk as a student. A lot had changed since that noon hour years earlier when he was making an excuse to get out of lunch hour embarrassment.

"Harland, sit down. We need to talk a few minutes." Irvin studied him as Harland perched forward on the edge of the chair. He had matured so visibly over the years in Tupelo School. Though he was still slender-bodied and now very tall, with a new toughness and a tan to his frame, he was a young man of purposefulness with an easy, relaxed pleasantness. Carter was bubbling with great news for this promising Senior, but he needed one more review to be sure he had done right by him. "Are you still determined you want to go on to college?"

"Yes, sir! I sure am. Don't know where I'll be going or how I'm going to pay for it. But I *am* going."

"Why is it so important?"

Harland thought a moment. "Maybe because no one in my family has ever gone before. Maybe 'cause my father thinks I can. But mostly, because I want to become a teacher, too. A really good one."

"Great!" Irvin smiled as he locked his hands behind his head and leaned back in his chair. "This has nothing to do with whether you become a teacher or don't but because I believe in what you're going to be, whatever it is.

"So, I've taken the liberty of speaking to the people at East Central Teachers' College in Ada, after talking with the rest of your teachers here. I have good news for you. You are going to be awarded a full four-year academic scholarship to the college there. Congratulations!" His hand reached across his desk and Harland shook his head in disbelief.

"This is wonderful, sir! But I don't understand. I'm not even first in our class. Gosh, I'm not the valedictorian..."

"No, and the Johnson girl who is, is going to do well, too. But you have the confidence of a lot of people, Harland." Carter cleared his throat. "Couldn't happen to a finer young man, in the minds of all of us."

"Wow! I'm really honored, sir!" He was half-way out of his seat when Irvin motioned him to stay. "'Scuse me, I'm just so excited! Wait till I tell Dad and Mother. They won't believe this!"

"And likely the first thing one of them will ask is just how you plan to pay for your room and board in Ada. See, the college is giving you a scholarship that covers all your classes and studies and labs and all that. But you have to figure out the rest yourself. Any ideas on that?"

Harland Stonecipher:
President
Honor Society
Junior Play
Tiger Staff
4-H Club
Boy Scouts

If the sensations rifling through his body could be measured, Harland was five feet off the ground. He had a full scholarship to college! It had been orchestrated by a teacher who believed in his future. How could a little thing like food and lodging be any kind of problem?

"I'm sure I can get a job there for after classes, sir."

"Well, why don't you see what you can find. To be able to carry your meals and dormitory, you'll need about sixty dollars a month."

Harland never flinched. So that was more than his father had been able to make a month from the farm in more than thirty years of trying. "I know I can find a job," he declared, reaching across the desk to shake his benefactor's hand again. "Thank you very much for the opportunity. I really appreciate your getting me this chance. I won't let you down."

Weeks had passed. He had been to what seemed every job possibility in Ada. Hitch-hiking into town, he had spent every morning and afternoon going from one business location to another, talking to the owner, explaining about his scholarship opportunity and asking their situation. *Was there maybe a job now?...Or possibly would there be for him in the Fall?...He'd be glad to do just anything and he had references...*

No, son, there wasn't any hiring being done right at this time, but we'll keep you in mind...Sure, and if we hear anyone else is looking for help, we'll tell 'em about you, Harland...

He had to find work or East Central was still just a dream. The searching itself was costly. Stella was getting a flood of calls now for the services of Steve and Harland. "I could buy the pick-up and go back and forth to class. Some of the students do that," he suggested one evening after another day of turn-downs. "I could get back out here and do some jobs every day and make the money to drive there and back every day, too."

"I don't believe that will work, son," replied his dad. "You're going to find you need lots more time for your school work after class hours and how can you do it here?

I can't see us gettin' any electric here at the house for some time yet."

The three were outside, cooling on the small front porch in the early evening, watching the last light fade off in the West. Soon the temperature would be breaking. A sudden barking from his dogs at the corner of the house announced activity down the lane.

"Now whoever might that be?" Viola stepped to the edge of the porch as a car turned off the road onto their entrance. Visitors to their farm could be counted on one hand in any given year and a strange car was an almost unheard-of occasion.

"Hey, that's Mr. Carter's car." Harland darted from the porch, waving excitedly.

Irvin felt a grab in his throat at first sight inside the Stonecipher homestead. It was exactly as he had guessed. Pride and neatness were there. Here was a family that held its head high. But it obviously was a scene of pride constantly pounded below the poverty belt. He was glad he was bringing the news he had. It had taken him several days of his own private searching, but now it was worth every bit of the postponed vacation time he and Nell had been planning. Alarm had grabbed when he saw Harland on the streets of Ada a week earlier and asked how the job search was going.

"Fine, sir. Fine. I've just got to keep at it. Something will turn up."

"How long have you been looking, Harland?"

"About a month. Every one I've seen is real polite, but they're not hiring right now. But I'll find something."

"Good boy. I know you will." Privately, then and there Irvin had begun his own search for someone to give this very promising local student a job and the chance to take advantage of a college scholarship.

It was obvious that goodwill was everywhere in Ada, but jobs were in short supply. Until he stopped by Bayless Drug Store. When he left, there was important news to report to Harland and he headed straight for the Stonecipher farm thirty miles away.

"Did you take a job in town yet, Harland?"

"Not yet, sir. But I'm still looking. I'll be back in there tomorrow."

"Good. When you go, see Mr. Bayless at Bayless Drug Store. He's always had one of the college students to deliver his prescriptions and I spoke to him for you. The one he has right now is a Senior. I believe the job will take care of your needs."

"Oh, wow! That's great!" Harland grabbed his mother. "Mama, you hear that? Now I can for sure go."

"I want to thank you for all you've done for our boy, Mr. Carter." Allen Stonecipher was feeling the impact of what had just happened through one teacher's caring.

"Say, we're proud of this young fellow. So's his whole class. You know, being the Senior Class President says a great deal about what all the others think."

A new door had just opened. Harland was offered access to the whole new world. A sharecropper's son...the kid who lived back in the pasture out of touch with the real world ...It didn't have to stay that way.

As Irvin Carter told his wife later, with this one everything was going to be different.

Chapter Three

Shock was the only word for it.

Gone were sixteen years of life back in the pasture — running in the night with Lake and Drive, riding bareback from the Breeds with Steve to go work for a farmer miles down a dusty, pitted dirt road. Gone was a year of getting into Tupelo — population, 365 — for Saturday night action with thirty-five cents for the movie and a coke afterward.

He wished Steve were here. The Breeds had been starved out with crop failures and had moved to Oklahoma City. "I'll be with you next year. Count on it. I'll just get a job till then and make some money," he'd said as they left Coal County.

Abruptly Harland was a new resident of the city of Ada. He had had no hint of the shock it would be to change overnight from country boy bathing in a cattle pond, using an outhouse, reading by an oil lamp, drawing water outdoors by a crude pulley system and carting buckets to his mother in the kitchen, raking peanut rows and picking cotton.

Suddenly he was a member of the Freshman Class in a college. There were more than fifteen hundred strangers as students around him. And there were indoor water fountains and indoor facilities — toilets and showers, an enormous student cafeteria and, wonder of wonders, electricity everywhere! Lights were everywhere he went. A light in the ceiling, a table lamp on the desks in the room he shared with another Freshman and lights illuminating the beautiful grounds at night, too.

He looked from his window in Fentem Hall at the campus around the dormitory. It really was beautiful. He never had seen sidewalks like these. He studied their graceful curling around the buildings. Magnolia trees were everywhere, too. So were people...Seven hundred and more, male and female, in his Freshman Class alone. Compare that to the twenty-eight in his Senior year at Tupelo. And females! Wonderfully attractive girls his own age were in abundant supply. The place literally was teaming with humanity and the whole campus would not have covered much more than his father's two hundred and twenty acres.

As the Assistant Registrar, Merle Boatwright saw that Harland Stonecipher was at East Central to get a Bachelor of Arts Degree in Education. His registration said he was on an academic scholarship and he was going to be a work student, too. Place of employment: Bayless Drug Store. He'd be working for the owner who had helped students for years with jobs in several of his stores around Central Oklahoma. Young at heart, Mr. Bayless at 75 cared a lot about these young people, especially ones who needed an extra assist to be able to go to college. Harland must be something extra himself, to win the job here at Bayless's. It was a coveted spot.

Merle had watched so many who had come to Ada out of similar rural conditions. Country youngsters all saw their school teacher as truly successful — by the only standards they knew. Nice clothes, a car and the outward marks of 'making it' said teaching must be a good profession. But right now 124 credit hours for that great degree were ages away. She had seen many like Harland come and go. An opportunity would surface in Ada promising higher pay, if only a student would cut short education and come now up the path to plenty.

She hoped this tall, bright-eyed, personable young man, somewhat unsure of himself, but carrying determination in the set of his jaw and friendliness in his smile, was going to be able to adjust and survive their foreign country called 'college.'

'Pop' Bayless confided in Ben, his young druggist, "Harland's going to be a good hand for us. Irvin says he's a hard-working farm kid and real smart. Guess I'll start him out checking those new shipments and you can have him deliver the prescriptions, too." (Pop always had seen to it that his customers who couldn't get around easily,

146

had their orders delivered right to their homes.)

Within days he had become so impressed with this new boy, he moved his working hours up to forty a week. It was a combination many collegians across America can parallel as their own career in higher education. Work a full work week. Attend sixteen hours of classes each week and equal that by two study hours for each class hour and you have a passing chance of doing average work.

It was pure challenge time for Harland. He was determined to succeed and since textbooks were not a part of his scholarship provision, he was going to have to earn them. There was no way he was going to swallow his pride and look for any shortcut to get them. Till he made enough money, he wrote down every lecture in every class. With his kind of dogged patience and his nose buried to a notebook, he could just about get what was needed to handle the quizzes and exams. But the pressure to take full advantage of the academic experience hounded him. One by one he purchased each necessary book.

Not that a one-at-a-time purchase, when he could afford it, was all that painful. Katey Knight Hall was far more interesting as the girls' dormitory than it was as the location of the college book store. Come the day of financial independence, it would be good to know his way around Knight. None too soon to start either, since guys outnumbered gals two-to-one at East Central.

Whatever the prime motivation in his drive for increased finances, Harland began to measure those dollars spent for his room and board. Talking to some other Freshmen in his same crunch, he began a search for off-campus housing that would cost each of them less than dormitory space and he found an apartment they could share.

It was upstairs on a side street. They split up the $35.00 a month rent between the four of them and climbed up a set of iron stairs to their two rooms — a kitchen and a bedroom with two double beds, with a small bathroom attached. They lived, studied and ate in their apartment and Harland would be staying with the three as his roommates for two years.

Everything was beginning to turn around for the better. He was doing well in his major in English and he was becoming more confident in the scene at every step.

Pop — who was always 'Mister' Bayless to Harland — noticed the gradual turnabout, too. His jack-of-all-trades was making himself more valuable at every point in the store. They used him just as many hours as he could work. Behind the counter he was learning the composition of drugs, listening as Pop and Ben counseled customers on prescriptions and over-the-counter items.

But it was as Merle had predicted about this personable country boy — someone would try early to lure him from the college years.

"You know, son, you would be great in pharmaceutical sales. Why not make yourself a pile o' money fast?"

Harland assessed the salesman to the drug store and listened to the promise of what would happen if he would quit everything and go on the road, representing the man's firm.

"Thanks, sir. I really do want to earn my degree first."

"Whatcha goin' to do with it? Be a teacher?"

"Yessir. I'm going to teach English and maybe some other things, too."

The salesman snorted. "Everyone to his own poison. You think about it. Guarantee you, you'll make at least twice your best-ever pay in teaching, if you come with me." The pitch ended abruptly as Pop approached down the aisle.

"Leave this young man alone now, Harry. If Harland has any interest in talking to you, you can see him after hours. Right now, he's mine."

A great difference in his independence began to assert itself as the first year moved over into the second. But he was both tantalized and terrified by public communication. He learned that Speech and Debating was a curriculum offering which could give him a chance to challenge the fear. If he was to be any good as a teacher, he certainly was going to have to stand before a classroom and think on his feet. And that was a long way from the only experience he had — reading poetry in a small high school class.

For some students the speech course and the debating course may be considered easy credits. But it was a tough, demanding discipline for Harland. His teacher sensed there was a lot more purpose to his unusual drive in it than just for a classroom grade.

"I don't know where I'll be teaching," he explained. "I've got to be able to stand up and think as I talk and I've got to sound like I belong right there."

"You're doing fine," Dr. Nabors encouraged. "In fact, maybe you'll want to stay with this and list it as one of your specialty fields when you graduate. Schools are always looking for this kind of teaching skill."

No way could he share the professor's confidence. "I wish I'd o' had some of this back in high school. I sure would feel a lot better about what I'm doing with it now."

The Thompson family was back in Lula. At last things were taking a turn for the better, after years of following the crops and struggling to get a toehold on some place of permanent living. Shirley was full time in school and in her years of going from one district school to another, for the first time she felt at home with her peers.

Her two closest friends were staring out the window with her when a car drove up in front of the school. She watched the tall one in the driver's seat unwind, stand and stretch beside the car. "Who *is* he?" she asked.

The girls exchanged glances. "Why, that would be Harland Stonecipher. I do declare, don't he look spiffy? They say he's a big-shot college boy now."

Shirley took in the two-tone black and white shoes, the black slacks and the white shirt and tie. "He looks very nice," she said quietly.

"Then you're going to have to meet him. C'mon." They propelled a captive Shirley into the hall just as Harland and Steve rounded the corner.

"Harland Stonecipher and Steve Breed! What a nice surprise. Have you come slumming from that big old college?"

Harland and Steve

Harland grinned. "First chance we've had to get back for more'n a year. I talked Steve into risking his life in coming down here in my old flivver."

"This is Shirley Thompson."

• • •

It was like coming home as Gladys King and Irvin Carter and other teachers popped into the conversation. And through it all Harland felt there had to have been a mysterious good reason that pushed him to put aside work and study and to act on an urge to drive out to Tupelo School. Going full throttle to create his own new world, he felt compelled to return.

And suddenly he was looking at Shirley — tall, slim, dark wavy hair framing her beautiful face, then tumbling across the back of her shoulders all the way to her waist. There was something very special about this meeting. She returned his smile and even if she was as shy as he, there was a special look in that smile.

Some love affairs are simply meant to be. Harland had timed his arrival for the end of the school day and Shirley should have already been on the bus going home. There was a delay. Their meeting was to happen that day and once they met, romance blossomed quickly.

A common bond was between them from the start. They were from the same world and had come from similar roots — the blood, sweat and tears of poverty and the love of their families. Both knew what it was to draw blood from the barb of the cotton boll and the sharp, rough stones on their bare feet...to sweat through unending hours in the field picking and digging and pushing and pulling... and the tears came when those times of resentment overflowed at the unfair cards life had dealt them and their loving parents.

No matter how bad it got, neither Allen and Viola Stonecipher nor Marvin and Sally Thompson ever let their tough straits interrupt their family love. Early months at college had given Harland contact with many students who knew no such love support. That his Dad and Mother were powerful motivation for him and that Shirley, too, felt so lovingly for her Mama and Daddy, told them a lot about each other.

He pulled his two-tone Chevy to the side of the road as they were about to round the final turn into Lula. It was only their second for-real date and they'd enjoyed being together for the Debby Reynolds movie and the coke afterward.

"Look, I know we've only known each other...well, for just a little while...but what would you think...how about us going steady?" Dr. Nabors and Speech 101 hadn't done anything to help him through this crisis of words.

"I think I'd like that very much," Shirley answered, watching as he peeled his high school class ring from his finger.

He had saved to buy the ring himself and it was an important symbol of achievement to him. "Would you wear this then as my steady girl?"

"I'd be proud to."

He put his arms around her slender body and kissed her gently for the first time. Her lips were warm and soft.

• • •

Marvin and Sally were pleased. They liked Harland's mannerliness in coming to ask for the privilege of dating Shirley. They liked his openness and relaxed air with them around their home where he and Shirley often spent weekend evenings. There was something special, too, about a college student who would make the time on some weekends to come home to work the fields with his parents. As far as the Thompsons were concerned, their daughter's steady was a welcome part of their family.

And so was Steve, who by this time had his own steady girl. The foursome found their fun together in the very simple things. At the wheel on a return from Ada and a student play on campus, Steve suddenly dove for the side of the road and leaped from the car..."Everybody out! I jus' found the perfect way to end this evening for Shirley and whazhisname."

They were in the middle of nowhere and Nowhere, Oklahoma, was well lit with a full moon. The mischievous Steve disappeared at the edge of a fence and reappeared an instant later bearing a big ripe-and-ready watermelon.

Shirley's parents

"Hey, c'mon, Steve!" yelped Harland, coming totally awake. "That's gonna get us a lotta trouble! Drop it. It's a dumb idea!"

Steve dropped it. Squarely in the middle of the road where it split wide and wonderfully ripe. "Dessert, Harland! We forgot to stop for dessert in town, girls, so here it is!"

By now they all were out of the car. "Oh, for Pete's sake! We're at Edgar's place. Okay, okay. So he wouldn't mind, but it's still stealing." He had to laugh at the beautiful mess by their feet.

"He always plants a few extra right by the road. Told me so himself...jus' for emergencies like this." Steve scooped a piece of watermelon from the center with his fingers and presented it to Shirley. "See, we really didn't forget. I just didn't want to disturb you lovebirds neckin' in the back seat."

"Now you're addin' lying to stealing," growled Harland. "Tell 'em the truth. We're a little short on cash tonight, girls."

"Never would have guessed, if you hadn't told," laughed Shirley, happily seizing the fistful of the ripe fruit. It was so good.

• • •

"Everybody, wake up!" she cried, dashing to the back of her home and bursting into her parents' bedroom late one evening, just after Harland left. "Look what he gave me for my birthday! Isn't it beautiful?" She pirouetted at bedside to show off a pink, shiny cotton dress with a full skirt, a matching belt and a fitted waist with an open, square neck. "Oohh, I'll never forget this birthday! I know I never will. Don't you just love the way it swirls?"

Marvin leaned on his elbow to study his daughter. "Well, now. It seems to me this is getting serious. You jus' don't go out and buy someone a dress."

"It is! Daddy, he wants to marry me and he wants to come talk with you about our plans."

"Any time he's ready, I'll be glad to listen, but I don't know's I can agree to it."

Marvin and Sally privately liked the plans Harland outlined. He had found a rental place called Barker's Valley, with little white cabins not too far from campus, where he and Shirley would begin their life together. He had already reserved one for their first home, if her parents would approve.

At first Marvin was more than a little skeptical, just as Allen Stonecipher had been. "Well, Harland, I appreciate how you two feel 'bout each other, but you got any idea how much it costs to be married? I'm right fearful it will put an end to your education."

"That's what my Dad said, too, sir. It's not going to be that way. I made a commitment when I took that scholarship. I'm going to graduate. Besides, I want to be a teacher. I promise you, I'll take real good care of your daughter. We thought we both could work through my college together and..."

"And where will she find a job?" Marvin interrupted. "Remember the hard time you had locatin' something for yourself and it'd be even..."

"We've already been working on that. There's a drug store in Ada that's right across the street from Bayless, and my boss spoke a good word for us, so Mr. Gwin's going to give Shirley a job over there. So, between us we'll be all right."

"If that don't beat all!" Marvin was impressed with what he heard. "Sally, what say?"

"I think we should say yes."

• • •

It was a very simple wedding service at a friend's home near the crossroads in Stonewall. That's between Tupelo and Ada. Kay Durland, a friend of Shirley's, was maid of honor and Steve, now a student at East Central himself, was best man. No flowing gowns and rented tux and no organist to pull the stops out and let swell the processional, "Here Comes The Bride." Two gutzy young people of the Twentieth Century met there in Olan Snow's home that Saturday. Shirley was beautiful in a pink jacket over a pink dress and white flowers in it. Her dark hair was

Stonecipher wedding

153

accented by a white flower and the dainty white gloves and white shoes were a perfect complement to a lovely bride. Her husband-to-be, sharp in a grey and white suit and dark tie, managed to hide any nervousness he felt as he stood at her side before the Reverend Waldroup of Stone-wall's Church of Christ.

Yes, Harland would have this woman to be his wife. And yes, Shirley would have this man to be her husband. The vows confirmed that a remarkable young lady of the Thompson line would give her love to this unique young man of the Stonecipher line...and now the curious chemistry of two whose bodies and minds and spirits were blended as one, was about to interact.

• • •

It was accident that these two would ever meet. Just as purely accidental as the meeting of everyone who forms that alliance-for-life called 'marriage.' Marvin Thompson should well sound his apprehension to twenty-year-old Harland — 'I'm right fearful it will put an end to your education.' In nine out of ten such youthful marriages, the world of experience knows it usually does slam the door on college or whatever early career hopes may have been in such a young man as Harland.

With this man and this woman something different happened at the moment they exchanged vows. It was the same mysterious mix that began for another couple six years earlier and three hundred miles South in a quiet little wedding at a military chapel at Sheppard Air Base. In both marriages no one had the least notion that incredible strength and purpose was being welded in the union. Their horizons were flung wider than either Harland or Shirley, John or Naomi would ever dare guess. Because two became one, they found strength to handle themselves singly in the events which were soon to follow. The world would be enriched because of two simple little ceremonies of exchanged pledges. It is safe now to prophesy that what was to follow would not have happened, if either of these two couples had not found love.

Harland and Shirley had no formal wedding reception either. With Steve and his girl they drove to their first home, a small frame cottage just outside of Ada, on a direct line to their families' farms.

"Come on Harland. She's a little thing! You gotta carry her over the threshold."

"Welcome to our happy home!" Harland flung open the door and led the parade into their first little palace...a compact living room, bedroom and kitchen...furnished. They already had done their first grocery shopping, laying in some extras for the after-wedding party. One jumbo pack of Oreo cookies, plenty of soda pop and a little home radiating lots of love. It made as unforgettable a wedding reception as though it had been a great affair at the Plaza in New York City. Beauty was there. Fun was there. Love was there. And all the trappings of wealth from a million other wedding receptions would never surpass the toast of Steve to Harland and his bride...

"Not beneath you...not above you...but beside you, because I love you. Here's to both of you!"

❖   ❖   ❖

Harland and Shirley

A few days later Shirley walked into Gwin's Drug Store to begin what would be a first for this girl of the little town of Lula, who had never known life in a city or been a part of any business anywhere.

"So you're Shirley Stonecipher. I'm Mr. Gwin and that's Dave over there. He's my brother-in-law, Dave Davis. We're glad you're going to work for us. Let's get you busy right away unpacking this shipment and putting it on the shelves."

It was a fascinating first. She had come from a home that never saw TV ads or the regular daily newspaper. The product names — Revlon, Eli Lilly, Max Factor, Johnson and Johnson...She had just been plunged into a strange, new world. She was itching to read the labels, too. And then as she worked down the aisles, finding the shelf marking that told her where to stack boxes and bottles and containers, she gradually became aware of another new sensation.

She had entered a world of incredible scents and odors. It was a mix of strange mediciny smells and colognes and perfumes. She never had come across such odors. Here was a pleasant smell...there was one quiet penetrating and disturbing. Over here was a curious vinegary smell, sold as something that was to make women smell better and there was a pungent bit of sickening odor sold as medicine to help arthritis, gout and a host of other ills which age experiences.

For a while it was entertaining. In fact, it was fun to move like Alice in Wonderland through a new world. And then it slowly became nauseating. The homogenizing of medicine and drug and perfume odors suddenly struck Shirley. She was positive she was going to be very sick.

"Mr. Gwin?"

He peered down from the drug counter at the pale face staring up in abject despair. "Yes, Shirley. What is it?"

"Mr. Gwin, I...I don't know how to say this. But I think I'm going to have to leave for just a little bit. I think I'm about to be sick."

Her boss stopped his counting of pills immediately and hurried to her side. "Whatever is the matter, child?"

"I don't know, sir. It's the way it smells here...Please understand, Mr. Gwin! I hope you won't fire me. Harland's counting on me...It's just...sir...I haven't smelled anything like all this...ever. Could I be excused for just a few minutes?"

"At home"

Gwin read the signs of the country girl and responded like the gentleman he was. "Good heavens, Shirley, of course you can! You take till tomorrow. Come back and try it again. You'll find we all get used to it." He walked back up to the prescription level, chuckling quietly to himself at the agony of a sweet young thing coming into the city with its harsh odors after a lifetime in the natural world of field and forest and farm.

• • •

Shirley was back at Gwin's the next day and the day after that and most every working day until Harland's graduation. It was wonderful to be able to help her man push forward toward his coveted degree. With her earnings at Gwin's and with his at Bayless's, they were living on a string budget, but they were used to that and now they were sure they could make it.

When they were able to spend a day with Harland's folks to help them work on the farm, she could feel the great pride of Allen and Viola for their son's nearing accomplishment. That may have had some influence when another serious effort came to lure Harland to pharmaceutical sales.

Harry waited till the degree was in sight, before coming with what he called his 'common sense offer.'

"I personally guarantee you two will be enjoying at least ten thousand personal income the first year you join Wayland Distributors." It had to be at least double the amount a first year teacher would earn. And it was so loaded with fringe benefits! It was tempting. "It starts right now, if you'll just sign right here, Harland. As a matter of fact, the firm wants you badly enough that, since you're so close to finishing, they'd prefer to see you complete your degree first before leaving here."

The two exchanged glances as he described the wonderful medical protection policy that would come with just signing this line right here. Had Harry heard they were very pressed for cash this month? Neither believed for an instant that word had gotten out of Gwin's about Shirley's recent miscarriage. But Harry, the veteran salesman, sensed he had their attention.

The pregnancy hadn't been planned, but it was there and in their thrill with the gift, they knew they could handle three as well as two. And in three months the miscarriage. Their hopes were dashed and medical expenses were hurting. Maybe this was the thing to do. Harland looked at his wife and there was that look he'd come to know in their almost two years together. Shirley knew he wanted to teach. She wanted him to reach that goal. To turn away now would always taint the memory of the precious baby who wasn't meant to happen yet. Dollars and medical costs were not what it was all about.

"Harry, I appreciate your thinking I'm the right man for you and both of us would sure welcome that kind of income. But I've got to teach. Guess you might say it's in my blood. We're going to have me graduate in two months and I want to put that Education degree to education, at least for awhile until I prove to myself it's right or not what I'm meant to be."

The graduate

Chapter Four

The blue-and-white Buick caught the attention of fifteen-year-old Joe Sam Vassar as it arrived in Chandler, Oklahoma. Hard not to notice, with the racket it was making. Joe pivoted his slender six-foot-five frame to follow the movement of the car and U-Haul it was towing. A chain had popped loose from the ball mounting and was merrily flailing the lower trunk lid. The driver was tooling down Chandler's main street in air-conditioned oblivion behind the car's closed windows. *Wait'll he stops,* thought Joe. *The guy's going to have a cow.*

At the moment, even if his windows had been open, Harland might not have heard the pummeling of the chain. He and Shirley had just arrived at a goal. For years he had dreamed of becoming a teacher somewhere and they were at the high school that wanted him. He was to be English teacher here and coach of the Speech and Debating classes. It was a little hard for him to absorb that in a few years he had come so far and he felt so ready.

A tall kid on the sidewalk was waving frantically as they passed. Harland threw a genial wave in return. They really were friendly, outgoing folks in these parts.

"There it is, Shirley. Chandler High." Her fingers locked with his and squeezed. He knew they both felt the same emotion. From country kid to classroom teacher. It was going to take some adjusting.

There were young people on the walk in front of the long, rambling, cream-colored building, even though it was still summer recess. Harland waved and the kids waved back and Shirley, looking at her husband, thought, *we look almost the same age as they do.*

Harland rolled down his window to yell back at the youngster who was cupping his mouth with one hand and pointing with the other. "What'd you say?"

"Your chain, mister! It's jumped loose or somethin'. It's whackin' the tar outta your trunk."

"Well, I'll be! Thanks for letting me know."

It was instant first test for teacher cool. He stifled whatever comments wanted to come out, as he matter-of-factly secured the chain in place and ignored all the damage to his trunk lid. He was conscious of the amused curiosity of the watching teenage cluster. Glancing toward the central two-story section of the familiar WPA era school structure, he suspected that more than a few faculty members were just as amused. It was Faculty Orientation Day and, judging by the cars in the lot, some were already on hand early.

Shortly Dave Phillips, Superintendent of the school system, was welcoming Harland as one of the new faces on faculty. "We're expecting great things from you, Mr. Stonecipher. You're going to teach English and handle the Speech classes, too, I hear."

"He's also going to take over the Debating classes and Drama and turn 'em into winners for us," added Melvin Skelton, Chandler High's principal. "And just to keep him busy, we're going to make him the sponsor of the Junior Class."

"I'm Bill Vassar, Harland." It was the President of the Board of Education whose hand reached for his. "I want to wish you the best here at Chandler. You'll likely see a lot of that son of mine and his buddy, Wayne Pounds, in your Debating class. Don't know if my kid figures to be an attorney, but, like his old man, he's sure gung-ho for debating. Do me a favor? Work him!"

Within months Harland had the reputation in the halls of Chandler High for doing just that.

Though English offered little in rewards and incentives, it was certain that he could offer the young people in his Debating, Speech and Drama classes good reason for accomplishment. Tough taskmaster from the first day, he won the accolade 'Boss' in the whispered conversations of those who opted to compete for debating team spots or dramatic roles.

The debaters came back from their first regional competition nursing the wounds of a thorough drubbing. 'Boss' Stonecipher spelled it out to the losers as the four rode home with their new coach. "You win or you work!" he announced after gently reviewing the points that had cost them the debate. "Connie, Shirley, I'm telling you and Wayne and Joe Sam that we can take the state championship and we can do it this year. If you four will work at it! But I'm telling you again right now, you didn't think well on your feet today and you're going to learn how. That is, if you want to win."

The kids did. They came back from their defeats — and there were more of those — and very gradually Harland's belief in them was paying off. They liked their young 'Boss.'

Harland with speech and debate team, 1961

He wasn't that far from them in age, so he had to know a lot of what they were thinking. He had that special way of getting mad over a loss, but still remaining absolutely loyal to everyone on the team-of-the-day. When one of them made hash of a spur-of-the-moment topic he'd demanded they debate, or fumbled an extemporaneous speech on a surprise subject, or forgot a memorized quote, Harland was always there to correct, but never to humiliate. Every student in his classes knew they had a friend in 'Boss' Stonecipher. He felt it. It was good. In those critical first months, the responses of his kids really working, told him he had chosen a profession that was right for him. And, as a fringe benefit, they were beginning to win their competitions.

Shirley loved the winning excitement she saw in their eyes. She was completely fascinated by a phase of education that had not been hers to enjoy. She went to all the competition tournaments and all the drama events as excitedly as any sports fan. These were very special sports — mental athletics. And her man was the coach. He made her immensely proud. There was something about Harland. Around him the teams always knew they had the winning edge.

• • •

But not always. There was a painful day he was sure he never would forget, early in his work with the Drama class.

With other schools, Chandler High had been invited to a one-act play festival. A highlight of the whole event was the presence of drama faculty from all the area state colleges. A special feature would be their private audience afterward with each of the casts and coaches and a critique of the work presented.

There was a certain look about the leader of the critique group as Harland walked his half-dozen budding actors and actresses, flushed with the applause of the crowd, into the private session. The thin-lipped curl of the spokesman's mouth warned of trouble. It came.

The panel of critics, or at least their spokesman, went without preamble to his pet peeve. "Mr. Stonecipher, we're very disappointed that you permit what can only be described as Okie talk by your students."

A ripple of surprise moved through the listeners.

"It simply is not acceptable in this day and age for anyone in a play to say 'eny.' The word is 'any,' Mr. Stonecipher." Harland felt the flush rising at his collar. "And it may be a way to move your mules, but in educated circles your people should learn to say 'get,' not 'git'!"

What could he say? The accusations were partly accurate, but a public whiplashing of his hardest working students was completely out of order. Even some of the others on the critic panel were squirming and one of the girls next to Harland was fighting sobs that had to surface.

Fury was the only word for the rage running through him as their tormentor took one last shot. "I suggest we're all proud to be from Oklahoma, but we don't have to sound so much like Oklahoma. Sheep say, 'Baa.' People say, 'Bye,' or perhaps even, 'Goodbye'...and so say I. Goodbye."

It was the last straw, But somehow Harland kept his composure. Dr. Nabors had worked hard with him in his years at East Central on this very problem of local dialect and he had largely licked it.

"Okay, people," he announced to the despondent cast, just before they left the building for the long ride home. "You heard the man. I'm mad and so are you. One and all you did very well. But I promise you, we'll be invited back here next year and no student of mine will ever have to listen to that kind of criticism again."

• • •

It was an accurate prediction of things to come.

In debating that first year, his debating team placed second in the entire State of Oklahoma in the finals competition. Everyone was impressed with what a high school of less than five hundred total student body, from a town of only 2500 residents, had done against cities like Tulsa and Oklahoma City with populations of a quarter- to half-a-million. 'Boss' was putting winners together. A year later his debating team moved even farther out in front, garnering nine trophies for regional and interstate wins.

The harsh critique worked wonders on his drama classes. In a repeat of the one-act play festival, most of the same young people went to Durant to compete against fifteen other invited high schools. This time it was a different show and a different critique. Chandler High — Harland's kids — earned the only Superior rating given for the fifteen performances and won highest praise from the Drama Department of Southeast State College.

❖ ❖ ❖

Two years sped by quickly. He had developed techniques that worked for him in his own first years of terror whenever he was forced to speak to a group and he had found new ways to help his young people win against the challenge of a dialect trademark. His students seemed to

163

enjoy 'Boss' and his theme, 'You win or you work!' And when he was a monitor of a study hall or in the midst of teaching a class, his warning, "Let's cut that out!" was backed by firmness and love in the same instant.

To move so soon to Okmulgee High, thirty miles to the East, was a tough decision. Another crunch of financial pressure had come when Shirley went through a second and then a third miscarriage. With the invitation to Okmulgee, they would have a salary increase that would take them over five thousand a year. Too, the administration there wanted to build a new competitive department in Debating and Speech and Drama. They were ready for innovation and so was Harland.

• • •

Over five hundred students made up the Senior High Classes at Okmulgee and with the other eight grades, they had classes in a big four-story, red brick building near the center of town. One of those five hundred seniors was Myra Rainey. She especially welcomed the arrival of the tall, good looking new teacher when she learned of his reputation for developing winning debate teams. Debating was a new department and she loved its coming before she was graduated. It could help her decide if the legal profession, which her dad loved, was for her, too. Mr. Stonecipher was dynamic and demanding of those who wanted to try out for his competition road teams. That was good.

Myra found herself in the six-hour class debate tournament, one of Harland's techniques to find which students were the toughest competitors. When the preliminary contests were over, the survivors staged semi-finals. And then the grand finale was before one-hundred-and-fifty classmates.

There was no matching the exultation that Myra and her teammate Suzy felt when they bested the boys' team on the opposite side of the question of Free Trade, all before the filled auditorium. For the rest of her life she would remember Harland's praise of her quotation from one of President Lincoln's addresses to Congress — " 'The dogmas of the quiet past are inadequate to the stormy present...' "

"Congratulations, girls! Myra, there's no question about it, you pulled the rabbit out of the hat with that quotation. I'll bet the ballot went to you just for the way you both performed. By the way, you're expected for lunch today at the Lions Club. They want you — and the boys — to explain what the national debate topic this year means for all the high schools in America."

Whatever else he attempted in teaching, it was always to make his students reach beyond the capabilities they thought they had. When his Seniors opted to attempt the play, You Can't Take It With You, many said it shouldn't be done. After all, the greats in acting had already made the play a well-known classic with the work of Jason Robards and others like him. Fearlessly Harland tackled the challenge and one of the better moments in the story of little theatre at Okmulgee High happened in the exciting production the students gave for an enthralled audience from around Oklahoma.

Shirley found his number in the phone book. They were new in town. He was tall and freckled. He was kind. He had reddish blonde hair. He was an obstetrician and that's all she knew about the man studying her chart.

"This time we're going to make it work, young lady," Dr. Hollis Powell informed Shirley when he decided that, yes indeed, she was very definitely pregnant again. He also found that all of her other three month miscarriages had been from a physiological problem. He'd help her with that and there would be a strict regimen, too, of diet and rest. This time would be different.

Shirley had at least two chaperones to make sure it was different. First Harland, who immediately, positively forbad her to collect his dogs after his regular weekend sport of a night of wolf hunting. The run for the wolf by his trained pack, scattered tired dogs across miles of country and to make it a play weekend for him, Shirley slipped out in the early morning to collect and bring home their canine family. That would stop now, declared Harland.

The second overseer of her pregnancy was her next door neighbor, Maxine Keck, far more a sister than a landlord. With Harland and Shirley, Maxine was determined this baby would arrive. Nine months later Allen was born, a much wanted child after six years of waiting. The life style in the little white house next to the Kecks was instantly, wonderfully changed to make room for three.

Maxine Keck with baby Allen and her sons.

Harland and Allen

It especially thrilled the Kecks that Shirley had had a boy. Parents of three sons, Charles and Maxine had suffered the agony of losing son Russell in Viet Nam in the service of his country. Nothing could lighten that loss, but the presence of a new life next door helped. And the ever-present cluster of students who loved Harland and Shirley and constantly sought out the always unlocked door of the Stonecipher home, helped too.

"Whatever are you mixin' up out here, Harland?" asked Maxine one morning as she came by his kennels from checking their herd of polled herefords in the back pasture. Curiosity had the better of her after watching his commitment to his dogs for an hour or more every day. She often marvelled at their total quiet and Harland told her he did the same as with students who sounded off. Just tell 'em, "Now cut that out!"

I'm mixing the best dog food ever," he said. "I've almost found the perfect balance of protein, carbohydrates, vitamins and trace minerals. Great stuff. Want to try it on the boys?"

"Thanks, anyway. By the way, Charles gets home from Egypt next week and wants me to ask if you could watch the herd during the Summer. He wants us to go with him on an assignment in Canada. Think maybe you...?"

"I'd love to do it. Maybe I'll try this stuff on 'em while you're gone."

"Don't you dare!"

The word was around that debate and drama teams created by Harland were worth seeing, worth hearing. One of his teams came home from an Arkansas tournament with a championship trophy from a four-state debating competition. Over four years his teams amassed four state championships.

Harland had an unwavering belief in those he taught and coached and a fierceness of loyalty. Even ones who were no longer his students felt his unswerving belief in them. Joe Sam came down from Chandler with Wayne and two other teammates to compete in a state debating tournament at Central State University outside of Oklahoma City. Unexpectedly they were treated to that loyalty in a dramatic way. The boys were formidable contestants. Nothing would please them more than to advance in the tournament to confront the team from Okmulgee, also heading for the semi-finals.

"You...Vassar! I want a word with you!" It was the coach of a good team from a much larger high school, just soundly defeated by Joe Sam and Wayne.

All motion in the hall outside the auditorium stopped. A crowd gathered to listen to the loser accuse Joe Sam of inventing a quote that was not a quote to win his final point.

"Sir, I never did that. You'll find it..."

"Don't smart-mouth me, kid! You cheated to win!"

A heavy hand clamped on the tense shoulder of the losing coach. "You apologize to these young men! I know them both. They couldn't...now quit that!"

Beside himself in a rage, the furious loser threw a punch at Harland that missed...and another one that didn't. Suddenly Harland was staring down at his stunned antagonist, sprawled on the tile, just as stunned himself that he had decked the bad loser, and hoping vainly that no other faculty members were around to see the scuffle of two teachers.

"Let's go, boys. I'm proud of you." Harland pushed the boys toward the auditorium. "I'll see you later. You won it fair and square."

"So did you, Boss! Thanks!" The Olympics that year had given Joe Sam a new signal for victory and he raised a clenched fist in salute of his former teacher.

Wayne chortled as they headed down the auditorium aisle to their seats. "You called him Boss! You never did that to his face before."

Joe Sam winked. "He walked out on Chandler, didn't he? So next we draw his Okmulgee kids to debate and do the number on them."

At almost that precise moment in 1966 a meeting was taking place in the offices of National Foundation Life Insurance between Nick Pope and his Oklahoma sales force.

Nick was NFL's Chairman and Chief Executive Officer and he had a reputation he liked. He was tough. He had built the company out of whole cloth. It was his idea and right now it needed new blood.

"So, man, it's as simple as this," he declared, surveying the dozen key salesmen from Oklahoma sitting before him. "You produce offspring or you perish! I want every one of you producing at least one new man by next week. It's a Get-a-Man Program. Until we get it going, we don't get going! We don't want just any man. We want *good* men who will turn on to this business." He looked across the two rows of men. "And be darned sure when they show up with you here next week, that you tell 'em I'm a tough bastard and I expect every one of them in white shirt and dark tie. And, by the way, at least one of you has a loose knot in his tie. It had better be squared away before we adjourn." All twelve fingered self-consciously to check.

"Charley, you figured who you're going to get for your new man?"

"Sure have, sir. I'm going for two fellows in Okmulgee who're teachers like myself. Figure if I can bring them in, we'll make Little Dixie hum like it never hummed before."

Nick smiled. Charley Walls was his heaviest producer and that didn't make a lot of sense. The territory Charley and his team of four took, was the Southeastern corner of the state, away from cities. And it wasn't a lot of little towns either. It was very rural. It was the dollar hurting section of Oklahoma. But somehow the inspiration of Charley was electric down there in what they called 'Little Dixie.'

A combination of three people made up one Charley Walls. He was a teacher, an ordained and working pastor, and a cattle raiser. For the moment he had a goal — a five-year goal that made him put aside the teacher, preacher, rancher in him temporarily till he had earned enough from insurance selling to have a thousand head of cattle. That would let him teach and preach and live happily ever after with his lovely LaVerne. Some of his envious colleagues were sure, at the pace Charley was rolling, that he would reach the goal well before five years were past.

• • •

"I can't do it, Charley." Harland shook his head, wishing he felt altogether as certain as he sounded. This was a former teacher from Antlers whom he respected. There was a definite lure, too, to what he had described. It was a business that Harland knew nothing about. "I made commitments to myself," he went on. "And there are other people who've counted a long time on me being a teacher and I think I'm a pretty good one."

"Look, I want only what you want for yourself, Harland. If this is the right thing for you for life, you should stay right with it. By the way, aren't you from down Tupelo way?" He went on as Harland nodded. "Thought so. I'm out of Antlers myself. Same kind o' country. Lots o' poor farmers."

Harland nodded again. "That's why I owe it to my folks to stay with teaching. I'm the first in my family to go through high school and college and, you know, the teaching profession means success like nothing else does. Besides, I love it."

"Know jus' where you're comin' from. And it *is* success, in my book. That's why I'm goin' back to it in the next five years. But you know something? Even with my Master's Degree, I was only earnin' five thousand a year teachin' history. And, too, school boards are always cuttin' staff, with these hard times. I jus' figured I'm gonna set myself my own security, so when I come back, I never ever have to think again about how much I'm makin' or about what happens, if I get laid off."

Harland's parents

"You think you're getting there in insurance? I mean, the thousand head and all that?"

Charley laughed. "I haven't bought a single head yet. But LaVerne and I are sure gettin' there. I made over twenty-five thousand this past year."

"Twenty-five thousand? That's something else! I congratulate you."

Harland knew his visitor well enough to be certain he wouldn't throw the obvious next question, What'd you make, Harland? Charley would already know Okmulgee paid less than a quarter of that.

He sat quietly and mulled the opportunity booklet Charley had given him. Privately he was thinking, *If Charley*

Walls can earn twenty-five thousand dollars a year, I'm at least half as good a man as he is. That would be well over twelve thousand a year and twice as much as I'm earning now. And all the options are wide open to return to teaching some day. "Tell you what...let me keep this and think it over. I want to talk to Shirley, too." They shook hands and parted.

That night he talked it through with Shirley. As she listened, she felt the new enthusiasm building in him. This was not the same temptation as the opportunity to go with a drug firm. It was obvious he had a lot of respect for Charley and his goals.

"You've got to do what feels right for you, Harland. If you want to do this, I know it will work for us."

Three days later Harland took his decision to the superintendent of the Okmulgee School District.

Harland and Allen on horseback

"Look, tell you what we do, Harland. I know your work in the classroom and it's almost summer break. There's no reason I have to put a new teacher in your place right away. You go try this insurance caper. If it doesn't work out, then you've got your place back here in the Fall."

Harland reached out to grab the man's hand and smiled gratefully as he shook his head. "I really appreciate that, but I've got to say no. If I don't burn all my bridges, I might not do my very best work. I've got to prove to myself just what I can do. I just can't let myself have an escape, in case it doesn't happen to come easily for me at first."

In June, 1966, Harland was a free agent, walking into a new world. Suddenly in stark, challenging black or white, he was where so many men and women find themselves in any year. Trained for one profession and abandoning that work, with no certainty of success in a new field and no way to return to what they have left.

Already, privately, he had taken stock of his decision to break with teaching and never thereafter for a moment, felt qualms of uncertainty. Fear, but never uncertainty. He had to do it. He tried to visualize what it would be like to go out and actually try to sell someone something. In the drug store years he had taken orders, delivered orders. In the classrooms he had given orders and shared knowledge. But what would it be like to actually try to *sell* a life insurance program to someone he'd never met?

• • •

It was a week before the training school was to start. Charley had assured him that he would have a solid week with an expert teacher; the same one who had gotten Charley himself off on the right foot. "We're going to have John Salter. The best."

Harland felt good about Walls as his sponsor into the business. He obviously cared. They had first met by chance, away from the atmosphere of home and teaching, at a fox hunting weekend. Harland and Shirley had collected the hounds, and headed for a meet near Antlers, Oklahoma. Charley, also an enthusiast for the sport, came to the same meet with his running dogs. So, without talk about their work in the classroom, but knowing of Charley's gradual shift of vocation to insurance, Harland had built a friendship and strong confidence in this man who had persuaded him to so radically alter his life.

They were together again the weekend after his decision; Harland with Shirley, Charley with LaVerne at another running meet. It was an informal meet with their dogs running, but mostly it was a chance for the wives and men to socialize. This time shop talk was okay. Charley liked Harland's burned bridges.

"I'll bet they tried to hold onto you," Charley observed. "The super try to talk you out of it?"

Harland shook his head. "No, we're good friends and it'll stay that way. He seemed to appreciate that I want to give it everything I've got, without any way to cop-out."

Charley pushed fresh logs under the metal grill. It was an early summer evening with a refreshing nip in the air and the coffee Shirley was pouring from the well-used traveling pot, smelled good. "Maybe it's the preacher comin' outta me," he said, "but I kept thinking when I got out o' teachin' for this insurance period of my life, it was like testing my capabilities. I know you read a lot, Harland, and I'll bet you've come across that line by Robert Louis Stevenson, 'To be what we are and to become capable of what we can be, is the only end of life.' It always grabs me when I'm runnin' low on courage. I just can't get over how Stevenson, who wrote such great stories, did that from the worst possible conditions — constant pain and confined to his bed. Yet he still kept reaching for what he had the capability of becoming."

Harland saw a little shiver travel across Shirley's shoulder and reached for her sweater. Maybe with the pregnancy so young, it wasn't good to have her outside in this night air. "Evening's getting a bit cool." He massaged her back lightly as he helped her into the sweater. "Should we tell them what Dad said about getting out of teaching?"

"Let's see if I can't tell *you*." Charley showed that contagious grin and his dark eyes glittered in the fading light. " 'Now son, I believe someone has addled your brains,' " he intoned. " 'You mean to tell me you're puttin' aside all that college trainin' and all your teachin' experience? You work with no salary and all risk an'...?' "

"...and kinda like that. Yeah," Harland interrupted. "But he'll back us all the way, if I can do half as good as you do. I'll tell you one thing about my dad. He wants to see us succeed. And he knows that to do that, I've got to risk. He would risk anything if there was any way he knew of to get out o' the back pasture."

"I'm sure he would," agreed Charley. "Prob'ly trapped there, same as my folks."

"Exactly. I was sharing with him something one o' my debators used to win a competition. I'd made a note not to forget President Roosevelt's words, 'It is far better to dare mighty things. The credit belongs to the man who's

Parents with Verman, Doyin, Harland, Vircle, (L. C. not present)

actually in the arena, whose face is marred by the dust and the sweat and the blood; who strives valiantly. Who errs and comes short again and again and knows the great enthusiasms, the great devotions and spends himself on a worthy cause. Who, at the best, knows in the end the triumph of high achievement and who, at the worst, if he fails, at at least fails daring greatly.' Dad smiled once and said, 'Teddy Roosevelt said that, did he?' He had started life about the time the President was national hero with his Rough Riders.

"You know, Charley, I told him I understood his respect for teaching and had it, too. But I also have a great opportunity in insurance to better our standard of living. I don't believe there's one thing less noble about that. In fact, the one you and I have a lot of faith in, said it for me. 'I'm come that they might have an abundant life...' That's why Dad smiled. He knows better'n any other man, I guess, that there's not much abundance in being poor."

Charley turned his attention to Shirley. "You feel good about this decision? You haven't said much, but I think you're kinda like LaVerne. Quiet, but with lots o' thoughts."

"I'm all for what Harland wants to do. I know whatever he sets his mind to do, he's going to succeed. I loved his teaching and I've enjoyed the kids so much. And I guess we'll probably have to leave Okmulgee, but I really hate to. My best friend lives here next door to us and my doctor..." Her voice started to break, then steadied. "But I want it for Harland. I'm all for it."

Harland was studying her. "About our doctor...We're going to have another baby."

"Oh, how wonderful!" LaVerne was on her feet, a hand on one hip and shaking an accusing finger at him. "You men and your dogs! She shouldn't be out here!"

"I wanted to. I hadn't met you and I hardly know Charley either. I'm fine, really."

"Your baby doctor is in Okmulgee?"

She nodded. "But it's all right. I expect we'll have to move to another open territory. I'll find someone else to take care of me."

• • •

It was a fast training week in Okmulgee. If anyone could get him off on the right foot, Harland knew John

Salter was the one. He made it all seem so very simple, too.

"Memorize your presentation book. Pictures, words, exactly how to present the program...no deviations...not one! Stay with the proven way and you'll make a sale at least twice in ten presentations. That's all you've got to worry about, for starters."

It was nearing the moment of truth, Harland knew. In a few days he would be going out with an experienced salesman for a demonstration of how to present the program. For a week he would be on the apron strings of a veteran salesperson and then it was *his* show. He alone would go out to sell a complete stranger. Well, it was not like going out cold. Some shareholder or friend had mentioned the insurance, or thought this neighbor might be interested, so he had a name and an address with him. But from there on he was on his own. Really alone. Harland Stonecipher — English teacher, Debating and Speech teacher who had always doubted he would want to be in any sales, or was even suited for it — was going to have to become a salesman. He had just burned all the other bridges.

• • •

It was *the* day. Charley came by Harland's home in Okmulgee to pick up the fledgling. Behind him in another car was John Salter, who had offered to drive to Okmulgee from Oklahoma City to take another teacher-in-training on his first sales rounds.

"Lucky for you, Harland," Charley informed his protege as they sat over coffee.

"We'll see about that," snorted Salter, a handsome six-footer with a formidable sales reputation. "You lads from Little Dixie are about to take some lessons. Right, Raymond?" The tension in Raymond's face as he tried to smile, told Harland he wasn't the only nervous newcomer.

"Okay, Harland, here's how we're going to do it. We'll probably be able to do four calls today and get in a little review after each one. I'll take the first few and you just watch and enjoy yourself with my mistakes. Just be sure you enjoy yourself!" Charley was a great coach. "You've got a product you believe in. I know you do. And you're going to folks who need it. You just watch me and you'll see I have fun, even while I'm workin'."

He used the same presentation book Harland had. He used the same words and the same approach and the only thing different was Charley's own contagious personality getting into the scene. He inspired confidence. You knew he was coming from truth and concern for the person.

It was not until his second presentation that Charley made his first sale of the day. He critiqued himself good naturedly, then said to Harland, "You notice he invited a return in a few months. We qualified him right then and want to be back there in about three months. Right now he wants the program, but he can't afford to start up. You get to recognize signals from the mate. But we have their interest."

The next call was different. Harland marvelled at what Charlie made look so easy. All through the training course Harland had been awed by the ease with which Salter led people to a positive decision for the program in a classroom setting. The thing they called "closing the sale" still seemed to him as something that separated the men from the boys. But watching Charley at work as he sold the next couple a small life policy, he was relieved. Closing wasn't the artistry of some slick salesman. It was just sensing when the mood of the prospect was ready, and asking for the business in one of a number of ways.

• • •

It was a week later. Charley Walls was back in Antlers; John Salter was back in Oklahoma City. And Harland Stonecipher was very much alone.

For once he was truly scared. He was carrying his briefcase. His presentation book was in it. He knew his lines from the classroom. He had made them his own so he would sound as much like Charley as he could. He was going to show his first prospect a participating plan that made dividends for the owner. He could do it. He knew he could.

It was be to a remembered turn-down. He got through the presentation and had the gut feeling the couple had no interest. A few minutes after their decision, he was on his way to the next prospect. And again he did it by the book, but now it was from his heart, too. Once again he had a "Not now. Maybe later."

He drove down the country road to his third stop and carefully reviewed those first two calls. *Had he been too eager to get on to the presentation? On the second, hadn't he tried to close too quickly? Scared 'em? There needed to be a little more time to relate to the prospect...to get them to feel comfortable with him.*

The tall antenna over the farmhouse caught his eye. He'd heard about the Citizens' Band...*'CB' radio. That was it.*

The youngish head of the house demonstrated the CB, "Breaker, breaker...Bois Dark...come in Bois Dark. This here's Red Rooster...Ya got yor years on?" He turned to Harland. "That's my neighbor's handle..." He chuckled at Harland's expression. "Handle's the name of every CB operator." His set squawked and a second later grunted, "Red Rooster, over and out."

"I'll bet your neighbor has a bunch o' the hardest wood in the world and that's why his handle is Bois D'arc."

"Well, Grace, we gotta be talkin' to an ole country boy. Roy sure has a bunch o' that stuff. Sells it all over the county. Y'ever try to cut bois d'arc? Roy claims he can do five hundred posts a day."

"He's got callouses to prove it, then," laughed Harland. "Folks, I'd like to take a couple o' minutes of your time to show you something that might be right for you..."

Two months later Harland and Shirley were taking stock of what had happened to them. In two months he had achieved far beyond the quotas first assigned him as targets for his initial sales months.

"I don't believe I'm really here!" Shirley exclaimed, standing by the floor-to-ceiling picture window of their suite at one of the finest hotels in Mexico City. "A week to see Mexico, all expenses paid, and now an invitation to have your own territory. Harland, I'm so excited for us."

His arms cupped gently around her waist as he stood behind her looking across the panorama of the beautiful city by night. "It *is* hard to believe. Do you want to know something even more exciting? We've made more this second month at National Foundation than I made in my whole last year of teaching."

"*You've* made more," corrected Shirley. "I'm your cheering section."

He hugged her close. "You really don't know, do you? None of this would be happening if you weren't doing all the things for us that you do every day. And it wouldn't be happening if I didn't feel as if you were right there with me, when I go to a strange house. I bet I'd have quit after my first two turn-downs, if I hadn't known it was all for you. I'm just so sorry..." he sucked for breath. "I'm really sorry about the miscarriage, honey. Next time, wherever we're living, let's go back to Hollis Powell again."

She nodded quietly, feeling the strength and resolve of the man behind her. There were hurts. And the two of them were apart all day and most every evening, too. But there was this overriding happiness when they were together. And she knew the commitment he had to succeed in his new profession was from his love for her and little Allen. Sometimes she wondered if his total dedication to bringing them "the good life" wasn't underlined by the name given their firstborn. It was a proud name from a courageous, honorable grandfather who had done all he could to give Harland the right start. Harland was going to do all in his power to see that his children had the same legacy. And to those important things he was going to add security — an absence of poverty.

It was a consuming drive. He was an achiever. As a teacher and now as an insurance salesman — she could feel it about him — he must become someone very important to this, their new world. Sometimes she wondered if they were just dreaming and hoping. It was really too early to have such anticipations. After all, he'd only been in this new work two months. This trip to Mexico probably was just an incentive builder and she was reading too much into it. But in her heart she knew his teaching role, the demands for stage presence and public speaking ability, and now the challenge of selling insurance and going to sell strangers... not one of these things came easily to her man. He had to dig for the courage to sell and to speak and to teach. But the thing that made him different from others, was that he *made* himself do it. Nothing he chose to do came automatically to Harland. He didn't soar quickly to pinnacles of high success. But when he was put down or knocked down, that was the time to look out for Harland Stonecipher. *He had something of the foxhound in him,* she smiled to herself. *He just doesn't know how to give up. How she loved that in him.*

She appreciated the things in their family's security that Harland found important. He already had begun a life insurance program and they had health insurance protection — things neither of them knew existed when they were kids. And since he was on the road constantly, he made sure both of them were protected with more than adequate auto insurance. "Never know, with these nuts on the highway," he'd said when he raised their coverage. "I think maybe Dad had the right idea. Twenty miles an hour and that was it. No need for all this rushin'. Anyway, we've got total protection, far's I can see."

• • •

It was only the beginning. Harland was convinced he could sell well above the average needed to make earnings that would put him on his way to the same independence Charley Walls had. And very shortly Nick Pope was seeing the potential in him for a company leadership role. A selection group laid the hand on Harland and a few others to take what National Foundation called its PDM training to become District Managers. Within one short year he was noticed and singled out as one who could be a special key person to the company.

Then it happened. Gradually. Those closest to Harland could feel a shift in his spirit, in spite of the outward signs of success. Something was starting to go all wrong in his relationship with National Foundation Life. The new blood that was being brought into the company through the recruiting effort of Charley and Harland and many others, gave Nick Pope such a handful that he had no way to notice a slow disillusion going on in just one of his agents.

Harland's sales were far above the average. As a district manager he had all the outward marks of a man on the move for a top spot somewhere waiting, if he continued to dramatize that one most visible characteristic — his tenaciousness for the goal. The only thing that could shake him from that quality was for someone else, over him and in control of his earning power, to be less than honest. Everything in him had always hinged on dealing from honesty. The key superior in this turning point moment was worse than a disappointment. He simply used people as things and truth as an urn to be drunk from or urinated into, depending on the need of the hour.

It was more than Harland could handle. There was no way in his forthrightness not to express his feelings when the times of deceipt and deception showed. It was obvious he was going to have to get away from this person or sour in his career. The offer from a national real estate company seemed to be a possible alternate course when the time came that he knew he could no longer continue under this man and there was no way to change his situation. Possibly an alternative might have been there, had his guide and mentor from the beginning been around to help him work it out. But Charley was gone.

Charley had reached his target of a thousand head of cattle and a thousand calves on a 2500 acre ranch, and had retired. He was back in Antlers, Oklahoma. National had been good to him and now it was 1968 and time to get back to the life he really loved. So it was Harland's dilemma alone to extricate from the bad relationship at the company.

A decision was made to go to real estate sales and to move Shirley and Allen and the life they had begun in Oklahoma to Springfield, Missouri. Shirley remembers that unhappy year as one well worth forgetting — except what happened for Harland because of it.

In the course of his year of traveling far and wide from Missouri in his assignments, someone else had been missing Charley Walls in the insurance scene and had gone to Antlers looking for him. Ed Held and Wayland Roberts, chief executive officers of Paramount, a life insurance company in Little Rock, got wind of his early retirement. They sought him out at his ranch to try to lure him back as a key man in their company. There was no way.

"Tell you what you do," Charley urged the disappointed pair. "There is a great guy for you up in Springfield, Missouri, who pulled out of life insurance just about a year ago. I'll bet you can get Stonecipher 'cause he loves the industry and something just went wrong in his old company."

• • •

Dilemma time again for Harland. His friend Charley had read his situation loud and clear. Real estate could never be for him, after the years in insurance, and he was unhappy with himself in shifting gears, even if there was no choice at the time, if he was to support his family.

What to do now with another new opportunity? He

listened hard to the two men. He had listened hard before. The opportunity was fully as interesting as that from National, except there was a difference. His record as a salesman was now established and Paramount Life was anxious to give him leadership. The invitation carried the immediate promise of overrides and a more comfortable quality of life than any he and his family had known before. Yes, there had been abundant promises in NFL, too, till they were blocked by one person he could not trust nor believe. There was just one way now — with a man he knew could really be trusted. He reached for the phone. He would, by golly, create his *own* superior.

Charley's accomplishments in taking an impossible part of Oklahoma for National Foundation and leading the nation with 'Little Dixie' sales, were legend. Paramount would like to make him Number Three in their company, if he could be persuaded.

"Aw hey, Harland, have a heart!" Charley responded. "I'm retired. I'm out of it now. I'm down here in cow country, doin' jus' what I want to do the rest of my life. That's why I sent 'em to you!"

"Charley, I want you to have exactly what you want." Charley grimaced silently to himself. He was getting the very line back he had often used in recruiting. He'd used it on Harland! "But do something for me before you say 'No.' There's a new twist. This is just too good an opportunity and I could not let it get by you without your hearing it first-hand. Now I'm way up here in Missouri and these two men, Ed and Wayland, are coming from over in Little Rock and you're down there in Antlers. Will you do me a favor, Charley? Come meet us tomorrow at McAlester? That's kind of mid-point for all of us. Just trust me that there's something new and it's at least worth your hearing about. I guarantee it, Charley."

There was an extended silence. Finally, "For you I'll come, Harland. But no promises. I figure on teachin', preachin' and ranchin' for the rest o' my days and this deal you're talkin' about jus' doesn't fit, I'll betcha anything."

"Wait till tomorrow, Charley. Just come with an open mind. Besides, preachers don't bet."

"They do when they're cattlemen!"

Next day the four sat around the dining room table, nursing coffee and cokes and exchanging ideas. Ed and Wayland had flown over in Paramount Life's plane and they knew what they needed. Harland was just the man to run Oklahoma for them and he had made no bones about it — he would only come if they could interest Charley in joining Paramount, too. The two from Paramount would like nothing better. Whoever persuaded him or what changed his mind, is not recorded. Charley was persuaded.

The stage was set for a new day for Harland. He would run the business of Oklahoma and Charley would take over as Director of Marketing and Senior Vice President. It was to make a tremendous difference in the lives of millions of people and it was all decided over a cup of coffee in a motel dining room in McAlester, Oklahoma.

Ed and Wayland left and as Harland and Charley walked to their cars, Charley said, "You said something about a new twist. That was exactly what they offered me before. What's the new thing?"

Harland chuckled. "Why, it's me. Now you get all that and me, too!"

Charley slapped him on the shoulder and strode away. "So make Oklahoma work!" he called from his car.

❖   ❖   ❖

He was Marketing Director of Oklahoma. It didn't mean that a thing was different in this career he had come to respect, but now he was recruiter and trainer administrator, as well as salesman for Paramount. He enjoyed it. Now he had his real opportunity to move forward both in leadership and in sales. He was sure that the gifts he recognized in himself would have the chance to surface, if the company grew beyond its four state region. Meanwhile, he now had every chance in Oklahoma to show what he could do and the company was a wonderful break for him to demonstrate whether or not he could.

The skills were there. He built his organization. He was leading the other states. The future was brighter than he dared hope it would be when he left teaching. His income was good and getting better. It was comfortable now to be a two car family, live in a larger home and enjoy a quality of life neither he nor Shirley had known before.

The best omen for the future as 1969 moved into Summer was that Harland had reached the certainty that he was able to lead, to sell and to build his organization. He had absolutely no interest in remaining at any fixed point of success. It wasn't possible, in the first place, and there was something as yet indefinable, needling deep at his subconscious level. There was more he was meant to do with his newfound skills.

Chapter Five

It was a beautiful early July morning in central Oklahoma. Harland was due at his sales meeting in Shawnee and it was a leisurely drive from Ada, where they now made their home.

Good to be back in Oklahoma, he reflected. It had been the right decision to return to insurance. Working his home state with Charley as his overseer, he was doing well as Marketing VP. The title wasn't important. He was involved again with a work he believed in. He had a good crew of salesmen up in Shawnee district and everywhere he went there was visibly a dramatic upturn in the Oklahoma sales. Most of all, he felt comfortable in the leadership slot. His people liked him and they worked together well and the results were showing.

Mile after mile of bois d'arc fences lined Route 13 and he remembered when Steve and he dug post holes by the hundreds on weekends. He wondered if some kids like himself and Steve had cut these he was passing. *Chances were they made a good bit more today than the nickel-a-hole he earned with his partner fifteen years ago.*

The weekend — it didn't seem possible that it was Friday again already. He'd promised Shirley he'd get that new kennel run completed on their land. It was the next step in his fun with the running dogs. Allen was of an age now to be more than a baby. At six he thoroughly enjoyed the dogs that his dad had at a hunting camp about twenty miles East of their home. It was going to be a big weekend, too. He'd been instrumental in organizing the Oklahoma

Hunter's Horn magazine

State Hunt for July and was secretary for the event. He smiled to himself as he remembered his early hunger to have his own dogs. Already Allen was showing that same enthusiasm.

Hunter's Horn, the magazine he had read so avidly since school days, now wanted to run a cover story on the young Paramount insurance executive and his passion for foxhunting. He was pleased they wanted his family on the cover, along with Minnie Jantzen, his nine-year-old foxhound. Minnie had produced many champions and launched Harland into what was becoming a profitable avocation of breeding hounds.

The country road was practically deserted. It was a nice time of day to get started...and it was a pretty, gently rolling route, up a low hill to a crest like the one he was approaching...

...and suddenly, savagely, there was a great blur of white directly in his face. A car! Cresting the hill toward him, swinging across his path in a violent left turn!...*No time to react!*...

 ...a *flare of white*...
  ...a *terrified face!*...
At the instant of impact there seemed a great rush of sound — then blackness...

Accident photo from Ada newspaper

184

· · ·

"You're a lucky man, Mr. Stonecipher." The speaker was a distant blur of white somewhere above him.

Everything else seemed white. Had the whole world gone white? The last thing he could remember was that sudden white blur...

"Where am I?"

"In Ada," said the gentle voice. "You're in Valley View Hospital. Let me go get Mrs. Stonecipher. She's outside and worried to death."

"What happened?...I remember...car...my side... was it...drunk...?"

"Not that we know. We just know you got knocked into the back of your car—into the one little place where you wouldn't have been crushed. Like I said, you're a very lucky man. You shouldn't be here, from the way they describe your car. I'll go get Mrs. Stonecipher. Harland? Harland, do you hear me?" Her patient was unconscious again. She reached for his pulse.

· · ·

It was almost a week before he was to begin to be able to put his world back together. Still in traction, his back injuries weren't under control but he was itching to be home with his family. Shirley was at bedside, making a valiant effort to keep his mind off the problems that had needled him all morning.

"You've got everything taken care of. Now, Harland, just try to relax."

She was right, he knew. It wasn't going to get him back on his feet to sweat out his worries. Worries that very well might not even come to pass. He had been hit hard by the visit from a lawyer friend and the assessment of what could eventuate.

"Don't want to worry you, Harland. But you are in quite a vulnerable position," Stanton Wilson said. "I'm just glad you're well covered with your health policy and it looks like you'll do fine as far as car replacement right away. We ought to have you back on wheels about the time they let you out of this place. Your main worry is probably legal. This very possibly could get sticky."

"What's that supposed to mean?" he demanded.

"Could mean any number of things. Just because you didn't cause the accident, doesn't mean you're out of the woods legally, you know. I don't want to scare you — certainly not here while you're trying to recover — but I think you should be aware. Just for instance, I suppose you know that if the lady would fail to survive this accident — and let me assure you, it looks like she's going to be all right — but your auto insurance would not protect you, not with one penny, if she were to die.

"And *so* it was a company insured car. You'd still be on your own for legal counsel, unless you wanted to risk it. See, any death on the highway is treated like any law enforcement. Always a potential murder. That's why they have homicide departments on the state police and highway patrol. It's not uncommon for a surviving driver to wind up with a charge of vehicular homicide or manslaughter, or even worse, till the case is tried in court."

"You're saying I would be completely responsible to retain my own attorney and pay all those costs, too?" He wished his visitor didn't look so grim. "What other legal problems? Hey, I wasn't the least bit in the wrong!"

"I'm afraid that doesn't matter. As it is right now, you're probably looking at some considerable costs in litigating this thing. Just call me, if I can help you with anything. I better let you alone. You look like you could use some rest."

"Yeah...guess so. I thought I had everything taken care of."

"Nothing you *could have* taken care of." The attorney shook his head as he headed toward the door. "There's no way to anticipate these things. And no such protection that would keep you ready for this kind of emergency. It's not like your medical insurance. You just gotta grin and bear it."

"How much would you guess I might be facing? I mean, you're saying the person who caused the accident doesn't pay my attorney costs?"

"Not usually. And your employer probably won't. We just need to hope the other side doesn't get into a court room and convince the judge or jury the accident wasn't like it seems."

"A jury? This could actually be a jury matter?"

"Of course. That's America. Anyone can demand a trial by jury for anything. Then it's Katy-Lock-The-Barn! Turns into a real crapshoot as to how it's all going to come out...who's going to win." The lawyer waved resignedly and opened the door. "Don't let it throw you. Just get some rest."

"Yeah. Thanks for the warning."

When he was alone, Harland took inventory. He had no idea of what the outcome would be. The main thing was that that woman survive, but there was now some very ominous potential in the picture and it was going to take tall figuring in the family budget if he was handed even half the legal costs his friend had intimated. "Sure...get some rest," he muttered to himself, resolving not to say anything about the likely legal hassle to Shirley. She'd already come through enough of this nightmare.

• • •

It was several months before he felt like himself again. He was really lucky, he told himself as he headed out to pick up the pieces of his career. Fortunately, there had been a great support team to carry over the hospital time and the months beyond. Charley was all over the Oklahoma scene helping train and recruit new agents for him and there was no serious loss of the momentum Harland had built.

As he drove toward Oklahoma City and his first sales meeting since that morning of July 11th, he counted his great luck. He had wonderful friends.

The problems out of the accident were far from over. There had been a replacement of his car that had been totalled. But there was sure to be extensive litigation. Whether it was the bad taste of the lawyer who called on him at the hospital or a feeling he had better go to someone a little more upbeat, Harland had sought out Ada attorney Frank Jaques. Frank's lawyering always carried a confident smile and Harland was sure he'd be needing smiles soon from anyone who could muster them.

He shifted uncomfortably in the driver's seat. The full length back brace was one of the reasons for his Oklahoma City run today. The sales meeting was just part of it. The therapy at the O'Donoghue Rehabilitation Institute was the most important thing at the moment. He had to get the compressed discs and injured spine back in shape, if he was going to go full steam again. At least that much was covered by a pretty good pre-paid medical.

He mulled the worries that had been set in stone in his head about likely legal costs. *He had been right. Already it had taken a large amount. Why wasn't there something like a pre-paid legal in America for such a mess? For any kind of mess! How could this country be so matured and yet have come no further than this for the average man? There were more lawyers than doctors, he'd bet, and that must mean there were as many legal problems as sicknesses.*

When his legal costs, apart from the bruises and breaks, were added up, it would cost the Stoneciphers thousands. To some families such cost might mean nothing much, but to many millions of Americans they would mean a disaster. For Harland and Shirley it was very costly and further sensitized Harland to a great gap in America's available protection. Something should be done.

• • •

"I've got to do it!" he shouted from the shower stall as Shirley brushed her new short hairstyle.

"Do what?" *Maybe she shouldn't have had it cut. He so liked it long.*

"This thing. This...legal protection thing. Somebody's got to do it. Nobody's ever heard of it."

Shirley recognized the sound. It was Harland with a mission. There was Harland the tease...Harland having fun with foxhunters...Harland the teacher...the father...and this was the sound again of him with his mind made up.

"The big problem is how we get it going," he mused at breakfast. "It'll take money. A good deal of it. I'll bet there's a thousand things we'll need, but for starters, it's going to have to be capitalized."

Shirley, keeper of the Stonecipher books, willing and enthusiastic hostess to the feeding and entertaining of

Shirley with long hair

188

foxhunters who dropped by every weekend to run their dogs on their acreage, now had two questions on her mind.

"You have to tell me why *you* have to do it. And with your back the way it is and just getting the pace again with your work, why is this so important?"

"Because nobody's even tried such a program seriously. We've had medical protection for over thirty years in this country. There's been legal protection in Europe from way back, but we just don't bother in America. Just seems to me a lot of families must be getting bankrupted by legal costs they haven't had a chance to prepare for."

"You mean you're thinking of starting this from scratch and then taking it...well, everywhere?

"We better think big or not think at all. I've found out that the only attempts ever have been little associations of lawyers from the same law school, recommending each other on a list and giving a discount for services if you have a problem in some other city in California or Florida. Their organizations all wind up in the complaint section of their local bar associations and have to stop. Nothing like what I'm thinking of. We've got to think big from the start."

"I'm glad you're thinking big, darling. So am I. That's why I'm going to Okmulgee this morning."

He stared curiously at his wife. "I don't understand. I thought you were going to see Maxine. And weren't you just there last week?"

Her giggle had that infectious excitement about it. "I'm really going to see another man. Best I tell you. His name is Hollis Powell. He called to tell me the test I took is positive. I'm very pregnant."

His hand slid across the breakfast table to hers. "How wonderful!" He squeezed. "The best news is you're with Dr. Powell again. This time it's going to be fine."

Seven months later Brent arrived, healthy, happy and vocal. He was a wonderful addition to the family, seeming to herald the coming of great accomplishment.

Allen with Brent

From the time the idea commandeered Harland that what America desperately needed was a legal protection plan, he couldn't let it go. It was on his mind almost constantly. He shared it with Frank Jaques, who immediately liked it and urged him to put it in the works. On New Year's Day, 1971, Frank called his friend Bob Thompson to his home to meet this Stonecipher fellow and listen to what he had in mind. He wanted Bob, a local businessman, to react.

"Bob, Frank here has been a great help to me in an accident situation I had recently," Harland began. "It kind of got me to thinking and doing some research. And I discovered something that really shocked me. At least seventy percent of the American middle class can't afford an attorney. That is, they don't *think* they can. Fact is, of course, as you know in your auto parts business, there's lots of times where the worst thing a person can do is to wait awhile on a problem, or just wait and see. Maybe it'll go away? Anyway, almost three-quarters of adult America don't believe they can afford an attorney. And a lot get hurt every day because of that."

Bob poked his glasses up across the bridge of his nose and shook his head in despair. "Course, ole country boy Frank here's 'nuff to make anybody swear off attorneys."

Frank threw a playful punch. "Tell him, Harland. Didn't I do all right by you on your little matter?"

"Some 'little'! But yes, you sure did. Worth every penny and a lot more, because you've given me a listening ear on this idea from a lawyer's viewpoint."

"Wait'll you get this bill," laughed Bob.

"No fair," growled Frank. "This is on me. I happen to think he's onto something we all can benefit from. The American Bar Association has pretty well concluded that even less than thirty percent of American adults use lawyers …ever. It's kind of a vicious circle. People hope the problem will go away, then go for professional help when it's in the crisis stage and it's expensive. End result: we wind up with a bad image and words like 'shyster' and 'crooked lawyer' come easy. But it isn't fair. Most of my friends in law are honest people. Now what Harland's working on has real merit, I believe. And I think he's one man who can make it happen."

190

"So what would you call this?" Bob's interest was up.

"Well, it's a pre-paid legal idea. I've been checking and we may have problems calling it that at first though. At least till the legislature can lay down some rules for us on it. That'll take time. But I've come across a way we can break into the field through a motor club approach. That's part of why I wanted Frank's opinion. But let me ask you, Bob, would you think, if people knew we'd protect them with a lawyer for about eighty percent of the problems they have, they'd be interested in a protection like this?"

"I know I would," he responded. "What do you guess it would cost?"

"It's got to be very little or we can't get the interest." Harland leaned forward in his chair, wanting them to really absorb his next point. "The way I see it, to get the support of both the public and the attorneys, we have to give them their choice of lawyer and keep the cost for belonging very low."

"You just got my attention," smiled Frank. "So, how do you propose to fund all this?"

"Of course, that's the big challenge," Harland replied. "The fact is, I don't know. I'd like to canvass some of the banks here and in a few other states where I know people. I'm going to look to my own resources at first, for starters. Right now, I'm going to let you fellows enjoy the holiday. Thanks for hearing me out."

"Listen, keep us posted," Bob encouraged. "I'm interested. I know my father will be, too. Looks to me like you'll want to incorporate. I'd be interested in passing the word when you're ready."

"You two are a great way to start the year. Happy New Year to you!" Harland called from the door. *That's it*, he exulted to himself as he hurried to his car. *That's the perfect thing to call his protection. Pre-Paid Legal. It says it all. But first things first. Let's get the means to make it happen.*

The next months all left major question marks as to when they would be ready to start, if ever. The canvass of the banks, local and national, all brought the same understanding, professional smiles from those who listened. Universally Harland received a bottom line response, "We would have no interest in getting involved in this kind of thing."

To make it possible to do business in the State of Oklahoma, for starters, was going to involve a lot more than just some legislators rewriting a few laws. It was going to need direct involvement with the insurance department, even though Harland saw this as something other than insurance. "Somebody's got to regulate you; you can count on that. I'll be glad to listen to any plan you come up with," advised Gerald Grimes, Deputy Insurance Commissioner. "If you go on with it, we're going to have to develop some kind of model act to regulate you. It'll help." Harland had the feeling from his first encounter with Grimes that this was a man of his word.

He made it a point to get to know Lonnie Abbott, too, representing the city and area in the State Legislature. Again more encouragement. It was obviously going to be driving a spade into untilled ground, but it was encouraging in the very early months of digging, to find people in public service who believed the dream had possibilities. They were willing to listen and to help.

It was back to a question of money. How to finance even the initial stages of a legal service company? He had good feelings about many of the men he worked with in Paramount Life. Of course, his first thought was good friend Charley, who had been such a backstop and inspiration. Charley was totally disinterested. "This time, Harland, I'm going to get out and stay out. I'm just about ready to retire and this ole boy is going to go back to Antlers and stay. I may even run some dogs. By the way, you're not gettin' to run yours much anymore, are you?"

"Not the way I'd like to, Charley. My back is still messed up with this brace. Allen is already into hunting, though. But you've just given me an absolutely great idea. You know a lot of my hunting friends like that dog food I mix up. You kinda like it yourself, too, you said. Well, you just gave me a great way to put together some capital for this program of mine."

• • •

The next day he walked into the law office of Barney Ward. He was bent on talking about his great idea for a pre-paid legal program to get another lawyer's opinion. But first he needed counsel on incorporating. Not incorporation of his legal protection plan. Too soon for that. First, the means to finance the start of it.

Barney Ward listened briefly as he described his want to incorporate to produce his dog food mix. "Better hold it a minute, Mr. Stonecipher. My specialty is criminal law. You need an attorney in general practice. Do you mind if I call a friend for you?" He was dialing the number and Harland wondered at the remarkable skills even in the little things, of this well-known Ada attorney who happened to be blind. He must have faced huge odds against success. "Ken Johnson, please. This is Barney Ward...

"Ken, I've got a friend here you can help. Harland Stonecipher is interested in trying to sell a product. Incorporating's part of your territory. Can I send him over?"

Harland walked into the offices of Johnson and Thompson. He knew from the moment he shook his hand he was going to like Ken Johnson. There was an immediate communication. Different men out of different disciplines — insurance and law — but each sensed a similarity in mindset in the other.

Ken remembered seeing Harland on the streets of Ada. Always moving with that purposeful stride and good-natured smile.

"I've got this dog food mix, Mr. Johnson, I'd like to package."

Ken leaned to scratch notes on his pad. "What do you plan to call this product?"

"Think I'll go with Stoney's Super Hound. I've been refining it with about fifty of my running hounds and it's pretty special. Lots of friends with dogs love it so much I've been forced to get a truck and hire one of my nephews to mix and pack it and run it around to everyone. Looks like it could be a pretty profitable business. But someone told me I'd best incorporate before we go any further."

"That was good advice. We can put it on through for you, but to tell you the truth, you're into a very regulated procedure. Costs add up for what might be little return. I'll spell it out and you decide."

He described the necessary legal steps for Harland and he watched the disappointed shake of his client's head. "Well, that's way too much for the return, as you warned. Where it's a food substance, I can understand all the regulations, but it's too rich for my blood at the moment. Thanks, though." He was disappointed. "I had really been looking for a way to generate some serious money for something a lot more important than the dog food."

"Well, if I can ever help you with anything else, just feel free to come by." Whatever the 'something more important' was, his client had decided now wasn't the time to broach it.

When the door closed behind his first meeting with Harland, Ken reflected on the similarity and the dissimilarity between them. They were close in age and Ken was sure they both came out of the roots of struggle. No doubt that this one had a lot of struggle going on still inside him. Ken knew something about all of that. Not long out of law school, he was part of a large firm and in a decision time about going it on his own with George Thompson. Could be good or it could be bad, in a city as small as Ada. There was security here where he was. Maybe even a move up. But he had a bigger goal.

Wasn't that all part of what his dad and mother had given up so much for? They wanted to see him go to the top of whatever he chose to do. Sitting still wasn't going to get it for him, anymore than for anybody else. The restlessness he felt in Stonecipher wasn't too different than what he felt in himself.

His glance traveled across the wall of his panelled office, pausing at the black framed certificates — the Bachelor of Arts from Oklahoma and the Juris Doctor from the same university. He smiled to himself, remembering how the chance to go there had all been planned by his father and mother.

When they were first married, his parents, Otis and Willene, pursued the life others in their family had followed. Red dirt farmers. It was that simple. They simply farmed forty acres. The couple had good reason to believe that was the only course for them in pre-war Oklahoma. Between their two families, his mom's in Corbet and his dad's in Wanette, there were twenty-one brothers and sisters — eleven on his mother's side, the Higbees, and ten on his dad's. For most of them it would be farming or nothing in this near depression economy.

Something turned on in Otis Johnson's mind about 1939. It was not going to stay that way for the children he and his wife had! Already there was the clear evidence of two seasons that the ground he was working was going to fight every effort to make it productive. No quitter, he hired out to other farmers, to keep his family from starvation. There was no way he was about to stand by and settle for this deprivation for his loved ones! And there was abundant evidence, from so many others right in his family, that if he kept all of the children he and Willene wanted to have, in this atmosphere it was likely to be the extent of their horizons.

It must have been a tremendous decision for the two to make, the day Otis brought up his conviction to Willene that they should move to a college town.

"My kids are going to have the chance I never had!" he declared to her. "We're sure to find some kind of work, if we just go to the biggest school in these parts and that's at Norman. There's where Oklahoma University is and that's where our kids are going to go!"

• • •

It was exactly what the Johnsons did. When they arrived with oldest son Robert, daughter Jequita and nine-month-old Ken, they knew they would reach the goal of giving their children what they hadn't had for themselves.

To make it work, Ken's dad worked for the University — at first for the Commissary, delivering food around the University eating centers, while Willene worked as a cook in the school kitchen. Both forced themselves to work incredible hours through the children's childhood and already by the seventh grade, Ken had caught the magic of the quest of his parents for all of them. At twelve and weighing 80 pounds, he followed his brother and sister into the family work team, finding his niche in the North Campus University cafeteria as a youngster doing pots and pans and maintaining the beverages at the counter.

It made a long day, off for school at 8:30 to 4:00, then to work in the cafeteria from 4:30 to mid-evening every day. It was good money at thirty-five cents an hour and there was a wanted goal.

From the cafeteria he graduated in mid-teens to the scrubbing crew, working the dormitories, and his pay was better. Always there was the target of one day being a student himself at this university.

Admission Day as a Freshman finally came. As it had been for the five years before, he carried both the work and the academic hours. Four years later, with a great deal of pride, his parents watched him receive his B.A. Degree at Oklahoma University.

• • •

It had been a struggle. It had been worth it. He had focused only toward the end of his Junior year on pre-law. He was a long way from admitted to study it. No way to forget the rule of the University that there was no way he could work and attend law school at the same time. It was not generally permitted and it took persuading. He gave it his best shot. He had become thoroughly convinced that law was for him. He had dropped his major in Accounting to switch to law and there was no way he was about to quit without a fight. In the end, he was admitted.

Allowed to enter law school, he did well. He married his sweetheart of the undergrad years, June Leibenderfer, just before he entered law school and with his job at Oklahoma Natural Gas often requiring many hours a week, he still had put it all together through the years of going long days on light sleep. The early years of his life had toughened him. No one was more pleased for him and proud of him at his graduation than Otis and Willene Johnson.

Ken recognized the same tenacious spirit in the caller who had just left. Disappointed, but far from anything like defeated. He wondered about the other project Harland had in mind.

It was many months before he was to find out. He had an inkling of something going on that made absolutely no sense. A client friend came by his office on a Saturday with a <u>Daily Oklahoman</u>. "Hey, what do you know about this Sportmen's Motor Club? Says something here about a million-and-a-half shares with Harland Stonecipher and your colleague up the street, Frank Jaques, and some other guy. You in on this?"

196

Ken shook his head. "I don't know a thing about it."

• • •

Some days later June Lawson announced on his intercom, "Harland Stonecipher to see you."

Harland dropped into a chair and immediately moved close to the edge of his seat. He was totally different than the man who had come to this office months before to talk about dog food. He leaned across the front of Ken's desk. "I've got two things I need you to do for me. One we can do later and that has to do with my vesting with my insurance firm, Paramount. I'm going to need every bit of dollar yield I've got coming from those years, to do what I've started now."

"I'll be glad to help you on that," said Ken. "What's the second thing?"

"Have you ever heard of a pre-paid way to pay for attorney's services?"

Ken puzzled a moment, then shook his head. "No, but somewhere back in law school a prof was saying someday in America we ought to be getting to some kind of way to pay for attorney fees."

Harland stood, paced, then stopped and faced him across the desk and drew a small brochure from his inside coat pocket. "How's this for starters?"

Ken examined the cover on the brochure. "Sportsmen's Motor Club. A client of mine mentioned he had read something about this in the paper."

"We *just* incorporated. Frank Jaques did it in exchange for stock in the company. So he wrote up the paperwork. But I need a real blunt appraisal. Just as blunt as you handed me on the dog food, if that's the way it seems. What do you think of this program?"

With lawyer's precision, Ken digested the brochure word by word. "Well, I'll be! Here I thought you were going into competition with Triple-A."

Harland still stood. It was obvious the opinion he had come for was tremendously important to him. "It's not

pretend. We're going to do all the motor club things —
maps, trip layouts, towing...But we're aiming to make it
into a pre-paid legal and the insurance department couldn't
allow us to use our first brochure, which said 'Pre-Paid
Legal Service' yet."

"Yeah?" Ken smiled sympathetically. "Say, here's a good
twist — this business of giving an annual dividend credit
at the end of the policy year." He studied the cover again.
"Sportsmen's Motor Club, Inc.," he read aloud. "Sportsmen's
is a Legal Service Motor Club. By golly, you are that!
You've got three out of four of your offerings really legal
services. Emergency legal protection and the right to pick
your own attorney for traffic court and criminal court...
Emergency bonding service...And I like this emergency collection service...I'm really impressed, Harland. Do you
know what you've put together here?"

"Tell me," demanded Harland. "What do you think I've
put together?"

"Well, in my book it's the first breath of fresh air on
the legal scene I've seen since I got into practice. I congratulate you!" He studied the brochure again line by line,
word by word. "This is just great," he murmured as he read.

Harland waited till he looked up from the reading and
said, "The things you've talked about — being so good — I
wonder if you'll help me get this off the ground tonight.
I've got a number of people we've passed the word around to.
We're not selling them anything. Not stock...not memberships...This tonight is just for their information. It sure
would help...I know Frank would appreciate it, too, if an
attorney of your stature could just share your candid re-
actions with the people who come."

Ken's hand shot out. "I sure will, Harland. I'd be honored
to help put this across." Now he was on his feet, too, feeling
the excitement of Harland's enthusiasm. "This can be a
great thing for attorneys and for clients. Do you know how
many times a lawyer has to turn people aside, just because
they have no way in the world to pay for the only thing
he can offer — his service? This gets a whole new opportunity
going for all of us."

Harland's beaming expression said it all. "Will you tell them just how you feel? We're going to be out in that back little meeting room behind the Village Inn. It's all we could get on short notice."

Curiosity was very high in the crowd who came out on that cold February night in 1973. Access to the room was blocked at the only side entrance, so everyone entering by the roll-up garage door on the end, brought a chilling, wintry blast inside with them.

Harland wasted very little time with preliminaries, once he had more than seventy in the room. "I appreciate your coming out to hear what this is all about. Sportsmen's Motor Club is the name we chose to give the new enterprise, until we can get certain legislation passed.

"Well, we're kind of a shock to the Insurance Commissioner. We're not really insurance and we're not really a motor club, as our main reason for existence. We know just exactly what we intend to be, soon as the laws can be set in place and the regulatory body can know how to regulate us.

"Meanwhile, we're incorporated, thanks to attorney Frank Jaques here, and I've asked another attorney, Ken Johnson — and I'm sure you all also know him — to come give you his impressions of what is going to become a national pre-paid legal service. Ken, come on up here and tell us how you see this enterprise."

Ken touched on every single point in the brief descriptive brochure Shirley had handed out to everyone. When he finished expressing his professional opinion, that this was a program long overdue in America, it was obvious the atmosphere in the room was charged.

"So, when do we get to buy in...or sell it?" demanded Charley Carroll, a watermelon farmer who had traveled fifty miles to hear out this new organization. Another farmer had phoned him that this was 'the biggest thing to hit Ada since the outlaws took over the city in 1900...and then got themselves lynched.'

"Well, we'll be by to see you, said Harland. "We're just wanting to tell you the story of what we're about to do. We appreciate your interest and hope you'll tell your neighbors. Just be sure you sign the guest book Shirley's sending past you and we'll be in touch."

Shirley moved from row to row, glowing in the excitement she heard in the conversations everywhere as she walked by getting their signatures and they lingered around the room having coffee and doughnuts.

●　●　●

Harland looked from Benny Prentice to his wife, Kathryn. It was obvious they were disappointed. Benny examined the check for $2500 which Harland had given back to him.

"But let me get this straight," he demanded. "You're giving us back our money because your partner exaggerated the promises you made?"

Harland nodded. "I'm breaking up the partnership with him and starting off fresh." He looked at these early investors with that infectious smile and open-eyed directness that had won them to his new business in the first place. Behind that smile they could sense a resolute determination that made clear he wasn't giving up what he had started. "The man went to every investor with the same wild exaggerations, after they were already with us. I'm not party to lies."

"So what's up? I mean I gotta tell you, me'n Kathryn are still behind you. You gotta be one honest guy an' that's enough for us. Right, Kathryn?"

His wife nodded enthusiastically. "Why don't you just keep the money and when you're ready with the new plan, use it?"

"It's not mine to keep, once I dissolve that partnership. When my lawyer gets the new plan set up, I'll come right back out here and present it to you. I hope you'll want to get back in."

Kathryn waved the check she had retrieved from Benny. "This will be here. We had to borrow it, to invest with you. We never knew you before, but you heard Benny — we know whatever *you* set up, will succeed. So count on us."

Harland smiled, grateful for her support. "I think we're going to surprise a lot of people, including the banks, when we do make it work. My guess is we'll sell about 200,000 shares of stock at a dollar a share. I couldn't borrow a dime from any bank, so believe me, I'm grateful to you for backing me. And you'll find we make good use of your money, once we're started.

"Well," he glanced at his watch, "I've got to go to Oklahoma City. We're starting to build our sales force now and there's a fine salesman I've been urged to contact. A car salesman."

"If he's smart, he'll grab the chance to work with you." Benny extended his hand. "Come back to see us soon."

• • •

As he drove the 90 miles to Oklahoma City, Harland puzzled at the couple's surprise when he returned their money. Others had also seemed unable to understand it. He knew one who wouldn't have been surprised, was his father. One friend mocked this notion of returning checks. "What are you concerned about? You've got your money," he laughed. "They don't need to know you're going through reorganization. All you're gonna do is confuse 'em. Keep the money and go do your thing. It's their risk. Why be concerned?"

Once Harland took that money from others, that's when his concern started. That's when he had a special obligation. When he gave shares of stock in a company yet to function and put a check in his shirt pocket, he knew he had cut off his source of retreat. Maybe some people could treat that lightly and see no moral issue. But to Harland it was a trust.

Anyone who invested in his company, ever, was going to know their money was safe and they were going to know his gratitude. With the banks giving him a unanimous turn-down, he was committed that the Prentices and the rest, with even less reason to trust his venture, would know they'd been wise.

Shortly he pulled into the lot where he had been told there was a salesman interested in Sportsmen's Motor Club.

"Haney?" The manager moved to the door and pointed across the lot. "There he is. Hey, Rick! Rick Haney! Come over here!"

• • •

It was one of those meetings that purely and simply was meant to happen. Harland outlined to Rick the opportunity with his company and frankly admitted to his prospect that Sportsmen's Legal Service Motor Club was scarcely off the drawing boards.

He liked very much the direct questions of this handsome, self-confident young man. Rick had to be about five years his junior. He liked the way he took care of himself, meticulously dressed as though he was going to an executive office, instead of to a car sales lot. He groomed hair and hands carefully. His flashing smile and the happy sparkle to his eyes said he had it all together.

There was an urgency about him that seemed a mix of hyperactive and a drive he was having difficulty holding in check. But it all added up to good vibrations between both of them.

After hours of conversation, Rick said quietly and thoughtfully, "I'd like to come with you."

Harland had a strong feeling that he and his pre-paid legal dream had just turned a very important corner.

Within weeks, Rick showed too, just how important he considered his decision to join the infant club. He seemed to eat, drink, breathe, sleep and even drive with the legal service concept foremost in his thoughts. With the kind of commitment that he reflected every day — constantly there to encourage Harland and Shirley, even as heavy clouds began to gather around the budding organization — Harland knew they couldn't fail.

With Ken Johnson and Frank Jaques and the fiercely loyal initial investors and a core sales force gradually growing, there was solid feeling in both Harland and Shirley that they now had passed out of the dream stage. It *was* going to happen. And when days and nights came that seemed to hold certainty that everything would be shattered, Rick of the flashing smile and the happy sparkle, the ever-present urgency and the relentless optimism, was at their door or on their phone to be sure their morale stayed high.

It was the end of their first year. Harland stood before a full room of shareholders, together for their first annual meeting in early March.

"Let me tell you how far we've come," he declared to the group. "Last year when we began, we had no sales force and almost no business on the books. We projected a thousand members during our first year. The fact is, we'll have over 2,000 members by next Monday and that means a premium income at present of more than $70,000 annually. And that's..."

A spontaneous explosion of hands and whistles burst around him and he smiled and waved for silence.

"That enthusiasm is just why we're off and growing. It gets better...

"We paid over one-hundred-twenty-five claims the first year, most all for legal services. We have sales people earning in excess of $500 per week, with the average earning of our full time sales force of over $250 a week. So you can see we have a product that is sellable and wanted by the market." (More applause and again he waved for silence.)

"Here's where we're going to put our emphasis for the indefinite future. Payroll deduction and selling to employers with a shop of more than five workers. We began last November to try to sell schools and since that time, in the last four months, we have enrolled fifty-four schools and colleges."

This time the applause stopped him and he relaxed to enjoy it, pointing to Rick Haney to come forward.

"I want to tip my hat to one of our sales force who has been with me since the beginning of this. You all know we are committed to becoming the first company in America solely involved in what we're going to call Pre-Paid Legal. There is one man who has made that goal a large, if not total, part of his life.

"You would not believe the number of hours per week he invests at much personal sacrifice. Through all the ups and downs, he remains constant. He's the man I lean on when the going gets tough. Let's let Rick Haney know we appreciate him!"

As enthusiastic shareholders came to their feet in noisy approval and his fellow salesmen chorused, "Speech! Speech!" Harland pulled Rick toward the podium beside him.

"Any time you ask Rick for a speech, it's a cinch you're going to get it! Well, I want that, too, and as soon as you're through hearing from your President, I'm going to ask Rick to deliver his first speech as our Executive Vice President."

Hard to match the wave after wave of applause that greeted the news. No one was surprised and not every one was in total approval perhaps, for Rick's personality would tolerate no one's neutrality. But one and all in that room that night would agree that Rick was the man who, next to Harland, gave everything he could muster in energy and conviction to a budding Pre-Paid Legal.

"I'm off for Tulsa, babe," Harland announced to Shirley early on a Fall morning. "We're having a real special day for our sales force. Fellow who's President of National Foundation Life now — remember National? Seems an age ago! — well, John Hail is the President there now and he's going to address our sales team North of Oklahoma City.

"You know, it's fantastic. We've got almost a hundred selling for us now and in less than three years. Anyway, I'm anxious to meet John Hail. He asked if I'd join him for lunch. He wants to hear more about our company. Seems like he doesn't know much at all about Pre-Paid Legal."

PART THREE

Chapter One

Harland appreciated John from the moment he met him. The lobby of the Tulsa Marriott was filled with the luncheon crowd, with check-outs and check-ins, and Harland was surrounded by a dozen of his sales force.

A stranger edged through the crowd and a hand extended. "Hi, Harland. I'm John Hail."

It was simple, unassuming and typically John. He was old-shoe but very much in charge of his space. He could easily get lost in a crowd, but once you met him, you knew this man never would be lost in any crowd for long. There was an immediate, understated charisma that communicated itself without a word.

If Harland felt that about John, it was felt in turn by John about Harland. Call it a collision of creativity, or whatever, both men felt an instant appreciation of the other.

"Rick, why don't you introduce these fellows to Mr. Hail, then he and I are going to excuse ourselves to go get acquainted before the afternoon starts."

Shortly John and Harland were comparing notes about National Foundation Life of the mid-sixties, with the way it had grown by the mid-seventies.

"Y'know, Nick Pope has a lot of admiration for you, Harland," John observed. "He says you did one whale of a job as a District Manager for him about ten years ago."

Harland smiled. "That's good of Nick. I really appreciate him. He gave me a lot of help right from Day One of my insurance career. I'll never forget the standards he set. Tough as he is, he always stands behind you. Say, I've been following NFL since you took the reins, John, and you've triggered an unbelievable explosion in sales."

"Just got a lot o' good people," he replied. "That's all."

"Oh no! It's a great deal more than that. You don't go from a couple hundred thousand in earned premium dollars to better than thirteen million in any three years, without someone special in leadership. We're mighty honored you're making time for us today. Now, if you'll just touch our men with some of the Hail magic, I'll be grateful to you."

"Harland, let me tell you something privately. Nick says you're the most determined guy he's ever known. I told him I was comin' up here today and he said, 'John, Stonecipher is going to succeed from sheer stubborn hangin' in there. I've thought of ten reasons he ought to give it up in his first three years of trying to making this pre-paid legal thing work. He won't listen to me. He just keeps saying that this is one dream whose time has come and nothing's going to stop it.'"

"He's right! I believe it." Harland reviewed the struggle he'd been having for three years, getting legislation in place that would let his firm run up its flag and show its true colors in its name — a pre-paid legal firm. He knew from the persistent questioning by his guest that he was winning a new enthusiast for his equal justice commitment for middle America.

"Be damned if Nick didn't have it right! You are one determined guy." John smiled. "I like that. Tell you the truth, I couldn't be sitting where you are today with that kind o' hassle. Let's see, a partner went and painted blue sky for your investors and you went back to square one. Started all over again. You're still waitin' a green light to call yourself Pre-Paid Legal, but you've managed to change from Sportsmen's to Professional and that's goin' somewhere. But from somewhere to everywhere is one helluva big trip! I'll guarantee you, you're traveling at very high personal risk. You've got a nice new home — I'll bet way over-mortgaged to pay commissions to your salesmen. And I'll bet your cars and furniture are on a note to meet your payroll. And the banks thumb their noses at you. Tell me, you still got a wife?"

Harland chuckled. "Sounds pretty bad, does it? Well, John, I've got Shirley and two wonderful sons. And that's why I'm going to make it. Shirley believes in me. So do Allen and Brent. Same as your family. I've read about Naomi. Shirley wants to get her to speak to our wives."

"Anytime." John nodded toward the energetic figure moving around the tables across the dining room. "That fellow you called Rick... He your key man?"

"That's the word for him. If anyone believes more in what we're doing than the Stoneciphers, it's Rick Haney. By the way, it was his suggestion that we change to *Professional* Motor Legal Services Club. We tried again to call it Pre-Paid Legal, but were turned down again. It'll come.

"You know, you're right about the mortgages. It tells me you've been there, too. It's part of the risk. We got overextended awhile back and Rick was out at our house. He's always out making sure we aren't discouraged. He was feeling rotten because it looked like we couldn't meet the payroll. Not sorry for himself now, but for the three office people. I guess that's about the lowest I've been. And I never have and never would think about quitting.

"I told Rick I thought maybe he ought to go find other work... that I probably couldn't make his salary that week or for awhile. Y'know what he said? 'Well, Harland, what're you gonna do yourself?' Of course, I told him I was going to stay on and see it through. I tell you, John, he's not a tall man, but he stands ten feet in my judgment. He just said matter-of-fact as could be, 'Well, if you don't mind, I'll pick my own work and I'm stayin' on, if you'll have me.'"

John shook his head. "I'm askin' myself, why does this man Stonecipher need the likes of John Hail here today? Man, you don't need any help motivatin' or anything else, from what I've..."

Harland reached over to his arm. "Oh, but we do! And we need it from you. We're survivin' and in a couple of years we're going public, if the Securities Department ever gets around to allowin' us to. But we're not looking for survival. We're going to cover America! I firmly believe that. I talked to Nick when I called to make our date today and he said it's all true—you are the very best sales motivator and salesman yourself in the USA."

Identification cards

209

John snorted derisively. "Don't you tell 'em that stuff in the introduction! You do and I'll tell 'em you just pretend to go fox hunting at night, but you're really the werewolf of...what is it?...Coalgate County? Here!" He dragged a checkbook from the plaid jacket and scribbled hurriedly. "Will you ask your investment people to sell me some of that over-the-counter stock, soon as they can? I'm gonna tell your people something about buying stock, so I want to get in on some ownership of one that's really going to soar someday. Will you let me in?"

Harland took the check and his smile broadened as he read the amount. "I can't tell you how much this will mean to our people, John, for them to know your confidence. But let me warn you fair and square. See this lady?" He fingered the gold figurine on his lapel. "Watch out for her! She can really trap you. She has me hooked and there's no backin' off...

"Well, we're about due to start. Shall we walk over to the meeting room? By the way, may I mention this?" He waved the check and folded it into his shirt pocket.

"Fine. No problem here. By the way, you really a fox hunter, Harland?"

• • •

Harland understated his guest's track record when he introduced John, recognizing a sharp sense of humor in the NFL President and not wanting to bait his guest. He focused on the three-year growth record John had at NFL and turned the platform over to him.

"I think it'd probably be pretty funny to a lot of people to hear that John Hail is president of a life insurance company. There'd be a few guys who used to pump gas for me in my station in Beavercreek, Ohio about fifteen years ago, who might want to introduce me another way.

"Let me tell you something. It's not the easiest thing to keep your head on straight when you go from where I was, to all of a sudden being the president of two insurance companies and being invited to speak around the country, like today, to tell people how *they* can do it. All of a sudden, here I am...never've been to college...almost didn't finish high school...and I'm the president of the company. It's good to have things that bring you back to the real world after introductions like Harland's. Back down to where you belong; where you should have been all along.

"Like the first event that happened to me after I moved to Oklahoma for NFL...right after we first moved into this big new house. Well, we had a leaky faucet. I was a life insurance company president, right? So I ain't about to fix leaky faucets. My wife knew that, so she called a plumber and this plumber came out and in about thirty seconds flat he replaced a washer in this leaky faucet and gave her a bill for fifty-five dollars for his time. Well, she looked at the bill. And she said, 'Do you realize that my husband is president of an insurance company and he doesn't make that much money an hour?' And the guy said, 'Neither did I when I was president of a life insurance company.'"

The roar left no doubt that one president had his audience with him. "There's some good things about my job. After you've been with it awhile, you get to know values. It takes you a little while, but eventually you catch on. Like when I came to Oklahoma City, I was offered the opportunity to buy 20,000 shares of stock in that company I was going to become president of, for $2,000. Ten cents a share; twenty-thousand shares for ten cents a share! Two thousand dollars is what I laid out and I felt like I got the greatest buy in history. Then I found out that nobody would pay anything for it was the reason they were willing to sell it to me for two thousand. Well, let me tell you, you may get your eyes open to a bad bargain and walk away licked, or you can do something about it.

"And the whole clue is not knowing *how* to do it, but to know inside yourself *why* you're doing it. I know *why* I'm in Oklahoma City at that insurance company and I know *why* we're lifting the value of that stock to a new story...It's because right now we've got a lot of good people out there knowing why they're selling our product. And you wanta know something about those two thousand shares? They're worth about a million bucks today.

"So let me tell you something about why *you* are here today. You're here because one bulldog tough, tenacious guy named Harland has known just *why* he's going to make a pre-paid legal company and that it's going to be big. That simple. He doesn't know how...but he sure knows *why*! He's got a product that nobody else has in the whole country. He's the only game in town that even comes near pre-paid legal. He's going to make it work because there's this blindfolded Lady of Justice who wants every American to have equal access to the provisions of the Bill of Rights and equal access to that justice we're *supposed* to have.

"Well, it ain't that simple. The only way it's going to happen, is if every person in this room knows *why* he's sellin' this product. And if you ever wonder, just look around till you find Harland Stonecipher. You'll know why this company of yours — which even my boss Nick Pope says ought to have laid down and died three years ago — is going to do more for America than anything in a long time.

"I'll tell you, this leader of yours is the kind of man I like, because he aims high. He's the kind of man who takes aim at the stars and he just might hit the moon. But he'll never just take aim at the moon, because he might hit the ground. That's the leader you have in Harland... and somebody better warn the moon!

"For myself, I want a part of what you're doing. Harland let me buy into your company for about twenty times what my own company let me come in for. And this time I know I got me a deal. You all wanta know how? Harland was telling me 'bout the time — and it wasn't too long ago — when he had to face the decision whether to go on or quit, with just about everything goin' wrong. What kept him in was he had made a commitment and he's willing to pay the price. He made a commitment to a lady and this time I ain't talkin' about his beautiful Shirley. He made a commitment to the Lady of Justice and he sealed the commitment by taking money for shares of stock from about four hundred people who heard about his affair with this lady and who believe that when Harland says, 'I'm committed'... he's committed."

• • •

A strange sixth sense needled John as he drove South on Turner Turnpike and neared the Northern limits of Oklahoma City. It was a curious discomfort. For no reason at all, his thoughts darted back fifteen years earlier to that dark drive another night back in Beavercreek. Then it had been the darkness just before morning. And the morning was the beginning of his gas station career which would open doors to the wealth he now knew. But this sudden rush of depression, gone almost as soon as it came, brought a feeling of foreboding.

How could he possibly feel any negative vibes? The world-as-hoped-for by John Hail had arrived...His worth was now into multi-millions — Fine homes in Oklahoma City and Baton Rouge and a summer home, more a mansion, on the Tickfaw River in Bayou Country, with an adjoining fishing camp for friends...a condo at Horseshoe Bay near Austin, a 53-foot Hatteras yacht in Louisiana...and much more.

His family was maturing and expanding and he inventoried his reasons for real happiness. Son Gary, now 23, had married and stayed in Louisiana where he was doing exactly what he had wanted to do from almost infancy — be a radio personality with his own show. He and his wife had two children and Gary was his own man. Denise, at 21 — was it really possible the kid who could hit him with her breakfast at two paces across the high chair, had made it through that stormy adolescence? She too, was in Louisiana, married and a mother, her husband Dennis the skipper of John's yacht, while groping for what to do with his future. And life was settling down for his youngest child, Vicki, also married and with a baby, and a student again with husband Andy.

So why the discomfort, John Hail? Closer than ever to Naomi and a hero with the founder of his company for leadership he'd brought to NFL, he probably was set for life, if this was the life he wanted. *Maybe that was the clue,* he thought. He remembered Nick's letter after his first three years with NFL.

Dear John:

On July 4th, one-hundred-ninety-nine years ago, thirteen Colonies declared their independence in order to pursue their way of life. Three years ago on July 17th, John Hail joined National Foundation Life and permitted Nick Pope to pursue his way of life. As you well know, I have pursued the little white ball and have reduced my handicap from twenty-seven (27) to fifteen (15). Thanks for shifting the responsibilities from me to you.

On a more serious note, John, National Foundation Life has been greatly enhanced from your leadership and direction. When one analyzes the Company's posture today and anticipates the future, we can all

Vicki and Andy

Vicki's Brian

Bayou Home

Denise, Dennis and Deanna

Gary in studio

become excited. Your leadership and performance are appreciated and applauded by all.

Sincerely yours,

D. N. (Nick) Pope
Chairman of the Board and Chief
Executive Officer

Already three more years had passed and the fortunes of NFL multiplied an unbelievable 60 times over in new business on the books for the year. It was nearing one billion dollars in insurance in force. It was another Hail leadership phenomenon.

But now the praise of 1975 was becoming tarnished, as pressure on the founder of the company from an unexpected source, was threatening takeover. All John, in the president's seat, could do, was want the best for Nick, but beyond that, watch and wait.

Involvement in oil, helping private companies go public, investment in real estate, diversifying the offering of his company to other insurance areas — all were part of the daily round of John's life. *But something was misfiring.* And he trusted his intuition.

Chapter Two

Shirley paused at the mailbox, perplexed with the envelope from the Oklahoma Securities Department. It promised to be some kind of problem and Harland was enjoying the only leisure he would know all day out on the grounds of their home. He had been through so much over the past year. Their company was now fully Pre-Paid Legal Services, Inc., but how long would it be permitted to operate?

Neither of them had even the slightest doubt that they were going to succeed. The question was, when would they clear the seemingly endless series of obstacles and be able to focus on their primary business? — selling memberships in Pre-Paid Legal. Already they had begun attracting media notice, and magazines and trade journals were publishing articles which made it obvious America was ready to hear about a program of legal protection at a very low cost.

Dr. Werner Pfennigstorf, a research attorney in Chicago and a scholar of insurance law, had praised the program after coming to Ada to visit and to study Professional Motor Service Club, as it had been called then. He had given such wonderful encouragement with his letter after his visit, writing so optimistically that he was impressed with what he saw and anticipating the company might become a model for the future development of legal expense insurance in the country. He had said that he would spread the word of this successful operation and would be very grateful if they could keep him informed on new developments.

All that was good. Even the most recent they'd heard was encouraging to their morale. Dr. Pfennigstorf was working with the National Association of Insurance Commissioners, who regulated and controlled insurance in the 50 states. The project was to develop a Model Act to regulate pre-paid insurance programs everywhere. It meant the day was coming when they would be everywhere, if they could just survive...today.

As she walked down the drive toward their kennels, she thought of the heavy disappointment Harland had received only the week before from one of his most promising officers. The man had taken what company funds he had access to and the plans for creating his own pre-paid legal in the Southeast, and had vanished. Shirley knew how that had hurt Harland and even though she expected his usual calm, it always surprised her that he could control what must be an inner outrage.

"Hon, I like the old geezer who said a long time before you and I were walkin' this earth," he had observed when the theft was certain, " '...the wheels of the gods turn slowly, but they grind exceedingly fine.' I don't believe you steal and get away with it in the long run. So I'm just going to leave him to heaven. We've got more important things to do."

She was afraid she was carrying one of those important things and if it hadn't been Harland's explicit request to interrupt him for *anything*, she would have waited till he came back to the house.

His face was grim when he finished reading the letter and he shook his head as if to wish another bad moment away. "Well, Securities Department is calling for a full investigation before we can go selling any shares in our company. They're requiring every man on our sales force to appear in Oklahoma City for interrogation. They just won't let go! It's obvious they want to put us out of business."

"But, Harland, how can they do that?"

"Simple. Just drag on the investigation. Try to find something we're doing wrong. Force us to go broke. Right now we're about to make the record as the longest Securities Department inquiry in history. And, Babes, we're going to make it, in spite of them!"

"I know we are. I hate to bring it up, but have you

any ideas on how you're going to be able to handle that block of stock that's being dumped?"

"I may. And don't you worry your pretty little head about all these things."

"But if someone doesn't pick it up, isn't it likely to do just what it seems the Securities Department is trying to do?"

"It could finish us. Our collateral wouldn't be worth a hoot. But it's not meant to go that way. You know it. I know it. And we both know Rick will kick our tails, if we forget it."

"That Rick!" Shirley reached for something that would turn her thoughts off a crisis she couldn't help solve. "I love that Lady of Justice statue he and Wanda are working on. He is *so* determined to make it just right."

"At the moment it's just about the only thing that's keeping him on his high. I'm all for anything that does that. *His* high is what's keeping *me* up there."

"The boys are absolutely hilarious the way they imitate him. When he left last night after two hours of non-stop motion, never sitting down and never ever stopping talking, I tell you Allen and Brent had him down to a tee."

Rick and Wanda Haney

Harland handed her the unwanted envelope. "Let's get Kathryn on these calls this afternoon. Did I tell you how she got so absolutely furious with Rick's temper and explosions around the office, that she quit a few days ago? I had to go bring her back. She's too good to lose. Rick's great, but he sure rides roughshod on a lot of people. When he comes off that elevator, you can hear him shouting a block away, if he's mad. But we know he wants everyone to like him and he's not really angry — he just demands everything to be perfect.

"I'm never going to forget Kathryn's second or third day with us. She was purely terrified of him. Remember, she actually ran to hide and cry in the ladies room? Rick got a tough phone call and needed help and he knocked on the bathroom door and called real sweet, 'Honey, you gotta come out an' help me! This guy won't talk to nobody but you! *Please* come out!' " Harland chuckled. "I bet she'll make it in spite of him."

Shirley nodded. "He's such an unusual person. The minute he gets on his feet in front of a meeting, he's absolutely marvelous. Yet he finishes and worries himself to a frenzy that he hasn't done a good job.

"And you can't sleep with him either, Ken Johnson says." She giggled. "You know when you asked him to go with Rick on those presentations in Louisiana last month? He said he simply couldn't shut Rick off when the meeting was over. Not even when they were back in their motel room. He just sat on the edge of the bed and kept up running on and on about Pre-Paid Legal, even after Ken had gone to bed and turned out the light. He says the last thing he remembered was dozing off with Rick still talking... And then waking in the morning with him still talking full steam ahead, still sitting dressed in the same spot!"

"I believe it," laughed Harland as he finished sweeping out the dog run. "I've got to go get dressed. Would you handle that Securities thing with Kathryn? Just get her to notify our people. They'll all be subpoenaed, too. I'm going directly to Oklahoma City to see John Hail."

"Give him my best. Naomi is going to speak to our salesmen's wives next month in Ardmore. You might tell him we're so glad she's willing to do it. I hear she's just wonderful."

• • •

Two hours later he walked into John's penthouse offices in the tri-building complex of the National Foundation Life Center. He wasn't there to talk about the Securities' latest investigation.

Ever since their Tulsa meeting, John had kept a close watch on what developed for this company that no one in officialdom seemed to want to let off the ground. If Harland was feeling hassled, he didn't show it, just as he never had before.

John remembered how, at the height of one crisis for cash flow, Harland had come to him and to the firm and asked them to consider buying a twenty-five percent block of the stock. The NFL people had agreed and John had promised him that when his budding company could afford to, he would see to it that they could buy back the block. And it had begun a very heavy daily routine for Harland.

He personally every day would bring the sales contracts from Ada ninety miles to Oklahoma City to John's office, and in exchange for the contracts as collateral, John would have a check cut for daily commissions for Harland's salesmen. Back he would drive the 90 miles to pay his men. For months and months John marveled at his dogged sticking to it.

One remembered day, Harland paused at John's door as he was leaving. He tossed an embarrassed look across the broad expanse of John's executive desk of hand-carved mahogany, at the occupant in the Peruvian ivory leather presidential chair. With a self-deprecating shake of his head, he asked simply, "John, could I borrow ten until tomorrow? I don't have enough gas to make it back to Ada."

"You bet." John knew he was looking guts squarely in the eye as he fished for his wallet.

• • •

This time it had to be another crisis visit, but you never could tell it from Harland's expression, John thought. *He had that pleasant air of the insurance salesman who'd made his two sales for the day and was ready to relax.*

"What's up, Harland?"

"Well, John, as you can guess, there's a problem. I've just been informed that there's about to be a flooding of the market with about $100,000 worth of Pre-Paid Legal stock. The fact is, it's overhanging the market right now and you know our size and what'll happen if that gets dropped, as it's going to be."

"Yeah, I guess I know," drawled John. "Just about be the kiss of death for you guys."

"Exactly. It'll reduce the value of our collateral to nothing with our creditors, and we both know what that'll do. So, what I wanted to ask you, even though it may look like a real bad investment, would you consider, maybe...?"

"Just let me know when," interrupted John.

"When? You mean you don't need more...I've got proformas and..."

"I don't need that crap, Harland! I understand the situation perfectly. Jus' let me know when. By the way, it's private, you understand. I think you'll want to come to my house when you're ready. I'm gonna be gettin' out of this job."

Harland was stunned. It was a time of transition for everyone. He extended his hand gratefully. "This is much appreciated, especially knowing you're obviously going through some critical times yourself."

"Naw, not at all!" John waved off the gratitude in a way that Harland had noticed before. *He's the absolute last guy in the world who feels comfortable with being fussed over,* thought Harland as he closed his briefcase.

• • •

The scene couldn't have changed more radically, he thought as he drove away from the Hail mansion, a check for the threatening stock in his pocket and a clean bill of health for Pre-Paid Legal Services to go do its business after a seven-year struggle. With this involvement by John, another major hurdle had been leaped.

Harland at home

As he swung down Route 3W from Shawnee, toward home and the chance to take a deep breath for the first time in many months, he remembered that in spite of all the holds and inquiries and frustrations, and as bad as these early years had been, there never had been a day when they had been forced to stop selling. No cease-and-desist order from some eager official trying to make his mark. Even if the sales effort had been slowed, as they were forced to give every bit of energy to finding a new source of mortgage funds, or appearing to answer another investigation — there always was the right to continue doing business. No one could find anything to justify closing down his new idea for America.

He shuddered at the memory of that three-day nightmare hearing by the Oklahoma Securities Department. Beyond a doubt, it was the worst seventy-two hours of his life. Every single one of his sales force had been subpoenaed and appeared alone before that panel of attorneys. It was obvious they were waiting, hoping for one of his men to answer just one question about his sales effort in a way that would justify a closing of the firm.

Ken Johnson and Frank Jaques and George Thompson had sat in the hallway outside the hearing room, powerless except to give encouragement by their presence. Cecil Atchley and Charlie Carroll and one after another of the rest of his sales team had gone before the inquisitors. And they had done nobly, every one of them. The battery of attorneys had found no cause for negative action. And finally, fourteen months after filing to go public, Pre-Paid Legal was given the green light.

Shortly the stock had climbed and there was the need to split three-for-two. And now what had been worth a dollar a share back in 1973, was worth ever so much more. He had good reason to be grateful to so many good friends who seemed to believe in him even more, in the worst of times.

As he drove, his thoughts drifted back to the way it had been when they were a tiny operation in the American Building in Ada...

How do you equal the friendship their new neighbor, Representative Lonnie Abbott, had extended from the first? He had an office twice the size of the two-room Pre-Paid offices and he wanted to encourage again the program he had liked from the moment back earlier when Harland had described it. He had no hesitation in saying, "Let me do anything I can to help you. Use my name. Use my office... here's extra keys, in case you ever get pushed for room."

That all had been very gutsy to let a brand new organization run around mentioning that this Representative to the Legislature liked the way they did business. And the use of the rooms was certainly needed, for the simple truth was that if Pre-Paid ever had a meeting calling for three extra chairs, it was in trouble for space. Many a time Harland had paraded visitors down to Lonnie's offices so they all could sit, or had sent Kathryn scurrying to borrow a chair.

And there had been enormous encouragement from the one place it could have really been tough, reflected Harland. *The Insurance Commissioner's Office.* Gerald Grimes had had to undertake a brand new concept, decide if it was insurance or a club membership, handle a whole catalogue of questions no one else knew how to ask or to answer. Very patiently and never going for the easy way out, he had walked the program through over five...six...seven...and more years since he had first seen it surface as an Oklahoma corporation. Somehow the department was able to find the mechanics within the existing mechanism of the Insurance Commissioner's Office to allow Pre-Paid Legal Services, Inc. to emerge a happy, healthy, bustling youngster doing business everywhere in Oklahoma.

As he turned South down the road from Ada heading to Centrahoma, Harland felt a special gratitude to John Hail. John probably didn't think of that $100,000 as anything but a drop in the bucket of his own wealth. He had walked Harland through the family playroom with its pool table and its huge indoor swimming pool and he'd smiled at the eagerness of guests playing the slot machine with Naomi. "The only chance she gets to win is with guests," he chortled and ducked as the towel whistled after him.

John's indoor pool

If any fellow deserved to have it, thought Harland, *it was probably John.* He'd been willing to pay the price for almost thirty years for greatness in the industry. Out of the insurance world now, he looked like a kid ready to play. They had lounged and talked for a short time in the den and when Harland stood to go, John steered him toward the empty mantel over the fireplace, asking, "Ever play hockey, Harland? I mean real hockey on ice?"

"Never even put on a pair of skates. Why?"

"Well, I want you to bring Shirley and come back here soon to see what I plan to put on this mantel. I've decided I'm too young to retire. Everyone else around here does oil — and I'm doing some o' that — but nobody else does ice. So, I'm goin' into the hockey business and have trophies up here. Just bought the control o' the Stars and we're gonna put hockey on the map in Oklahoma."

"That's great! Good luck to you." Harland meant it. It was the kind of step he could expect from this man of many talents.

Allen with some of his
trophies

I'll watch with a great deal of interest, he thought, as he pulled to a stop outside his own comfortable, rambling ranch and stepped out into the country night air. This was for him. All about him was the Oklahoma he loved. His acreage was expanding year by year and his horses and mules, and of course, his dogs were still a great pleasure, though Allen was doing almost all the running with them now and had filled two walls of their den with his trophies from nationwide competitions. Their kennels were large and they were still breeding Walkers. Brent probably was never going to be a hunter like his older brother, but he had an incredible set of talents in inventiveness and with machinery. And both boys had been pure pride to him in their academic work at the same Tupelo school he'd attended.

So different, he thought...*he and John.* But, while he never could see John in his environment, or imagine himself in the environment John enjoyed, he had the greatest affection for this man. There really were similarities between them and it had nothing at all to do with money or the amount of it...or who owed what...or what tomorrow held.

This was their day.

They both were men of vision.

They both had a strong love of the abundant life and of whatever gave them the drive to go for it.

Brent in his workshop

"Hail Pumps Excitement Into Hockey" read the headline in the Oklahoma Sunday paper January 20, 1980. The full page story told of the purchase by John of the Oklahoma City Stars.

At forty-nine he was out of insurance and feeling no pain from leaving the career to which he'd given everything. Now his interests were hockey, oil and real estate — the real estate on which he lived and played.

He and Naomi had always been so close and yet often so far apart, as the claims of his office and her popularity as a speaker seemed to fill day and night. Suddenly, wonderfully, they were by themselves again; doing what they wanted to do, going where they wanted to go.

A friend from the Beavercreek days was made President of John W. Hail, Inc. Typical of John, the break with NFL had not been without pre-planning. Old associates on whom he can rely, friends and family who understand his Ready ...Fire...Aim! assault on life — no bad decisions, just decisions that need fixin' — never are forgotten by John. Such a one was Lefty McFadden.

Back in the years of Beavercreek High when Lefty, then just retired from the Cleveland Indians, had admired Johnny Hail's swing at the ball and his swing at life, he saw another

Lefty McFadden

side of John he admired. In his Senior year Johnny gave up his third baseman position to a youngster named Bobby Durnbaugh, destined for Baseball Hall of Fame immortality in a few years. Lefty liked the grace of Johnny in stepping aside for a gifted Freshman and he liked everything about the man John Hail when he came back from Korea. Johnny Hail's Home Furnishings was one of the first and best sponsors of Lefty's Sports Show on Dayton television. And Johnny always made time for Lefty's Eager Leaguer baseball training for the sandlot kids. Lefty had made frequent tracks to the Knollwood Sohio, too, to plot some new campaign with him for the Dayton Gems Hockey Team which Lefty had founded, owned and led to six International League titles in ten years.

It was only a partial surprise when, twenty-five years later, John called him to Oklahoma City as his assistant at NFL. Lefty served in public relations and community relations and as kind of watchdog of some of John's interests outside of insurance. One of those was his limited partnership in the Oklahoma City Stars Hockey Club.

No surprise then when John, after resigning from insurance, bought out the controlling interest in the ice hockey team. If anyone needs to go down in the hall of infamy, it may be Lefty for whatever encouragement he gave John to buy this franchise. And John, as consistent at fifty as he was at five, when he took full responsibility that the salve he was pushing in door-to-door sales would cure any achy people in the house, also to this day takes full credit for the decision to bring professional ice hockey full blown into Oklahoma.

It was not long before it was apparent that the costs of retirement were high. The costs of nightly games in Oklahoma City, building an ice rink at the fair grounds for the team to practice, dealing with disappointments in oil development on numerous fronts, all this and more were costing him thousands of dollars a day. And beyond all that, the incredible Penn Square Bank disaster in Oklahoma was taking shape with innocent investors like John about to be hurt. The cost of his newfound sport peaked in the season when, under Lefty's expertise, the Stars hit the playoffs and the nightly loss for the honor of being the best was tens of thousands of dollars for salaries, for the arena, and ballyhoo. At the very same time his oil enterprises were following a statewide, nationwide skid toward disaster.

Always by his side and encouraging him through a period of mounting disappointment with the efforts to fix decisions that defied fixing, was Naomi. She was ever the optimist, sure there was a way they could work out from under their mounting financial crunch.

A feature story about the millionaire Hails was written one evening with John in his usual spot in the owner's box above the Press. The reporter was pressing for what made John Hail different. Talking about the drive by the Stars' front office to achieve season membership sales of more than 10,000, (*that might pay the rent*, thought John), the reporter asked, "You seem to be trying to attract the working class family. Do you still identify with the non-wealthy?"

"I have a very simple philosophy," replied John patiently. "Everything I think about is, what if I were that guy who worked at GM and sat down in row 23? I remember when I was sitting there in that row. Many people have an inability to remember where they've been.

"The biggest thrill of my night is when I walk through the arena and people come up and talk to me. My father never got a paycheck over $125. It makes me appreciate all this. I've seen hundreds of guys who, when they make it big, all of a sudden don't know other people exist. That's a crime. Everybody at the hockey games has noticed where I sit up here every night and they're startin' to come up to me. It's a big thrill.

"You know what they all wanta know? They all ask the same question: 'When are we gonna win a game?' "

Even when the clouds were building, no one was ever going to steal the Hail humor.

It was a Red Letter Day at Pre-Paid Legal and enthusiastic salesmen from four states met in Ada to hear the announcement Harland had as the year 1980 got underway.

"Ladies and gentlemen, we're very pleased to tell you that you are no longer limited to a membership that offers two major benefits of half-hour consultations and twenty-four hour automotive protection. I am very proud to report to you that now you also can offer all members a Legal

Defense Fund. If your member is personally named in a suit, he or she will be personally protected by Pre-Paid Legal.

"I'm going to ask Ken Johnson, who worked this out with Frank Jaques and me, to come tell you the exact way it works. But keep in mind, this is the first major addition to our program since we started up in business as a Legal Service Motor Club. We think it's a great breakthrough. The only people who don't need this benefit are preachers."

An exuberant crowd of over a hundred salesmen let their leader know they were just as pleased as he was with the new offering. As Harland looked across the crowded room and saw friends who had traveled to Oklahoma from Louisiana and Arkansas and Georgia and from Texas and New Mexico and Colorado to hear this announcement, he felt the special glow of knowing his dream was coming alive.

In the audience for the first time as a newly recruited representative was a young grocer, Wilburn Smith. A lot of thought had gone into his decision to change vocations. Manager of a profitable supermarket in Holdenville, Oklahoma, he had caught Harland's eye years before when Harland was selling insurance for Paramount and recruiting as he covered Oklahoma. He happened into Holdenville the day after Wilburn's market had burned to the ground. There was something remarkable about the sight of his outdoor market spread out on the parking lot next to the still smoking timbers of his once-large store. This was a man after Harland's own heart. And he said, "No thanks," to Harland's effort to bring him into insurance.

Finally Wilburn opted to change vocation when he saw his next move up in a grocery career was to own his own store. With earnings of $30,000 a year, there was no way he could capitalize a million dollar outlay for his own venture and he wouldn't go small. His cousin who worked at Pre-Paid Legal, talked him into a lesser investment — a block of twenty units of a special stock offering by this Ada firm that had just won an okay-to-go from Oklahoma Securities. The $500 those twenty units cost had rolled over in a three-for-two split within the year and again in a five-for-one split a year later and suddenly Wilburn was looking at six hundred shares instead of twenty. It was serious talking money to take to the bank as a down payment on his own grocery.

But now there was something that he wanted even more. He wanted it badly enough to quit his job and go out on his own as a representative of Pre-Paid Legal with a likely income of about one-third his grocery salary in his first year as salesman.

The same decision had been made by D. E. Romines a few years earlier. He heard that Harland Stonecipher had attended school at Tupelo, too, and one day in the school hallway D. E. turned back the old graduating class flipboard to see the picture of this fair-haired son of the town who had done so well as a teacher and now was an entrepreneur for himself.

D. E. had gone from school into cattle raising. And that had gone well — for a time. The time ended when someone in Washington persuaded a sizeable chunk of American citizenry that red meat was bad for your health. The cattle market was instantly in more trouble than the oil market. It was time for a change. After fifteen years, D. E. sought out the business that Harland Stonecipher had created.

It was a good decision for D. E. and a break for Pre-Paid Legal. In short order he had moved through the ranks that Harland had created for his team — from Representative to Regional Manager, to State Manager, to Regional Vice President.

"D. E., will you see what you can do with this green grocer?" asked Harland as the meeting about the new third benefit came to a close.

D. E. looked at the newcomer to his team. He liked what he saw and what he'd heard about this latest recruit. Smith had given up comfort to go for a new career and that pleased Romines. The successful people in Pre-Paid Legal were the ones who *had* to succeed. They were always the ones who wouldn't give up. There had to be something of a Stonecipher-tough tenaciousness to make it work for each new salesman.

• • •

A week after the announcement of Title Three, Harland called a hurried meeting in Ada for those who could come and sent out a memo to those who couldn't. The main purpose of that meeting: "Please disregard my comment that the only people who don't need Title III, the Legal Defense Fund, are preachers. I meant that facetiously. Furthermore, it has come to my attention that in our society even our preachers are frequently sued. Of special interest to us is that many ministers are becoming an active part of our sales force and have caught the vision of a society with equal access to justice for everyone. One of these ministers asked me to correct my comment."

A pastor who needed the Legal Defense Fund, if he was to afford legal counsel, was a pastor in Denver, Colorado, who had been asked for guidance by the wife/victim of spouse abuse. The minister counseled with her at his church office. Ultimately the woman sought a separation.

In the wake of a nasty divorce trial, the minister was named in a malpractice suit along with several counselors and he also was accused of sexual misconduct by the ex-husband. Both charges were dropped eventually, but not without the professional destruction of the pastor, who could not afford an attorney and attempted to appear alone in his own defense.

• • •

Harland was given to slipping leads from private conversations to salesmen he knew would follow through. He wrote a name on a slip of paper and gave it to Wilburn a few months later, certain that this bright newcomer who had made regional manager in two months would follow through. "This man needs his membership updated with Title Three, Wilburn. He's also a good friend and stockholder. Stop by and see if you can catch up on him for me and maybe you can even bring his personal company in on a payroll deduction. At least get me the news of what he's doing now."

Wilburn glanced at the name on the memo — John W. Hail. "Oh, he's the fellow who owns the Stars. You bet, Harland. I'll try to see him Monday."

It wasn't to happen Monday or any time thereafter. At the fairgrounds ice rink, Lefty was sure Hail wouldn't be back for weeks. "Tell you the truth, I don't know just when he'll be back. His wife's into some kind of multi-level selling of a diet food and John's gung-ho about it now, too. They're all over the country in their motor home building a big organization and I guess makin' money. You ever hear of that multilevel stuff?"

Wilburn hadn't and wished John Hail hadn't. It would have been good to bring back a payroll deduction from the Stars. The kind of mayhem they made on ice, any one of them could be needing the legal defense benefit anytime. Meanwhile, the lead to John Hail was stuffed into his pocket. Maybe some other time.

"Y'know, Naomi, the only problem with this operation is their marketing plan. It's lopsided as all get out. It gives all the edge to your upline. Look at this." He reached across the aisle of their motor home with columns of figures he'd sketched out. "See, your earnings last month for all this runnin' around are still less than $2800. And your immediate upline is raking in over $75,000 for the same month ...mostly on our sweat. I looked at all that turkey's downline and ain't nobody else doin' the work we're doin'."

"Well, it's going to come our way, too. You know, John, I hear that Claire what's-her-name is making over half-a-million a month and got upset when her income dropped by $10,000 last month. By the way, did you ever get hold of Curt?"

"Naw, sure didn't. Let me take a shot at catchin' him home right now." He lifted the mobile phone off its base. "Curt Wilson, please. This is John Hail," he said to the answering voice.

"John? Johnny Hail! Well, my gracious! This is Ruthie. Remember me? Last time you were in Dayton, you completely ignored us, I heard."

"Heck I did, Ruth! I'm comin' back out next month with Naomi and we'll all get together then. So tell me... is Curt still fat?"

"Not to me. But here he is. You ask him."

"Curt! John. You still fat?"

"Hell, you sure know how to hurt a guy! Yeah, why?"

"Man, have I got the thing for you! It'll get you back to size and fatten your wallet at the same time."

"Tell me about it."

"Un-nnnnh. First you gotta try the product. I'll send you some from Oklahoma City soon's we're back tomorrow.

I'd turn around right now, but we're due at dinner with a bunch o' boosters who're going to Tulsa in a couple o' nights. Want us on board, too. Listen, I'll get the stuff in the mail tomorrow."

"Good to hear ya, John. I thought you retired and all that good deal."

"Not me, buddy. I'm too young, I decided."

Chapter Three

"Harland! Hey, ya got a minute, ole buddy?"

It was Ernest, a long ago friend and early skeptic of Harland's idea of a pre-paid legal plan. These days he was mostly a bar-fly. Some of the boys at the bar had just opened his eyes to the phenomenon called Pre-Paid Legal started 'right here in Ada and now spread into half-a-dozen states.' Rumors had it that it was going to all fifty pretty soon. You could bet, his bar buddies declared, that meant round the world, too. "You talkin' 'bout that cockeyed notion my ole buddy Harland had about ten years ago?" Ernest asked.

His friend nodded and Harland's 'ole buddy' had exploded in disbelief. "Man, he was sellin' his stock for peanuts then! Tried to get me involved."

"You missed it, pal. That stock is as safe as Fort Knox."

Now the long lost 'ole buddy' was jaywalking hurriedly across the wide street toward the tall, dark-suited man about to enter the building at 321 East Main. "Shay, Harland, gotta ask ya question." He shook Harland's extended hand and stared perplexedly over his shoulder. "Wha' the hell's this, anyway? Thought this was the Chrysler dealer." He scrutinized the simple window lettering..."Pre-Paid Legal Services, Inc."

"It's us now, Ernest. So what can I do for you?"

"Lemme ask ya, Harland. 'Member that stock you was sellin' for a dollar-a-share? I'd like to buy some o' that.

You got any left? Say, 'bout a thousand or so? No big deal."

Harland slowly peeled the cellophane from his cigar. *He should be keeping count of the folks that wanted into Pre-Paid Legal at that first dollar-a-share, over-the-counter price. Better yet, he should swear off his cigar habit before he felt contempt for Ernest's drinking habit. Oh well, he'd get rid of this one vice soon enough. But then maybe he'd just find another. Besides, he wasn't even lighting them anymore; just making believe, so he wasn't smelling up the offices as he prowled around his staff, listening and learning from what they were doing.*

"Hey, Harland...didja hear me? Got me 'bout a thousand shares o' that dollar stuff you're sellin'?"

"No, Ernest. I'm afraid not. I can get it to you for about eight dollars a share now."

"Hell! I heard you was doin' good, but that's too good! Man, that's too rich for my blood."

Harland couldn't resist it. "I'm sorry to hear that, Ernest. You might be makin' another mistake. You know that thousand you want? Well, if you'd bought that when we last talked about six years ago, you would have owned some of this company through a couple of splits and your thousand would be worth seventy-five hundred now. Sorry you missed out. Right now would be a good time to still come in though. See, we're just getting started."

"Did you say seventy-five hunner...doll..." Ernest backed an unsteady step and fingered his chin. "I'll be double-damned!" He shuffled toward the curb.

"Watch yourself, Ernest," warned Harland, turning to the door and smiling at Bob Thompson, his stock transfer agent who was hurrying across the lobby toward him. Bob was the refreshing other side of the early picture of investors who had risked so much with him. The Thompsons, father and son, were among the first to buy that 'dollar stuff.' "Harland, you might want to look in on Rick and Mike. They've been goin' at it pretty hot and heavy since they came to work."

"What is it this time, Bob? Could you hear?"

"Just about from one end of the building to the other. I'm not a salesman. Seems to have something to do with the way one of them is promotin' this Career Guidance System we're tryin' and they're scrappin' how the salesmen are supposed to handle it."

"I'll look in," murmured Harland, going toward the stairs. "Thanks, Bob." He really appreciated Bob and the way he fit in and was growing with the organization after coming from a background in Thompson Auto Parts. He'd moved ahead on top of years of serious illness, to become very efficient in the administrative matters Harland was passing to him as he tested his abilities. It was Harland's way as his home office scene and sales force was expanding. Give each member the chance to show their ability with hands-off management from himself.

He tried to avoid the head-on confrontations, but this thing between Rick and Mike was getting worse. He smiled to himself climbing the stairs as he remembered Bob's gratitude for hands-off management from himself back at the start when Bob and Kathryn worked in a tiny room by the fire exit, with one of them often using empty cartons for a desk top. There wasn't room for any third person in those cramped quarters.

As far as Rick and Mike were concerned, they both were strong-willed and sooner or later they'd find their level with each other. Harland wanted to keep his distance, but he'd better go see, since Bob had asked.

The Hails were surrounded by the boosters as the rink emptied in Tulsa.

"C'mon, John! You'n Naomi promised. You'd be comin' up by car and goin' back with us on the bus. Besides, we won!" howled the delighted spokesman. "So we got two seats reserved for you in the back. You promised now!"

"Sure did! Let's go, Naomi. Be right with you folks. Gotta make our excuses." He grabbed Naomi's hand and headed toward the couple they had traveled with from Oklahoma City. "We'll see you in a few days," he told them. "Our booster crowd is going bananas with the win and we better go along to keep 'em under control."

They were heading down Turner Turnpike and excited chatter from the boosters, animated by the Stars' victory, rocked noisily back and forth down the aisle. *It was a good crowd,* he reflected appreciatively. *A nice family bunch.* That was one of the few positives he could think of, coming out of his experience with the Stars. It had been the public relations job of Steve Michael and others. Son Gary had left his radio work in Louisiana to come help and sometimes their son-in-law Dennis was there, too. He wondered if those two characters would ever get their marriages together. Up again, down again.

Meanwhile, Steve and Gary and Dennis had been building family participation in the Stars booster crowd. Family rates; children at giveaway prices; the chance to mingle with the players. *Maybe too much mingling!* he thought, mulling the sudden departure for Ohio of Lefty, whose blood pressure had sky-rocketed from his manager/coach duties. That was a tough loss.

John peered through the rain-drenched window of the bus. It was an unholy mix of sleet and heavy rain out there and this man at the wheel was starting to high-ball for home. "Y'know, I'm sure this thing is hydroplaning!" he exploded, straightening in his seat.

"What's that?" asked Naomi. "I thought only boats did it."

"They do, too. But a bus can, with this heavy a rain. You get a wedge of water between the tires and the road surface and you're flat out o' brakes or any turn control. He's gonna get us in trouble!"

John shoved from his seat and headed to the front of the bus, seeing the lights of Oklahoma City on the horizon a few miles ahead. It was a blistering downpour now, with sheets of water whipping across the highway on a horizontal blast as the wind intensified. He could feel the mushiness of no traction under the bus wheels and he was almost behind the driver when it happened...

Slowly at first...then a sweeping, yawing turn almost like a pilot moving into a twisting chandelle...and suddenly...
savagely...
all control lost...
the bus was a steel and glass monstrosity...airborne at the edge of the highway...
plunging through the guard rails at the edge of the cliff and...

> tumbling...spinning...
>
> totally out of control

as it spewed glass and steel and people

in its mad rush to oblivion...

Everything went instantly black through the coach.

John was tossed from front to back and ceiling to floor and back to the front again as they plunged through trees and plowed against boulders...till finally, with an incredible surge of pressure and the sound of crushing metal, they careened to a stop a hundred feet below the highway.

• • •

Frantic cries and the moans of terribly hurt and others near death were all around him in the darkness. The slippery feel on the floor and seats had to be from rain — but as he pawed his way toward the rear, John wondered if it wasn't a sea of blood.

Where was she? "Naomi...Naomi!"

He finally found her back in the rear. There in the well under the seat, with the great gaping opening in the roof letting through a little light in the night.

"Naomi, my God! Darling, what's happened to you?" There was no answer. Then he made out the glitter in the darkness. *A seat pole! Driven into her? My God, was she...?*

"John...John, you're here!" Her voice was a whisper. "What happened?"

"Bus went off the road. Everyone hurt...Don't move!" He pressed her arm back to her side.

"Cold, John...It's so cold!"

He tore the coat from his back and wrapped her. She was shivering uncontrollably. She had to be in shock or going. *The roof...insulation!* He stretched for the shattered roof and peeled sheets of rock wool from the airspace. She was covered. "Don't move!" he whispered. "Help's coming! Gotta go see who else..." He crawled to the seat in front. It was too late to help the man. No pulse. He moved forward, stopping at any forms that moved. He wondered why *he* had been spared. He'd been airborne in the aisle and should have sailed through a window. But nothing even hurt as he moved in helpless desperation from one victim to another.

• • •

Help finally arrived. Ambulances from every direction up on the highway. Fire trucks and emergency units were there. And expertly the rescuers were able to separate Naomi from the metal that impaled her through the hip. And then everyone who was alive was out.

"You can come with us now, Mr. Hail," said one of the stretcher bearers as they secured Naomi in position for the climb to the highway above. "Mr. Hail, are you all right?"

John, still in a kneeling position, was unable to comprehend. Minutes before he had felt no pain as he struggled through the destroyed bus. Now, as he tried to get up, he couldn't stand. His back was a searing furnace of hurt as broken ribs and crushed spinal vertabrae came alive with sensation.

He was strapped onto a stretcher and transported up the hillside behind Naomi. Soon they were in two Oklahoma City hospitals, separated, but only for as long as it took John to get into braces and tape and get free to be with his wife.

A tremendous cheer went up from the crowd for the Stars owner when he appeared for the game some weeks later. Some of the family were furious with John for forcing himself out for the first home game he could navigate.

"Listen, I have to be there! The accident and all those people in it...team morale is down and the public can really get the wrong impression. They can think we're licked and we're not!" He glared at the family members who had descended on him to protest his going. "I gotta do it my way. I'm goin'!" He went.

At Mercy Hospital Naomi went through plastic surgery and many dramatic procedures in the operating room as physicians and surgeons teamed to give her back her health. It was working, but something was different. There was a change, perhaps brought about by the shock and trauma. Subtle. She covered it with pluckiness, worrying about John and the children's concerns, but those who were lifetime Naomi watchers, saw a difference.

As the months moved on, the storm clouds of the costly hockey venture and the uncontrollable skidding of the oil involvements they had entered, made it clear financial disaster lay just ahead for the Hails. John stayed at home a great deal, reading a lot and drinking and sleeping little. He tried this way and then tried that way, but nothing wanted to turn for the better. He definitely was at the edge of going broke.

❖ ❖ ❖

In Ada, Harland sat puzzling the problem of the sudden lethargy in his Oklahoma ranks. He understood the cyclical nature of the sales business. He should. There had been many personal up and down times in selling in his years of insurance, and probably especially when he was the lone sales force of Pre-Paid Legal. How easy it had been to get those down-cycle sales challenges and the only answer was simply to *get out and sell.*

So why was his Oklahoma organization slipping off so badly? They had built to a remarkable 1200 sales a week, particularly to education and small businesses as payroll deduction and fringe benefits. And the servicing of those group business accounts alone should have kept the gross up to at least 800 in a down-cycle time. But for weeks it had plunged to 400 sales a week. They couldn't stand a two-thirds cut in new memberships processed. Something very strong had to be done. He reached for the phone and sent out the word. A sales meeting would require the attendance of everyone marketing Pre-Paid Legal in the State of Oklahoma. He didn't want to do it, but it was a time for forceful leadership.

Meanwhile, get it off your mind, Harland. Think about the wonderful growth of your company with a strong subsidiary in the Southeast, National Pre-Paid Legal Services under the leadership of Tommy Bush. In a dozen and more states, they were definitely growing. But what if the word got out that the home state itself was sagging seriously? It could have a domino effect.

• • •

Sunday came. The sales group assembled. It was clearly a key meeting. The room was tense.

"Well, ladies and gentlemen, let's get right down to brass tacks. Any sales organization goes through periods that are slow. That's understandable. But something more than slow times has to account for our drop over recent weeks from an average 1200 sales a week to 400 and under, from the State of Oklahoma. That's a two-thirds drop in production.

"Now, many of you have done your best and have moved into position as regional managers and higher. You must understand that these are *not* permanent positions and are controlled solely by your production capability and the production you inspire in the area of your responsibility.

"Some of you are *not* maintaining that level which will enable your company to remain successful. I'm announcing, therefore, first of all today, that overrides and bonuses are *hereby cancelled* in this state for all leaders until we see a move back upward in production."

A murmur swept the room and shortly became more defensive and argumentative. It was taking the opposite of the direction Harland needed in this critical moment. One of the men was on his feet. But it was nothing other than the same headquarters action he'd watched frequently in his years with Paramount. He listened quietly as the threats began. Ties were loosened and shirt sleeves rolled as the heated exchange intensified.

"Tell you right now, I'm not about to stand for this!" snapped one angry manager, grabbing his coat. "You can just stick this organization, as far as I'm concerned!"

Others followed. And still others. Rick and D. E. and Wilburn and dozens of others stared in disbelief as many left the room. It gave everyone the feeling that a house was tumbling and there seemed no way to stop it. Half the team had walked out.

One long-timer in the sales force from Ada, Ulysses Grant, shook his head incredulously at the defection. "Harland, we're with you. But you better believe this is goin' into the books as Black Sunday."

• • •

It was a lonely Sunday evening as Harland sat morose at his desk. He had made the move as a positive thing, fully intending to follow the usual program when such a disciplinary step is needed and pay every penny of the back earned overrides and bonuses the minute Oklahoma production began its swing upward. But something — whether the economy or the catalyst of that first angry manager's walk-out — had started a chain reaction. It was grim. He waved away Rick's attempt at enthusiasm-in-spite-of-it-all, and sat alone with his thoughts. *How to break the gloom? How to take the feelings in his heart home and hide them from Shirley?*

Thoughts of his wife and all she had been through these years surged around him. *How often had she known terribly low times and somehow kept them to herself? Plenty,* he knew. He sat quietly for long moments, then reached for the pad in his desk...

"Shirley," he wrote...

SHIRLEY

To those who don't have a Shirley, they should have. Shirley has always let me be the hero. Not only has she let me be the hero, she has always worked to make me a hero.

She believed in me when others didn't and when I doubted. She is probably the most unselfish person I have ever known. She has and is still willing to stay in the background and let me have all the credit.

About the only reason I have ever missed a meal at our house was because I wasn't there. Many mornings I have gotten up at 4 or 5 a.m. in order to be somewhere for an early morning meeting. I never left without breakfast that she prepared. This in itself is not a big deal, but it is just one of the many ways that over the years she has shown that she cared. It's one thing to say it and another to prove it. She's proven it in hundreds of different ways.

As a mother to our two sons, she is unequalled as far as I'm concerned. One could not expect, want or ask for more.

I've known a lot of men whose wives called them to tell them the sink was leaking or the washing machine just quit. Shirley handled and still handles those type problems, and in most cases I never knew they happened. She has always worked to make it as easy as possible

Harland and Shirley

for me. She has never interrupted me in a meeting to tell me about a crisis that just occurred at home. There have been plenty of crises at our place, just like for everyone else, but she handled them and let me concentrate all my attention on the business.

Shirley is my business partner and I couldn't have had a better one. She has devoted over 25 years to making it easy for me to do my job. Because of this, many people underestimate her ability as a business person. Those who really get to know her, realize she understands Pre-Paid Legal Services, Inc. as well as any, and better than most. Most importantly, she understands we are in the people business. She appreciates and respects those who make it happen, the sales associates, every bit as much, if not more, than I do.

Many times in the life of this company, she has given me the answer or the help to make a decision that I was having a problem with. Very few people know this because she seldom ever comments in public on company issues and only does it in private when I ask. She also has an ability to occasionally bring me back down to earth, in a nice way, when I get a little carried away with myself.

As I look back at my life, most of the things I have done I would do a little differently, if I had it to do over. Shirley is not one of those things.

• • •

Harland slipped the sheets into his desk and leaned back in his chair, feeling the quiet and enjoying the shift of his thoughts to his reason for being — Shirley. He glanced around the room. *All this energy and busyness and all these constant crises and challenges, like the loss of those good people... If it had come about from some mismanagement of his, so be it. He was a human being. But he had a cause here in what was emerging as a wonderful thing for America. And if it felt sometimes like a battle, it ought to and he'd better remember a battle brings casualties. Besides, nobody told him he had to do it.*

He sighed. *There had to be a better way to make his program grow more effectively. No way could this mission of his be held to such inefficient growth ways. It just couldn't impact on America in any significant way, if the controlling element was the moodiness or the temper or emotion of a few. There must be some better way to market.*

He headed into the hall, flicking off lights as he moved. Halfway down the stairs a voice caught him from above in the darkness he'd just left. "You okay, Harland? We're still up here doin' some recruitin' planning. I'll put out the rest o' the lights."

"Thanks, Rick." It was his always-on-hand, second-in-command. He considered joining their conversation, then decided he really wanted to be with his family for what was left of Sunday.

The Stonecipher home

Chapter Four

In Oklahoma City an aura of disbelief filled the room. Family and friends were at the Hail home. Sympathy was there. But at the moment John didn't want either family or friends, if what they had for him was sympathy.

"Look, everyone! I appreciate what you're saying...know how you're feeling. The real world is, there ain't nothin' can be done to save the hockey team or any other stuff that needs savin' to get out o' this mess."

Naomi was watching quietly from the chaise near the pool. It was not a comfortable day for her. She had seen this coming. As the crisis had worsened, John had told her by bits and pieces and had done it reluctantly. She knew why. He'd been worried about her personal physical condition and hated that she should have anything on her mind but complete recovery from a surgery that had brought only inconclusive findings. Something wasn't right. She shared the dilemma of her discomfort with a close personal friend, but didn't want John to know the extent of it.

Not that he needed any babying. She knew he'd face the world with any crisis — hers or his — pulling no punches and feeling no embarrassment. It was just an unfortunate crunch from several directions at once, over which he had no control. They were going to go under financially. But she wasn't afraid. He had more than enough strength for both of them and unless something changed inside her, he was going to need it.

This day she was especially sure of him. She caught his eye on her in the family room from time to time and she knew he was privately most concerned about how to help her. As the crisis had mounted and his equity and leverage to cope with problems shrank, for a time he had seemed to shrink. His early morning think times had turned into all day meditation. Sometimes sullen, other times buried in a book she suspected he wasn't reading, and sometimes drinking too much when she was sure it was more anesthetic to a growing agony than really wanted as a drink. Then she saw him take command.

The phone had rung the day before and it should have been the worst of all possible news. Their lovely home on the Tickfaw was lost and the yacht had been impounded. "I understand," she heard him say to his lawyer. "I know... you're doin' everything you can. Jus' keep me posted." His voice had seemed frighteningly calm.

She braced as he turned from the phone but when he smiled that crooked special way, she knew something else was going on in his head. And it wasn't anything like giving up.

"You know, Naomi, I think I'm on to something great for us. Remember my telling you that that diet marketing idea is a lopsided deal? Loaded for high honchos and screwin' the little guy?"

"I heard you." There was a different note in his voice. "But I knew you were just helping along and not going to do much with multilevel." She reached out to him. "I just want you to know I appreciate all the traveling, with all you're going through..."

"Aaaaahhh...ain't nothin' but a few bad breaks. I got nothing against multilevel either, with the right plan. S'long as it gets money to the workers fast...and doesn't top-load the rewards for the few who make the top. And s'long as it don't allow the downline you recruit to walk around and pass you up and then you never see a dime from them again...Bunch o' stuff I been thinking about..."

"Johnny, that's wonderful! If we had a program like that, we'd be making lots more."

"I'll tell you who's got the best product for multilevel with the right kind of plan. Harland Stonecipher. I'm absolutely convinced. I've studied every inch of what he does.

He's stymied from growing much till something really revolutionary turns on their marketing. I got the revolution!"

"Shall I run up the flag and warn them?" His contagion was music, once again sounding like himself.

"I've got an appointment with Harland tomorrow, so we'll see if he'll give it a shot."

• • •

Harland listened carefully to his proposition, wearing that impossible-to-read expression throughout. *He'd be one helluva poker player,* thought John at one point. Finally he sensed a small spark of interest when he interrupted with a question, but that was quickly dismissed as a rare furrowing tightened his forehead.

"What's your reaction?" John asked. "Think it might have some possibilities?"

There was silence. Harland seemed to be at a loss for words. "All right," he said finally and very deliberately. "Here's how I feel. I am tempted to say, if you think for one minute I am going to take all the blood, sweat and tears of the last ten years and flush it with some mickey mouse multilevel messin' it up, you're crazy!" John braced as he took a breath. "The truth is, I've got too much respect for you, to believe for one second that you'd be sitting here with anything that would mess me up. I think you've already proved that many times." He sighed and spread his hands, palms upward. "What I want to say is simple. If you believe in this thing, it's got something to it that I apparently don't understand yet. Tell you what I'm willing to do...

"We'll allow this multilevel experiment and we'll work out the details of dollars with you. But I want your promise on one thing. I want you to take this notion and work it at least five hundred — no, it ought to be at least a *thousand* miles away from Oklahoma. I don't want any of my salesmen to be involved!"

John cracked that wide grin and let the relief show through. "You wouldn't reconsider and make that five hundred miles, would you? Hell, I might have to borrow gas money from you and back and forth a thousand miles would be a ton o' gas."

"Five hundred, then." Harland smiled, remembering. "I'm not forgetting where I've been. And I consider Pre-Paid Legal lucky to have you involved at all. Guess I'm trigger-happy for what may have been a mistake." He described the debacle of Black Sunday. "I'm down by over half my sales force in this state and I sure don't want the word out that I'm switching to a brand new marketing idea. You know Oklahoma is already multileveled to death."

"You got nothin' to worry about. I'm gonna show you a whole new ball game for marketing Pre-Paid. It's got nothing to do with any o' those other multilevels, like soap. No inventory. No downline passing. No bookkeeping by your salesmen."

"You've got my support, John."

He stood and the two shook hands. Not a word had been said about the collapse of John's empire and he knew he wouldn't be hearing the subject broached by John. "And how's Naomi?"

For an instant John's expression changed and Harland caught it. "Tell you the truth, she doesn't seem herself these days. You know she got hurt about a year ago."

"We heard. That terrible accident! You're doing all right yourself, are you? You got banged up, too."

"I'm fine. We had her back in for surgery in October. Something's still giving her pain, and getting her to admit to that is next to impossible. But I'm watching her."

"We hadn't heard. Give her my best, will you? Shirley's, too. She still talks about the way Naomi inspired our wives." He chuckled. "Maybe with the big defection we can get her back to turn the wives into our sales force." Harland looked him directly in the eye and went on. "I feel I want to say this because I know I'll never hear a comment from you, but I'm just very sorry you ran into a threshing machine on your financial affairs recently."

Appreciating the concern, John knew there was a bond between them that made any comment by himself unnecessary. He grinned. It was a thin smile. "You know, they say water and oil don't mix. And ice is a form o' water. Anyway, it was interesting. Some guy was telling me you can't get people who never grew up on ice to appreciate ice hockey.

But you win some; you lose some. This is a country that let's you succeed or fail, but doesn't make you stay there. I'll be back. Watch me!"

"Yes, I *know* John Hail. You will be. Now tell me what I did wrong. How did I manage to blow half my salesmen out of the box? You know people behavior like no one else and you know marketing like nobody I've ever come across."

"You did what you had to. You had to kick ass. Some people just bruise easier than others. Maybe it was the wrong day. You know how it is...you get surprises. Just got to roll with 'em and *you* sure can. I been watching you a lotta years."

"I'm mighty glad we're going to work together." Harland meant it. "I'm not sure about multilevel. Frankly, it scares me. But I'm sure about you."

"Okay, buddy." John's hand was out again and both knew that was all the contract they would ever need. "I feel the same way. And you're about to see something fantastic happen."

He was anxious to get back to Oklahoma City. He couldn't pry the admission from Naomi that she wasn't feeling well and he suspected she didn't want another trip to the hospital to add to his problems.

• • •

That night he was alone in the game room of their home in Quail Creek. The room felt empty. He glanced at the bar. No interest. He walked toward the pool table. Even less interest. Naomi had retired, worn out from the day, but excited with the report of his meeting with Harland.

He walked toward the mirrored wall and stared at his reflection. "Hail, you look like hell!" he muttered, starting to turn away from the late night stubble on his chin. Suddenly he turned back, fingering his chin and smiling. It had been quite a trip since that day in Cabin Creek when his father waited with the truant officers on the old parsonage porch while Johnny in the bathroom studied a smooth chin and wished he was old enough to go punch out Nazis.

And now he had a new battle on his hands. This one beat them all. He looked at the man in the mirror. John

W. Hail. Chairman of the Board...Chief Executive Officer...
Total Multilevel Sales Force Himself...a Team of One!

Harland Stonecipher had incredible confidence when he said, "You've got my support, John."

He fingered the little cellophane packet containing the gold Lady of Justice. Neither he nor Harland were worth a damn at making pretense, so he had simply thanked him and dropped the figurine into his pocket as he left. Now he peeled the cellophane and studied the Pre-Paid Legal emblem. Held it to his collar and shook his head. *Not there.* Tried it at his shirt front as a tie tac. *No, not there. He'd wear it on his lapel.*

And he'd wear it proudly because the little metal lady with the scales and the sword had really gotten to him with her cause. Hail was just the man she needed to push the right buttons and give her an army. That much he knew for certain. *He'd do it because he'd done it before...and current problems be damned! He'd do it all over again and do it right this time.*

It was almost exactly the same hour of the very same day of John's meeting with Harland that another discussion about multilevel and Pre-Paid Legal was taking place in a closed door session between Rick Haney and D. E. Romines. Newcomer to the Pre-Paid Legal scene, Virgil Coffee, had just left their meeting to return home.

"Listen, D. E., correct me if I'm wrong. Wasn't Coffee brought onto Pre-Paid Legal staff a few months ago with instructions that he was to train sales force and teach recruiting?" Rick was on his feet, legs spread, hands on his hips and acting like a martinette as he stared accusingly. at D. E.

"This has got nothing to do with why we took him on. He's got a marketing concept that he's tried on the field with Travelers Motor Club and he believes it will work here."

"Well, I don't want to hear about it and..."

Rick started to speak, but D. E. waved him to silence. "No, Rick, I respect any man's right to a new idea. You got some kind of thing against this multilevel," he said. "And I'll just betcha I know what it is. You been moonlightin' with it and it don't work for you and you're stuck with a garageful of soap and tapes."

"Like hell I am!" snapped Rick. "I got no interest but making Pre-Paid Legal get to all fifty states!"

"Maybe you need some other interests," drawled D. E. "So you don't want to let him show us how this marketing plan works with his experiments in the field?" he persisted. "Take you ten minutes."

"There'd be no point to it just with us," Rick said. "But I think he ought to show it to Harland. I'll see if I can get him an appointment tomorrow."

"That's a deal! I hope you can listen in."

"You better believe it!" murmured Rick as he headed toward the door. "You can't make that stuff work here. I just want you to know I'm not on his side."

D. E. grinned that direct and honest way that could never leave an enemy. "Just as long as you know I'm on yours," he replied, as Rick beat him through the door.

It was a longer-than-usual ninety-four miles back to the city, thought Virgil, as he tried to relax for the tired last fifty in the comfort of his Lincoln. It wasn't too long ago, he remembered, that he'd been chasing around West Texas in another career beginning his first in sales.

He remembered how high his hopes had been for football, even perhaps as a career when he took the scholarship to Hardin-Simmons. It was wonderful, those four fun-filled high school years and the chance to play in three Texas play-offs for best of the Triple-A schools. Reigning #1 would have been wonderful, but getting there and the thrill of the team work and a lot of other things he knew he'd never forget, were an even bigger part of the meaning of football to him. And his football scholarship was the start of a dream coming true. It was rudely shattered when Coach Sammy Baugh left the college to create the Houston Oilers just as Virgil arrived. The college shut down all athletics and he transferred to enroll at Texas Tech.

End one dream...enter another. She was simply lovely. Linda Langston of the Baptist Church in Andrews, where Virgil's dad was Minister of Music and Education, captured his heart on sight. Her enrollment in Baylor was intercepted by one of Virgil's better sales promotions. Two-and-a-half months later the newlyweds set out for Lubbock and Texas Tech. Without a chance to play football there, he found his major field of study, chemistry, was not his keenest interest. As his third, then fourth year wore on, the excitement of sales grabbed him. There was something that intrigued him about taking a product in which you already believed and selling someone else on its value.

He couldn't wait for graduation to get into a sporting goods business with two good friends. All with last names starting with "C," they formed Triple-C Sporting Goods and Virgil set out for the conquest of Southwest Texas high schools as a sales force of one, ready to corner the Fall market that late Spring. Shortly Triple-C held the corner on more than half the high school athletic clothing and equipment sold in West Texas.

Two years flew by. He grew excited by the possibilities of sales of services. Recruited as a salesman for Traveler's Motor Club, over a decade and more he moved from salesman at the beginning rung of the corporate ladder to climb to the top. He had enjoyed the five years of President and the chance to lead the company, which had been a young one when he came aboard, and which, under his direction, moved from nine states to forty-eight.

He remembered how the notion of multilevel for Travelers began to form in his mind as he looked for ways to lead the company to serious head-to-head competition with AAA. The more he wrestled with what others had done in multilevel and how it might be done better, the more he was sure it was right for this company. Ownership agreed reluctantly. They'd let him give it a trial. They weren't impressed by what one of them called the 'rogues' who go into multilevel. But the willingness was there to allow it a trial run. He had drawn up a marketing plan, acceptable for starters.

The trial run became more of a runaway...sizzling to 4000 new salesmen over a few months. There was a cry to halt...starters were stopped...Multilevel would not give the company persistency of member renewals — that was one certainty of the skeptics among the owners. There was only one place to go — to new fields.

No way could his dream be squashed. He remembered his search for the right vehicle that would really give the chance to dramatize his conviction about the wave of the future. From coast-to-coast the search went and finally he confronted the hard truth that his family was the prime responsibility and he'd best become a breadwinner again.

He grabbed the opportunity to go to Ada and act in the consulting role as a trainer of sales people. It was his specialty. But multilevel of the right product remained his dream. It never went far away. And suddenly, when he thoroughly understood Pre-Paid Legal, he knew his conviction fit like a glove. He had tried the glove on for size in what had begun as a casual conversation with D. E. and Rick. It hadn't died with Rick's hostility. He'd have his chance sooner or later and if Mr. Stonecipher would listen, it just might fly. And Rick Haney was a man in love with doing business for Pre-Paid Legal the most successful way.

• • •

Harland listened patiently to Virgil's presentation and when it was done, there was a curious light in his eye. "I don't know whether you're a believer in extra-sensory perception, Virgil, but I can see you're convinced of the value of multilevel for this firm.

"I've got to tell you that only yesterday I committed the exclusive privilege of a multilevel experiment for this company. Do you know John Hail?" He studied Virgil's face as though looking for a clue that would clear the strange coincidence of back-to-back requests.

"I've heard of him, but I don't know him personally. I believe he still lives in Oklahoma City, doesn't he?"

"That's right. He's the man you should talk to. He may be interested in working with you."

• • •

"This is John Hail."

"Mr. Hail, this is Virgil Coffee. You and I have something we've got to talk about."

That was the springboard.

In John's living room they exchanged views about their mutual interest in multilevel for Pre-Paid Legal Services. Both sensed they could work well together.

Afterward John talked to Harland. "Is Virgil for real? What kind of a job has he done for you?"

A few questions later and a few meetings later, they decided. Two could get the company off the ground better than one. John would work with Virgil and make him his second-in-command.

They would call it The Vital Connection, or TVC Marketing Associates, because that was what it was all about... Making *the vital connection* between this fabulous product that hadn't begun to dent the market and 140-million adult Americans — the people who most needed its services. Middle class Americans, trapped in a land that had justice for all as a cornerstone, but had long since lost the capacity to offer it.

The thrust of TVC Marketing would have to be to that mass of disenfranchised citizens who believed an attorney could not be afforded, whatever their predicaments. It had to reach out to the millions who were increasingly embittered that 'in the land of the free and the home of the brave' their rights as citizens had been stripped away simply because they couldn't afford to fight for those rights and therefore didn't have them at all. Too much law for those who could afford it; not enough for those who could not.

Multilevel had begun for Pre-Paid Legal Services.

Chapter Five

It was a chilly, windy day in Oklahoma City when Virgil and Linda arrived in the early morning hours to begin putting together packets of marketing materials with John and Naomi. It was almost ten years to the day — and the same kind of day — since Harland and Shirley had had their first Sportsmen's Legal Service Motor Club meeting at the Village Inn in Ada. And now the men were readying to go out on the field on their first TVC recruiting run.

They had pooled their marketing concepts in the planning weeks and had set their techniques for getting started. John shared his convictions on how they should recruit and develop salesmen and how they should present the product to prospects. They'd call it an 'Opportunity Meeting.' Virgil pulled out the dog-eared marketing plan he'd been working and reworking for the best multilevel impact. John liked it. It was a good model for TVC. Above all, they had to get started. Now!

They split in different directions, carefully putting five hundred miles between themselves and any Pre-Paid Legal Career representatives, just as Harland had asked. Two weeks later they returned to Oklahoma and compared notes. It was a start. That was about the most that could be boasted for it. Here and there each had turned up early recruits in the state they had chosen to work. And for John, with more than three decades of selling experience, and Virgil with more than two, their combined half-century of professional know-how gave good reason for enthusiasm. The program was starting to move — loaded with bugs to iron out and new and better materials to be developed — but it was off and running. Optimism was high.

• • •

The wives were back again to help with the packing and sorting of the paperwork for the next week's trip and two of John's men from NFL administration had been brought in to help organize. As they listened to John and Virgil discuss what had to be changed and improved, Linda and Naomi had silent thoughts about what starting up TVC was meaning to them in their kitchens and in their private lives. The costs of traveling and of printing huge quantities of sales aids and brochures were coming purely from their personal family resources. The Printery was advancing much on credit, but it still was a massive drain on dwindling dollars. And the most drain of all was the uncertainty of just when the magic, which the men *knew* they would generate, would take serious hold.

• • •

Back again from the second trip...and then a third... and then another and still another. Now they were bringing back to Oklahoma reports of exciting things starting to happen. Working only with their own communication skills, talking about a program that would be coming to that state but wasn't officially there yet, dealing with the problem of getting past suspicion that the price of the Pre-Paid Legal protection was too low to be real...and how could anyone be sure this wasn't just a dream by some slick country boys from Ada?...And whoever heard of Ada?... and the catalogue went on...but here and there and everywhere there were those who immediately saw that *if* this was for real, it had the potential of being something wonderful for America and they wanted in.

John called people whom he knew in Louisiana and North Carolina, Ohio and South Texas and points over 500 miles away, asking them to fly as his guests to Oklahoma City for a business meeting about a wonderful new opportunity. Eighteen came. It was a daytime meeting at the Tradewinds late in January of 1983, and it was the first time Harland had had the opportunity to tune in on how the multilevel marketing of Pre-Paid Legal was presented.

John and Virgil explained the product and the marketing plan. Even though the up-front return then with TVC was only six dollars on a sold membership in Pre-Paid Legal, and Associates had to buy in advance the memberships they planned to sell, there appeared a positive response from those listening.

Harland shared the experiences of the decade of growth of his company and told of its great strength and the dramatic earnings of those who dared to believe and invest in it from the start. Enormous credibility grew visibly with the first time listeners when he told of the stock split three-for-two and then five-for-one and it brought a roar of appreciation when he talked about those, other than bar-fly Ernest, who still came up to him in Ada wanting some of that 'one-dollar-a-share stock.'

One of John's guests was Sue Hooter.

"You go hear what that man's up to," her husband Leon told her. "If you like it, come tell me when we should get involved." A computer salesman, Leon was unable to come from Louisiana to hear this new thing that had John Hail enthused. He and Sue had long been admirers of John.

Sue was one of those eighteen who immediately became a TVC Associate. Another who was fired with an intense interest as he heard John and Virgil share the opportunity for any who would become early TVC leaders, was D. E. Romines, who had come partly as a Pre-Paid Legal observer and partly out of his own personal curiosity in this new multilevel marketing.

Naomi excused herself from the packaging of supplies. "I'm sorry to be goofing off," she apologized. "I just have a little tummy upset."

The pallor and tension in her face frightened Linda. "Shouldn't we get you to a doctor? You know John would have a fit if he could see you right now."

"No, I'll be all right. Don't let him know. He's taking today in Indianapolis with his brother to rest and to get his energy back. He called David from the road two nights ago and said, 'I got a bug. Can I come sleep?' His sister Dorothy is coming next week to be with me...Our men are going *so* hard. When's Virgil get back from California?"

"He's in New Mexico tonight and he'll be here tomorrow. Did you know that Leon jumped into the car here with him and rode all the way to California and back just to find out everything he could about TVC and the marketing? He's ready to start selling in Louisiana now."

"They're all so optimistic." Naomi's voice was lower and Linda rose to leave the room. "What's the latest count on recruiting?"

"It's getting close to a hundred."

"It seems slow, doesn't it, compared to what they're both used to?"

"It does. But it'll take hold. I know it."

• • •

Their men knew it, too. When they compared notes next, they were ready to make projections of what they could expect in the first year of TVC. It would look like an impossible goal to many who could only measure one-hundred-and-nine Associates after several months work and great expense.

But to John and Virgil the one-hundred-and-nine gave every reason to expect that by the end of the calendar year 1983 — ten months away — they would see ten thousand Associates in action. By the end of 1984 there would be twenty thousand and by the end of 1985 there would be forty thousand TVC Associates selling Pre-Paid Legal memberships.

"I think that's a pretty conservative guess," John observed as Virgil scrawled the figures on the marketing whiteboard. No way to guess they would double those goals in '84 and '85.

Cancer was there and it was very bad. In exploratory surgery there was no doubt that it had gone beyond arresting. For three weeks Naomi lingered and then mercifully her suffering was ended. In early May God called her home.

There is no way to measure the pain in such a parting. John, Gary, Denise and Vicki, whose lives had been so deeply entwined with Naomi's for so long, felt the incredible loss of one who had steadied each of them with her love through so many tumultuous, but beautiful years. Ten others were very close. Mates Becky and Dennis and Andy and seven grandchildren knew someone very dear and very special had left them.

All across the family and friendships there were heavy hearts. John's brother David came from his parish in Indianapolis to share the funeral service with the pastor of the Nazarene church where John and Naomi had worshipped together over the last twelve years. Pastor Gilliland felt personally the hurt his good friend John was enduring. He had been at Naomi's bedside every day.

Silence is sometimes the better way in such a time. John invested some of the moments after the graveside pain in silence and some in the need for conversation with one of his most loved and trusted members of the family. In his own special way it was his manner of honoring Naomi's memory to carry forward a program in which she had invested the last ounces of her own energy.

"Fred." He plucked at Fred Morgan's coat sleeve and drew him aside. "Like to talk to you a few minutes. Let's walk. There's something I want you to consider when you get back to Florida." He described what he had started, with Naomi's help, in Pre-Paid Legal. He told Fred that it would honor him if he would seriously consider giving up his church building career and join him and Virgil in the TVC leadership. It was said simply, then characteristic of John, he walked away from the subject to let Fred think about it and get back to him, if he was interested.

• • •

It was over. It was done. There was absolutely nothing to be gained by sitting in Oklahoma City mourning what could not be changed. He had a commitment to Naomi. He had a commitment to Virgil and to Harland and already to a great many other people to help them get started in a much needed business. There was urgency. His greatest honor to her would be to move it...to get going...to make this thing happen all across the land.

For twenty-eight days he pushed himself. Thirty-one meetings and training through every day of the frenetic month. It had to be! It was absolutely necessary to get up the momentum and go for it! Establish credibility with those early recruits...sustain their sales effort with marketing materials...answer their problems by phone into the wee hours of the morning...deal with the initial one or two crackpots who come into such an opportunity with delusions of instant riches and with determination to get them, no matter how many get hurt with their blue sky promises...

...and then finally, as another month wound down and John was seen by one of the family who knew him well, the call went out to Chuck Cannon. "Chuck, you *have* to break his mad rush! Try to slow him down or he'll burn out. No human can take this pace!"

Chuck responded from California and John was at the point to listen and put the brakes on. Several days of rest... some golf...some conversation...and lots of quiet...the strength was coming back.

• • •

And strength was entering the program as word was moved from town to city to crossroad villages and county seats that something new was surfacing in America to give all men and women equal access to justice through equal access to the attorney of their choice.

It was a word that got out not by any advertising program or radio, magazine or TV hype. In fact, there was no commercial advertising at all. The genius of the multilevel marketing way as used to perfection by John and Virgil, two graduates of the arts of selling, was to depend primarily on word of mouth to present the product.

They had all the ingredients to make this program for a nation succeed and Virgil boiled it down for those he first drew into the business. "There are five simple rules to be successful in creating the desire for a Pre-Paid Legal membership...

"First, you have to really believe in the product. Know that its benefits cover approximately eighty percent of the legal threat areas of most American lives. Obviously, for the low cost of the membership, we can't cover 100% of all costs, but we do cover approximately 75% of the bill in the areas we protect. But, number one, you need to *believe* in this product you're talking about.

John and Virgil

"And next, you should always wear the Lady of Justice pin that we give you when you become an Associate with TVC. People are going to ask you if you're a lawyer and that opens the door for you to talk about this wonderful product of ours.

"Then, always live by the Three Foot Rule. Our business is built around the most successful method of advertising in the world. Your mouth. But you've got to open it, to be successful. When anyone gets within three feet of you, find a way to start talking about Pre-Paid Legal. Remember, relax and just be telling a friend of something wonderful you've discovered.

"When you're asked what Pre-Paid Legal is about, share what we call, 'If You Were My Attorney.' Our product is brand new to over 95% of America, so it has to be demonstrated in a way that makes them know its value. The best way to do that is by role-playing with a prospect. Have him or her pretend to be an attorney. Describe some of the services you and your family will need on a monthly cost basis, naming some of the Pre-Paid Legal coverages...and ask what the attorney would charge you per month.

"And finally, you're going to want to bring at least one guest each week to an Opportunity Meeting to hear from others about a Pre-Paid Legal membership and the business opportunity."

He and John were masters at sharing the program and the benefits for the listener. Most important, they created a presentation that could be shared by the rankest amateur who was certain, as Harland had been a few years earlier, that they had absolutely no sales ability. The method was good.

It was good luck for TVC Marketing that even as the growing army of TVC Associates was honing skills in selling the product, Harland was developing an enlarged and dedicated home office staff, and securing the finest in computer technology. As the firm spread to 10...12...15...18 states, then passed 20 with John and Virgil recruiting and leading a growing army, there was no doubt that TVC and multi-level marketing had Harland's complete support.

One absolute must that he insisted on as he guided the enlargement of the company, was to keep it simple for the attorneys who serve Pre-Paid members. Pay that professional promptly without requiring claim forms or deductibles or special status to qualify. Any attorney who was a licensed, practicing attorney in their state, and spelled out briefly the specifics of services rendered, was paid the covered amount at the going rate for the area, usually within ten days.

The word was getting around. Juris Doctor, the professional magazine of attorneys, Newsweek, US News and World Report, Time, and countless other magazines and newspapers were carrying stories overwhelmingly favorable to this new opportunity for access to the attorney of your choice for all Americans. If some criticized this or that minor point, the overwhelming testimony of the press was that America was ready for Pre-Paid Legal and that Pre-Paid Legal Services, with headquarters in Ada, Oklahoma, was the firm with the longest clear track record able to bring this hungered-for opportunity most efficiently to the nation.

Harland and Ken

Harland looked at the collection of eager, receptive faces from all across America, sitting before him in the Justice Room at National Headquarters in Ada. These were the new leaders, strong men and women from across the nation, who were among John's and Virgil's first picks for leadership of states in which Pre-Paid Legal was now allowed to operate.

"The first thing I want to tell you this morning is that Pre-Paid Legal Services now has as its President, Ken Johnson. Ken is one of the oldest friends of Pre-Paid and I want you to know that he has closed a highly successful law practice of more than twenty years in Oklahoma, to accept this invitation to become our President."

An enthusiastic crowd of TVC's newest leaders cheered and whistled for the popular appointment. For over ten years Ken had been helping Harland on the field with appearances for this program of legal protection to which he was personally, totally committed. Now he could help lead full time.

The room quieted. Harland surveyed the visible high quality of these relative newcomers, many of whom had given up other successful careers in their sense of mission for Pre-Paid. He wanted to put into perspective what he felt were the real ingredients to the success he had found, and wanted for each of the newcomers.

"I ask myself," he said, "why have we succeeded and continued to grow, while others that have begun along the way no longer exist or have accomplished little? I believe there are three key ingredients in any company's or individual's success. Two are not enough. It takes *all three*.

"There is no magic to it or no secret mystical formula. The first and most important quality or attribute is *persistence*. I cannot over-emphasize persistence. I do not believe anyone can succeed in a major way who is not persistent. Persistence makes up for a lack of capital, lack of knowledge, lack of education and the lack of almost anything else you can name or think of. The ability to keep on keeping on. There is simply no substitute for persistence. You are never beaten until you quit. Most people quit at the first sign of opposition.

"It could be said that Rick Haney and I didn't know when to quit or have enough sense to quit. We got up every morning with the idea, *something good is going to happen today*. Then it was up to us to make it happen. One's degree of persistence determines the degree of success. If I could give one quality to my sons, it would be persistence.

"The second ingredient for success is to attract quality people. To recruit and attract quality people, you must constantly talk to quality people. There are only two ways in the world to legitimately earn money. One is to have *money* working for you. The other is to have *people* working for you. The better quality of people, the higher the rate of return. Talk to quality people to recruit quality people.

"In getting quality people, always remember you can have anything you want in life, if you are willing to help enough other people get what they want. You must help quality people get what they want in life. It then follows as night to day, you will attract and recruit quality people to your team.

"The third ingredient that is also absolutely necessary to success is to not only know the Golden Rule, but to practice it. I am totally convinced that sooner or later you will reap what you sow. We have to ask ourselves on a regular basis if we want or would be happy to reap what we are sowing. Treat people and deal with people fairly, always. Not just most of the time.

"All of us have a problem with greed. It is a part of our nature. Uncontrolled greed destroys people and companies. You can only get and keep what you want from life by helping others get what they want. You cannot get what you want from life by *taking* from others. It only comes by *giving* to them. Be firm and fair in all business dealings. Attempting to take from others that which does not belong to you or at a price less than what it is worth, is stealing. That makes you a thief.

"There is nothing wrong with driving a hard bargain, as long as it is fair. We at times find ourselves dealing from a position of strength and at other times from a position of weakness. In each case, 'Do unto others as you would have them do unto you.'

"Be persistent. Attract quality people. And do unto others as you would have them do unto you — and you will be successful. In fact, as soon as you master these three qualities, you *are* successful."

❖ ❖ ❖

"John, I have got to salute you and Virgil for what you've done for this company. I want to be the first to admit I was absolutely wrong in my opposition." Rick Haney raised his glass in salute of the founder of TVC.

"Thanks, buddy," John grinned. "Just keep the opposition comin', if that's what you call it."

A dozen TVC and Pre-Paid Legal staff were guests at John's new home and conversation paused while everyone waited for him to go on. "Your kind of opposition is why we just signed in our 20,000th TVC Associate and that's six months ahead of when we planned for him. We never could be where we are right now, without the Ada team backin' us and Rick is the ramrod. We know it and we appreciate it."

Shirley leaned suddenly to Harland and whispered, "Rick is not well. Look, you can tell!" A glance told Harland she was right. The pallor, the expression...definitely not Rick.

"I'm just fixin' to go home," he admitted when Harland leaned across the table and questioned him.

"No, I don't think you should do that. Let me take you right to the hospital." Rick acquiesced with a quiet nod. "John, will you lead us?"

"You bet! We'll go right down the street to Mercy."

At the Emergency Room the doctors checked for signs of the cause. Harland went to the waiting room to tell the cluster of worried friends what he thought they'd best do. "I'm sure they'll want to keep him overnight for watching," he said. "I'll stay with him and likely bring him home tomorrow."

Pat Davidson, his personal secretary and ever the steady one through so many crises, was standing nearby. "Pat," Harland said, "you take Shirley and the other women back to Ada and we'll...why, Rick! What's happened?"

Everyone stared as he walked toward them smiling that confident Rick way. "The doctor says I'm fine, as far as he can tell, and I can go home. I'm sure I'll be great now. Thanks for worrying. I'll see you in the morning."

•   •   •

It was not to be. His girl friend drove him home to Ada and worried by his discomfort having returned, went inside to convince him to go to Valley View Hospital. He sat on his living room floor, dawdling aimlessly with his collection of little bottles.

"I'm going to be very sick," he said abruptly. Savagely the attack seized him and he crumpled unconscious. In less than an hour at the hospital Emergency, he was gone, stricken at forty-two by a violent heart attack.

It was a tremendous blow to everybody at Pre-Paid Legal Headquarters. For Harland and Shirley and their sons, it was the loss of one who was family to them. For staff members, from Kathryn Prentice to Bob Thompson to the newest secretary of the eighty now forming the office staff, it was a grim loss. Harland Stonecipher was the founder and the personification of Pre-Paid Legal. Rick, who always pressed the point that Harland was Number One, also always insisted that *he* was Number Two. He would invariably always see that Harland took the number one parking spot and that *he* took the place at his side.

He left the indelible stamp of his presence. Quietly Harland had a bronze plaque mounted in the Staff parking lot next to that reserved for the Chairman of Pre-Paid Legal. It reserves in perpetuity that space at his leader's right for Rick Haney. There was no doubt in anyone's mind that Rick truly poured out his life on the altar of the worship he felt for the goal of Pre-Paid Legal in the home of every American.

⬧ ⬧ ⬧

Helen was really rather annoyed. Her Scottsdale friend simply insisted she *had* to come by their house and meet this really neat man from Oklahoma. He was head of a marketing firm. They'd all have dinner together and then, just for kicks, she could tune in on a TVC meeting they were leading.

Dinner sounded okay but the TVC meeting sounded like the pits of an idea. It had been a long day at the water company office she managed and TV without the "C" sounded better.

"I'm not interested, Ann," she said. "I've met so many people in the past two years that I *really* am not interested in meeting anybody."

Ann and Terry prevailed. Helen went with them to dinner at the Pointe and then to the meeting after.

"Hello, Helen. I'm John." That was nearly the extent of their conversation as Terry Dunlap, alarmed at some new developments for his TVC organization, bombarded John with questions.

At one point Helen winked at Terry's wife. "Ann, I'm glad we're with each other tonight or we really would have been bored."

"Let's go to the meeting, girls." Terry was already enroute for the door and a reluctant Helen followed.

Half-an-hour later her first TVC meeting was underway and she stared at the man on her right as the video short introducing the TVC Pre-Paid Legal program presented John Hail. She punched the man beside her. "I thought your name was John Tate!"

"Hail," he muttered without moving his head.

• • •

It was 6:30 the next morning when her phone rang. "Helen, will you do a dear friend a favor?" It was Ann. "I am absolutely stuck with some early morning things to do and someone has to get John over to our place. Would you be a darling? He's got to be here at 8:00, so you won't be late for work."

If she had the slightest notion of protesting, Helen would never give a hint. The four of them had visited after the meeting when everyone else had left. She discovered she really did like John Hail. But she'd have to hurry. As she wheeled her Olds through the early morning commuter traffic, John sipped quietly at coffee.

"Oh goodness, that's your street!" She whipped the car around the corner and an explosive cry sounded from her passenger. She had totally forgotten the cup in his hand. A very sharp Hart Schaffner Marx jacket was decorated from lapels to lower extremities with John's coffee.

"I'm so sorry!" she exclaimed.

"Happen to anybody." He was quietly wiping in a futile effort to make the coat, tie and shirt usable.

Well, scratch the neat guy, she thought. *Who would want to bother anymore with a dolt who can dump coffee that efficiently?*

John Hail did. Lovely Helen with her auburn hair and contagious joie-de-vivre, statuesque and proud and very independent, alone herself after almost as many years as John with a marriage partner, was impossible for him to forget.

• • •

A year-and-a-half into a building of TVC, there now was no question that the firm was on strong footing. Harland was so sure of it, the decision was made to bring the entire force of career salesmen and saleswomen into the multilevel marketing of TVC. John Hail and Virgil Coffee had indeed carried off a modern day miracle in marketing.

And if there was a miracle happening in marketing, there was as beautiful a one happening between Helen and John. Loners both, and with their aloneness of more than a year confirming their contentment not to be bothered with thoughts of remarriage, they were awed by the discovery of each other. They were in love. They wanted to be together and carve out the rest of their lives as husband and wife.

In October, 1984, on the sweeping green of Oak Alley Plantation in Bayou Country, Louisiana, Helen and John were married, with the pastors of the Hail family, Lloyd and David, officiating. The two-century-old oaks that line

Helen Hail

the green have been witness to many a wedding moment, but none that brought to scores of children, grandchildren and close friends from every part of the country more pure joy to witness than to see two loners-in-love, stepping into the first moments of their new life together.

John and Helen's home

It was incredible, thought John, scanning his audience at Atlanta's posh Waverly. *More than a thousand in the ballroom.* The rally had been a four hour event — training seminars, recognizing achievers in Vice President Dave Roller's territory of Georgia and Florida, and John Hail was the featured speaker for the finale of the event.

He smiled down at Helen in the first row, marvelling at her ability to look so fresh and unruffled after a week like the one just finished. Four cities in three days and two more before the weekend was over. It was impossible not to stay pumped up wherever they went, with the Associates as enthusiastic as they were.

"...First of all, how many of you would like to own 1,600,000 shares of Pre-Paid Legal stock today at nine dollars a share?" he asked. "All you have to do is to be willing to do what Harland did.

"You know, he didn't get that yesterday. He got that in 1969 when the concept first came and he decided that nothing was going to stop him until he got this company started. And I can tell you, it didn't happen easy, folks. He'd already mortgaged everything he owned — his furniture, his house and everything that was worth a dime down there on his forty acres in Coal County, Oklahoma, just to be able to meet the payroll and do whatever he needed to to get this concept started.

"One day he walked into my office when I was President of National Foundation Life and put the question to me. Would our company be interested in talking to him about helping finance his company for a time? Harland's a pretty good salesman and convinced me we should and we worked out a deal. He would drive back and forth every day to Oklahoma City, 94 miles each way, to bring applications from his sales force so's we could cut him a check and he could pay his people. Then they'd go out and sell more memberships...Had to borrow from me more than once to get together gas money for the return.

"Sure, we'd all like to have 1,600,000 shares of any stock at nine dollars a share. But how many of us would be willing to do what Harland did? My favorite saying is, 'The highway to success is always under repair.' I've got news for you. They threw up every stumbling block there was in the world at Harland...but he wouldn't listen.

"And I want you to know that in December of 1982 I called Harland Stonecipher and said, 'I'd like to meet with you.' And when I proposed I would like to start a company to multilevel Pre-Paid Legal Services, I thought I was going to get thrown out of Ada, Oklahoma!"

The ballroom reverberated with the response of the delighted crowd.

"Naw, he didn't really even threaten. He said, 'If it were anybody but you, but because I've known you for so many years and know your reputation — I know your integrity — if you'd like to try it, we would love to have you associate with our company...But I don't want any of my friends to know!'" Again the ballroom threatened collapse. "'So, if you would like to do that, I want you to promise me you will not sell within 500 miles of Ada.'

"We did what we were told, Virgil and I, and today 120,000 Associates are able to go to the mailbox a few days, not weeks, after they make a sale and get a substantial check for their work. And that army is going to sell more than $50,000,000 in Pre-Paid Legal memberships this year."

❖ ❖ ❖

Two thousand miles West in Denver's Stouffer Concourse Hotel, Harland was facing an equally enthusastic Saturday Rally. He acknowledged Bruce McColl, Vice-President of Marketing in Colorado, who had just introduced him. *There was a lot of John Hail in McColl,* thought Harland. He knew the man and the story of how he had toughed it out when his business had fallen apart. He and his wife and the kids were for a time reduced to desperation of living in their car, as they struggled for a foothold. Now he had taken hold and turned his life to success. His state was consistently in the multi-millions of dollars in new sales each week.

As his moment was nearing to address the TVC audience, it had been impossible for Harland not to think of the hard route John Hail had traveled to reach the point he now enjoyed. John often said there would have been no Pre-Paid Legal, if it had depended on John Hail to weather those turbulent first ten years that Harland had to deal with. And Harland knew there would be no Pre-Paid Legal this day so widespread and on a growth pattern so breathtaking, if it was not for John. The merger of their talents had been the perfect business marriage and it was only just beginning.

John playing golf

"Only that which takes root in the mind can become a fact for the world," Harland said to his audience a few minutes later. "If TVC Marketing had not taken root in the mind of John Hail, it could not have been a fact in the world. That's a basic fact of life.

"Let me say to you today, I don't really believe that life was ever meant to be a gentle thing. I don't believe that life was ever meant to be something you could approach with dainty fingers. But I *do* believe that if you think you are beaten, you are. If you think you dare not, you don't. If you'd like to win, but you think you can't, it's almost a cinch that you won't. If you think you'll lose, you've lost. It's all a state of mind.

"If John Hail had said it was no use to try when it appeared that everything was against him in 1983, you never would have heard of him and you wouldn't be here today. The fact of the situation is, that you should never have heard of John Hail. John Hail was not supposed to be heard of again after 1982. Life had been cruel and rough and vicious to him.

"The last time I visited with John Hail at length prior to our visit in 1982 about TVC, I had gone to see him about buying $100,000 of Pre-Paid Legal Services shares of stock that was overhanging the market. If that stock had dropped on the market in that time when we were so small — and we expected it would be — you never would have heard of Pre-Paid Legal Services. John said, 'Yes, just let me know when' and in 1980, $100,000 didn't mean very much to John Hail. Because John was a millionaire.

"But you know, when I saw him during the Christmas holidays two years later to talk about TVC Marketing, he was broke. The home was gone, the cash, the boat and he had a car and an apartment. And in January 1, 1983, John began as a TVC Associate. That's what he was — a company of one. You know, about the only positive thing that probably could have been said at that time was...'John, things can't get much worse. They gotta get better.'

"Truth is, and you know it, they got worse. And from 1982 through 1983 the only thing John could control in life is the very same thing you and I can control in life. And that's how he thought about it; how he reacted to it. And only he could determine how he was going to think. And John Hail is living proof that — as a man thinketh in his heart, so is he.

"I want to close with this that tells, I believe, what's really required to take advantage of the flood of opportunity that exists in what I believe we have been privileged to give you in the program from Pre-Paid Legal and in the opportunity made possible for you through TVC — But it's still your choice...

"One ship drives east, another drives west...
With the self-same winds that blow.
'Tis the set of the sails and not the gales,
Which tells us the way to go.

"Like the waves of the sea or the waves of fate,
As we journey along through life;
'Tis the set of soul which decides the goal
And not the calm nor the strife."

...AND THAT WAS THE BEGINNING

271